THE DAKOTAS

OFF THE BEATEN PATH®

OFF THE BEATEN PATH® SERIES

TENTH EDITION

THE DAKOTAS

OFF THE BEATEN PATH®

DISCOVER YOUR FUN

REVISED BY MIKE WHYE

Globe
Pequot
Guilford, Connecticut

All the information in this guidebook is subject to change. We recommend that you call ahead to obtain current information before traveling.

Globe
Pequot

An imprint of The Rowman & Littlefield Publishing Group, Inc.
4501 Forbes Blvd., Ste. 200
Lanham, MD 20706
www.rowman.com

Distributed by NATIONAL BOOK NETWORK

British Library Cataloguing in Publication Information available

Library of Congress Cataloging-in-Publication Data available

ISBN 978-1-4930-4418-4 (paper : alk. paper)
ISBN 978-1-4930-4419-1 (electronic)

♾️™ The paper used in this publication meets the minimum requirements of American National Standard for Information Sciences—Permanence of Paper for Printed Library Materials, ANSI/NISO Z39.48-1992.

Contents

About the Reviser. viii

Acknowledgments ix

Introduction x

Northeastern South Dakota **1**

Aberdeen Area 1

Sisseton Lakes Area. 11

Land of Laura Ingalls Wilder 21

Southeastern South Dakota. **27**

North of Sioux Falls 27

Sioux Falls 32

Vermillion 43

Missouri National Recreational River. 48

Mitchell. 52

Along the Missouri River **59**

Lake Francis Case 61

The Capital. 65

On Lake Oahe 70

Pioneers and Walleyes 76

Western South Dakota **80**

Southwestern Reservations 82

Heading into the Badlands. 85

Rapid City 89

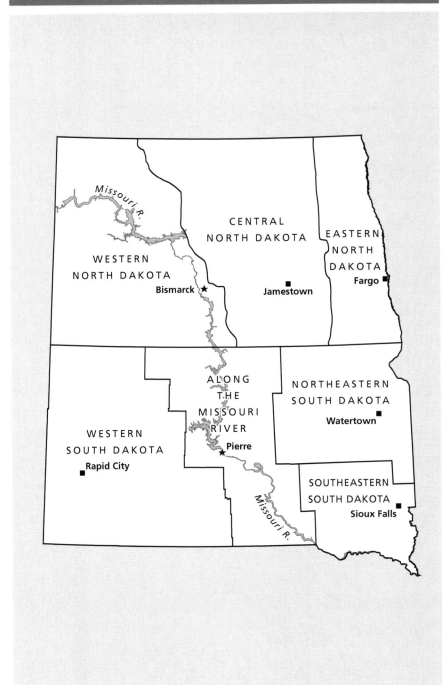

Mount Rushmore and Keystone Area. 95

Hill City and the Black Hills. 97

Custer State Park and Norbeck Byway 103

Southern Hills and Hot Springs. 107

The Northern Hills. 110

Northwestern Corner 118

Western North Dakota **126**

Medora. 128

Theodore Roosevelt National Park 132

North Dakota's Boom Towns. 135

Lewis and Clark Trail 140

Fort Lincoln and the Capitol 146

Central North Dakota **152**

Jamestown and James River Valley 155

Devils Lake and the Rendezvous Region 162

Minot 164

Turtle Mountains and Border Region 167

Eastern North Dakota **174**

Icelandic Communities 176

Grand Forks Area. 179

Fargo 182

Sheyenne Valley 189

Index 193

About the Reviser

Mike Whye developed his wanderlust as a member of a military family that moved often from when he was born until he graduated from high school. Although he did not plan to be a writer-photographer while earning a bachelor's degree in architecture at the University of Nebraska at Lincoln, he sold his first story and photos in 1974 to the *Magazine of the Midlands*, published by the *Omaha World-Herald*, during his junior year. He continued freelancing on the side while working on a master's degree in journalism at Iowa State University and then administering the public relations for a 150-person engineering-architecture firm.

Since becoming a full-time freelancer in 1985, he has supplied stories and photos, mostly about the upper Midwest, for publications including the *Omaha World-Herald*, *Des Moines Register*, *AAA World,* and *Motorcoach* magazine. In 2005, he also became a part-time instructor teaching journalism and photojournalism at the University of Nebraska at Omaha. He and his wife, Dorie, live in Council Bluffs, Iowa, where they raised their children, Graham, Meredith, and Alex. He has been a member and officer of Midwest Travel Journalists Association and its predecessor, Midwest Travel Writers Association, since 1989. Read more about Mike's works at mikewhye.com.

Acknowledgments

Thanks first of all to my wife, Dorie Stone, and our children Graham, Meredith, and Alex, for going on trips with me across the Midwest as well as putting up with me when I disappeared into my home office to write or edit photos (and for some years, working in a darkroom, too, until digital photography ended that task). Dorie deserves much thanks for reviewing what I wrote and helping with research.

Thanks also to my parents, Dorothy and Harry Whye. My father was an officer in the Air Force which meant the family traveled a fair amount, including two years in Grand Forks, North Dakota. We treated any place we lived like long-term tourists, visiting natural wonders and historical places on trips lasting from a weekend to a few weeks.

I appreciate the help of the offices of South Dakota Tourism and the North Dakota Tourism Division, plus many many people at the sites mentioned in this book. I also appreciate Jill Callison, William White, and Constance Hoffman for introducing me to places I might not have otherwise visited. Special mention goes to Jacquie Fuks, formerly of Southeast South Dakota Tourism, and Camie Lies, of the Bismarck-Mandan Convention and Visitors Bureau.

I especially want to thank Lisa Meyers McClintick for providing a terrific base to work with in revising this book.

Introduction

If you've had the privilege of admiring Mount Rushmore in person, you know it's more than an Eighth-Wonder-of-the-World kind of monument. It's a place that hums with national pride with an entrance that waves the colors of all 50 states and offers an unforgettable look at presidents representing American ideals such as independence and strength, freedom and equality.

You'll hear languages from across the globe and see kids who've gleefully hit the jackpot for the license plate game in Mount Rushmore's parking lot.

Truly this is a place powerful enough to draw people from around the world, but travelers who are wise know to stay, to linger, and to explore. No matter what road they take—east, west, north, or south—it's easier to ditch crowds and get off the beaten path. Travelers can discover places that feel as authentic and pristine as they were in 1804 and 1806 when Lewis and Clark and their Corps of Discovery made their historic journey through the Dakotas and across the continent.

In the eyes of some, South Dakota and North Dakota are far off the beaten path. They're two of the country's least-populated states (which include Alaska, Wyoming, and Vermont) and, with this much area, they rank 46th and 47th in terms of population density, or less than 12 people per square mile here. Still, you'll find some of the nation's more popular attractions here, such as Mt. Rushmore and Badlands National Park. Or you can find yourself kayaking solo down a stream or riding horses with some friends on trails in western North Dakota. There's a lot that people can see under the big open skies of the Dakotas.

You'll find Native Americans who proudly share their heritage with vibrant powwows, music, and artwork that continue their traditions and legacy of storytelling. You can stand on a bluff above the Missouri River to picture vast villages from the 1700s, tour an earth lodge, or sleep in a tipi that lets you watch the stars at night.

At South Dakota's Custer State Park or North Dakota's Theodore Roosevelt National Park, feel the power of a buffalo herd thundering across grasslands, watch a mother nuzzle her cinnamon-colored calf, and marvel at the resonant grumble of a one-ton buffalo as he ambles in front of your car—then disappears in a cloud of dust when he takes a dirt bath in the ditch.

Both North and South Dakota proudly celebrate their remarkable past and a rich cast of characters from Crazy Horse and General Custer to L. Frank Baum and Laura Ingalls Wilder; neither of these states has hit the pause button.

While much of the country has quietly ridden out a national recession and tough times, the Dakotas have boomed and thrived. Every city is growing—and quickly. North Dakota's population grew by more than 18 percent since 2000. In South Dakota, the rate is more than 21 percent in just three years. Construction of much-needed housing is catching up. Both states have added hotels and hotel rooms.

Much of the growth is driven by North Dakota's oil boom. New technology makes it possible to tap the Bakken and Three Forks formations that spread across the northwest part of the state and into Montana and Saskatchewan. North Dakota has risen to the No. 2 oil-producing state in the country, behind Texas and in front of Alaska, by pumping out about 4.4 million barrels a day.

The two Dakotas already had an energy legacy with lignite coal, hydroelectric power from dams harnessing the mighty Mississippi River, and wind turbines that pinwheel across the horizons, especially on the prairie coteau that rises along the eastern edge of the states.

Agriculture, including farming and ranching, also anchors the economy, continuing the dream of pioneers who settled the state and worked tirelessly to put down roots and claim a homestead. Their rural warmth and welcome, an echo of Old World heritage, a get-it-done work ethic, and a sense of pride still ripple through small towns (and cities, too).

The Dakotas are two of America's best states for hitting the road and slowing down, for hearing yourself think and soaking in sights such as a V of geese gliding into a prairie pothole lake gilded by a sunset, or wild horses roaming among buttes or plains. You can see a storm build from miles away before it thunders dramatically across wheat fields and then slips away, quietly spreading a rainbow across a pasture of black cattle. Word of advice: Keep your camera handy. These moments of beauty make it easy to understand why the Dakotas are so popular with birders, wildlife photographers, artists, campers and backpackers, hunters, and fishermen.

sizeandgrowth

South Dakota ranks 17th in the nation for its size of 77,116 square miles. North Dakota ranks 19th with 70,698 square miles. While both states are thriving and growing, they rank almost at the bottom nationally for population. South Dakota sits at 46th, North Dakota at 47th.

Geographically, North Dakota and South Dakota are generously endowed with pristine lakes, clay-streaked buttes, thick forests, blue-tinged prairies, and, of course, the mighty Missouri River. The Mighty Mo splits both states into East River and West River, with the flatlands of East River coveted for their agriculture, and the hills and forests of West River praised for their beauty and frontier inspiration. The states were

didyouknow?

As one can easily guess, South Dakota and North Dakota were named after the Dakota branch of a nation whose members were living in what are now the states of Minnesota and Wisconsin when they first began to encounter Europeans. In particular, they were coming into contact with the French who had formed alliances with the Anishinaabe-Ojibway. As the demand for fur grew, the Ojibway competed more and more with the Dakota and Lakota, forcing them out of their native woodlands to the west. The French picked up the Ojibway word for the Dakota and Lakota—*Nadouwesou*—which meant variously "enemy" or "snakes." The French shorted the word to "Sou" or "Sioux." Although the name became widespread among the incoming Europeans, it's a name still not liked by many present-day Dakota and Lakota. In their languages, Dakota and Lakota mean "ally" or "friend."

almost split into East and West Dakota, but a north and south division prevailed as statehood was approved for both Dakotas in 1889. That decision years ago ultimately offered them both diversity in landscape and economy.

In those early years, Germans, Scandinavians, and Czechs flocked to South Dakota. Germans from Russia, Icelanders, and Scandinavians headed to North Dakota. Both states also are home to many tribes of Dakota and Chippewa.

Some American travelers still snub the Dakotas (and the Midwest in general) as fly-over land. But those of us in the Heartland, as well as growing numbers of European and global travelers, know better. Yes, the drives to get from here to there can be long—even mind-numbing—but the reward is an authentic American experience.

It's here, off the beaten path from most of the country, where you can also walk in the footsteps of Laura Ingalls Wilder and Sitting Bull. You can excavate mammoth bones, spelunk in some of the world's longest caves, mountain bike a world-class trek through the North Dakota Badlands, find your inner cowboy, and enjoy some of the nation's best bird watching, hunting, and fishing. You can dance to Norwegian fiddles, polka with Germans, tell stories over a crackling campfire, or lose yourself in the brilliant splendor of a powwow where rhythmic drumming echoes like a dozen heartbeats.

This is a land rich with the history of explorers, treasures to be discovered, and adventures yet to be lived. Enjoy finding yours.

North Dakota Fast Facts

Population: 760,077
Capital: Bismarck
State tree: American elm
State flower: Wild prairie rose

State bird: Western meadowlark
Nickname: Peace Garden State
State drink: Milk
State fruit: Chokecherry

BIGGEST CITIES

Fargo: 122,359
Bismarck: 72,865
Grand Forks: 57,056
Minot: 47,822

TOP INDUSTRIES

Energy: Oil, gas, lignite coal and coal gasification, wind power, and ethanol fuel production
Crops: North Dakota ranks first in the nation for producing flaxseed, canola, durum wheat, dry edible beans, dry edible peas, spring wheat, pinto beans, navy beans, and honey.
Livestock: Beef and dairy cattle, bison and hogs
Tourism: 22.6 million visitors enjoyed North Dakota in 2018.

SPEED LIMITS

You can cruise up to 75 mph on interstates, 70 mph on four-lane divided highways, and 65 mph on two-lane highways.

ROAD CONDITIONS

Get updates on weather-related road conditions, closings, or work zones at dot .nd.gov/travel-info-v2.

TIME ZONES

Most of North Dakota uses the Central time zone, but the southwest corner goes by Mountain time. North Dakota also observes daylight saving time.

HELPFUL INFO

North Dakota Tourism
(701) 328-2525
ndtourism.com

Pride of Dakota
Locally made gifts and products
(701) 328-2231
prideofdakota.nd.gov

North Dakota Grape and Wine Association
ndgwa.org

North Dakota Bed and Breakfast Association
ndbba.com

South Dakota Fast Facts

Population: 882,235
Capital: Pierre
State tree: Black Hills white spruce
State flower: Pasque flower
State bird: Chinese ring-necked pheasant
Nickname: The Mount Rushmore State
State animal: Coyote
State fish: Walleye
State insect: Honey bee
State fossil: Triceratops
State mineral: Rose quartz
State gemstone: Fairburn agate
State sport: Rodeo
State dessert: Kuchen

BIGGEST CITIES

Sioux Falls: 176,888
Rapid City: 74,421

TOP INDUSTRIES

Agriculture: In the country's top 10 states for hay, sunflower, rye, honey, corn, soybeans, wheat, hogs, sheep, bison, and cattle production.
Tourism: Nearly 14 million people visit South Dakota annually.

TIME ZONES

South Dakota has two time zones: Central for its eastern half, Mountain for the west. Daylight savings goes into effect on the first Sunday in April to the last Sunday in October. About three-quarters of North Dakota are in the Central Time Zone and most of its southwest area is in the Mountain Time Zone.

SPEED LIMITS

Travelers can drive up to 80 mph on the interstate. Most other highways are 55–70 mph.

ROAD CONSTRUCTION

Call 511 for information
safetravelusa.com

HELPFUL INFO

South Dakota Tourism
(800) 952-3625
travelsouthdakota.com

Bed and Breakfast Innkeepers of South Dakota
southdakotabb.com

South Dakota Specialty Producers Association
Farm market products, meats, honey, and wines
sdspecialtyproducers.org

Winter Driving Tips in the Dakotas

- Listen to the forecast before departing and postpone travel if inclement weather is expected.

- Check winter driving sites such as safetravelusa.com for construction and road condition updates or call 511 for current driving reports.

- Carry a fully-charged cell phone and maps.

- Avoid traveling alone. Inform others of your timetable and primary and alternate routes.

- Keep your gas tank near full to avoid ice in the tank and the fuel lines.

- Adjust your speed to the conditions and increase following distances.

- Remember that bridges and overpasses are usually more slippery than other parts of the road.

- Always carry a survival kit in your vehicle. Your kit should be equipped with a can of sand or kitty litter; tire chains; flashlight with extra batteries; candles and matches; an empty coffee can (to be used to burn the candles for heat and to melt snow for water); caps, mittens, boots, and sleeping bag or blanket for everyone; nonperishable foods, such as granola bars or dried fruit; booster cables; battery-operated radio with extra batteries; and first-aid kit.

Weather

Summer: Warm (sometimes hot) days and cool nights are the norm from mid-June to mid-September.

Fall: Comfortable warm weather through September and crisp cool weather into November is typical.

Winter: Below freezing from December to early March, alternating with milder weather. Snowfall is prevalent, providing excellent conditions for winter sports.

Spring: Mostly sunny days late March to mid-June with scattered rain showers or the more rare snow showers through early May.

Restaurant and Accommodation Pricing

The restaurant cost categories refer to the price of entrées without beverages, desserts, taxes, or tips. Those listed as inexpensive are $10 or less; moderate, between $10 and $20; and expensive, $20 or more.

Places to stay listed as inexpensive are $100 or less per double per night; moderate, $101 to $200 per night; and expensive, $201 or more per night.

About South Dakota's State Parks

In 2019, some state parks in South Dakota suffered severe damage from floods, and some campgrounds had to be closed. Authorities estimate up to $9 million will be needed to repair the parks. Also, because fewer visitors were at the parks due to the weather in 2019, income was down. This situation caused the state to raise fees for people visiting the state parks. Daily visits are $8. Annual passes are $36. Prime campgrounds will be $26; preferred sites, $23; modern sites, $20; and non-electric tent-only sites, $15.

Northeastern South Dakota

By a fortunate accident of nature, the northeastern area of South Dakota, also known as the Glacial Lakes Region, features prime boating and recreational areas, with 16 state parks and two national wildlife refuges. Serendipity appeared in the form of glaciers some 20,000 years ago, and more than 120 lakes and miles of prairies were left when the glaciers retreated. This area is referred to as the Young Drift Plains by geologists, but residents simply call it the Lakes Region. For the most part, the area is swampy plain, dotted with lakes and marshes. The notable exception is the wide, flat valley of the James River. I-29, which runs north–south, and US 12, which runs east–west, help keep travel and commerce flowing from Sioux Falls, in the southeastern corner of the state, to Rapid City, in the west.

Aberdeen Area

We'll begin on US 12 in the northwest corner of the James River Valley, anchored by *Aberdeen,* which was first settled by the Arikara, who introduced farming to the region. Established Americans from the East Coast and newly arrived pioneers from Scandinavian countries, Germany, Russia, and the British Isles were to follow by train and wagon and on foot.

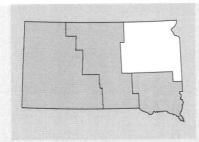

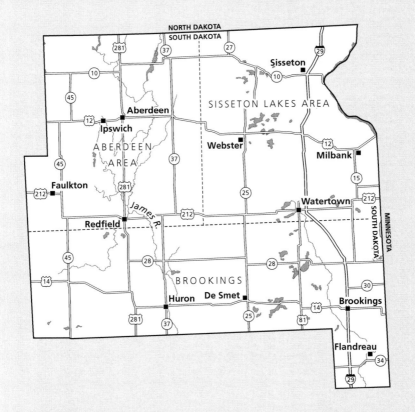

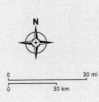

Established in 1881 near the Milwaukee Railroad, the town was named for Aberdeen, Scotland, the hometown of Alexander Mitchell, president of the railroad. Aberdeen soon became known as the Hub City in recognition of the rail lines that converged here—at least nine of them in 1890—like spokes on a wagon wheel. These days the community has more than 1,400 businesses and more than 28,000 residents, making it the third largest city in South Dakota. Agriculture and manufacturing still anchor the economy, while the city provides a regional hub for services and education. Northern State University, a public university established in 1901, and Presentation College, a small four-year Catholic college, bring history, higher learning, and the arts to the Aberdeen area.

You can wander through the whimsical world of *Wizard of Oz* author L. Frank Baum's imagination at Aberdeen's **Storybook Land** on US 281. It includes **Land of Oz** with Dorothy's farmstead (complete with special effects to simulate a tornado), a petting zoo with farm animals, a Yellow Brick Road that leads to Munchkin Land (a small cornfield that is planted and harvested annually), the Scarecrow's and Tin Man's homes, the Haunted Forest and Lion's Den, and the Wicked Witch's Castle. The Wizard Balloon Ride offers a view of the park from about 32 feet in the air.

Other larger-than-life exhibits at Storybook Land were inspired by fairy tales and nursery rhymes, such as "Jack and Jill Went Up the Hill," "Cinderella," "Jack and the Beanstalk," and "Humpty Dumpty." Kids can climb aboard Captain Hook's ship, ride a 30-horse carousel, slide down the Tin Man's giant metal legs, crawl through a tunnel to watch prairie dogs at the zoo, and explore a medieval castle. The zoo includes buffalo, elk, sheep, deer, and geese.

Admission to Storybook Land is free, although rides have fees, including a trip aboard the scale-model replica of the 1863 C. P. Huntington that chugs and whistles its way around the park. The **Visitor Center** stays open 10 a.m. to

BEST ATTRACTIONS IN NORTHEASTERN SOUTH DAKOTA

Bramble Park Zoo	Ingalls Homestead
Children's Museum of South Dakota	Redlin Art Center
Dacotah Prairie Museum	South Dakota Art Museum
Fort Sisseton State Park	South Dakota State Fair
Gladys Pyle Historic Home	Storybook Land & Wylie Park

9 p.m. between Memorial Day and Labor Day weekends, with shorter hours in the spring and fall (roughly Apr 15 to Oct 15). Call the park at (605) 626-7015 for more information or go to aberdeen .sd.us.

rollthrough
thepark

If you're seeking a whimsical way to get around the sprawling Wylie Park, *Rollout Bike Rentals* provides choppers, surreys, traditional bikes, tandem bikes, pedal go-karts, and John Deere Tractor bikes. Call (605) 226-1773 or go to rolloutbikerentals.com for details.

Surrounding Storybook Land, you'll find *Wylie Park,* with 200 acres of recreation that includes a lake, picnicking, paved trails, and golf. With *Thunder Road* (605-225-8541; thunderroad.info) you can race go-karts, play in the Lazer Maze, or minigolf past a volcano spewing flames. Events are held throughout the year, including *Haunted Forest* the third weekend in October. Visitors are guided through 13 spooky scenes led by ghoulish guides. A matinee walk-through is available for younger children, who are invited to wear costumes and collect candy at every scene. Visit aberdeenhauntedforest.org for more information.

Lake Minne-Eho, Wylie Park's man-made lake with more than 1,000 feet of shoreline, features an unsupervised swimming area and is stocked each year for those under age 16 to try their fishing skills. You can rent paddleboats or canoes to get onto the water. On a few Saturdays in the summer, you can catch the *Aqua Addicts Ski Shows.* Check the Parks and Recreation guide at aberdeen.sd.us for specific times.

Kids craving a cooler destination on sizzling summer days can shoot down a 350-foot-long lazy river, 280-foot raft slide, a 215-foot body slide, 30-foot-tall water slide tower, or an enclosed 125-foot slide at the outdoor *Aberdeen Aquatic Center.* The large complex includes a 50-meter, 8-lane lap pool, diving boards, and a lazy river. Day passes are $5.75 to $7.75. Call (605) 626-7015 or go to aberdeen.sd.us/aquatics for more information.

Wylie Park Campground offers paved roads and camp pads, 105 RV campsites, 17 tent sites, 15 camping cabins, 2 larger cabins, and a 3-bedroom deluxe cabin that sleeps 8 and has kitchen and bathroom facilities. For reservations, call (605) 626-3512 or toll-free (888) 326-9693.

You can learn more about author L. Frank Baum and about life in Brown County at downtown Aberdeen's free *Dacotah Prairie Museum,* tucked into an 1880s bank building rising grandly from Main Street. Walk through the luxurious brass-ceilinged, velvet-curtained Pullman passenger car, watch model trains chug through old Aberdeen, peek into an Arikara earth lodge and

The Man Behind *The Wizard of Oz*

The area's best-known resident was **L. Frank Baum**, author of numerous children's books including a 12-book "Oz" series that inspired *The Wizard of Oz,* one of America's all-time favorite Hollywood musicals. *The Wizard of Oz* movie debuted in 1939, 20 years after Baum's death, and his stories are still influencing popular culture with *Oz the Great and Powerful* hitting movie theaters in 2013.

L. Frank Baum moved to Aberdeen from New York in 1888 and opened a variety store called Baum's Bazaar that fall. Unfortunately, he was lacking the necessary business skills and had a track record of barely supporting his wife, Maud, and their sons. The daydreamer who loved to act and entertain didn't always please his formidable mother-in-law, Matilda Josyln Gage, a famed suffragist.

While Baum often bounced between jobs in his younger years—and he stayed in Aberdeen only until 1891—South Dakota was where he found a way to let his writing skills flourish. After closing the store, he bought the town newspaper. He renamed it the *Aberdeen Saturday Pioneer* and proved to be a top-notch journalist. Baum's stories were witty, satirical, and sometimes controversial, but the town's happenings were always reported with great passion. Writing let Baum tap the storytelling skills he would use with his boys at bedtime and lean on his love of playwriting and acting.

By 1896 and at the age of 40, he was writing *Mother Goose in Prose* and *Father Goose, His Book* and on his way to becoming America's first successful children's author. By 1890, when his first "Oz" book was published, it became an instant hit. Scholars suggest that the populist prairie might have inspired the Land of Oz, a fairyland where the common man and woman become hero and heroine and self-reliance saves the day.

He died in 1919, leaving the world a legacy of Yellow Brick Roads, ruby slippers, winged monkeys, and a dreamy land somewhere over the rainbow.

a Lakota tipi, and marvel at a 7-ton African elephant in the wildlife gallery. If you have kids in tow, print out a scavenger map before your visit. Museum galleries are open from 9 a.m. to 5 p.m. Tues through Fri and 1 to 4 p.m. Sat and Sun. Visit brown.sd.us/dacotah-prairie-museum/home or call (605) 626-7117 for more information.

From April 15 to October 15, the museum also opens the ***Granary Rural Cultural Center,*** where you can look at artwork in the 1928 granary and walk the grounds where sculptures and interpretive signs tell about life in the fertile valley where the James River squiggles across the landscape. To reach this historic farm, which also includes a 1912 town hall, head west on Highway 12 and north on Highway 10 until you reach 128th Street. It's about 20 miles northeast of Aberdeen. For more information on the granary and Dacotah Prairie Museum, call (605) 626-7117 or go to dacotah-prairie-museum.business.site.

aninsidelook atfarms

If you can plan ahead and travel in a group of 10 or more, Aberdeen's Convention and Visitors Bureau puts together special tours of wheat farms, cattle ranches, a pheasant farm, sculptor Ben Victor's studio, or a chance to visit the area's *Hutterite Colonies,* a self-sustaining rural community that has changed little in more than 400 years.

If you love history, leave time to stroll the *Highlands Historical District,* on North Main Street between 12th and 15th Avenues, encompassing 17 homes built between 1907 and 1969. The district earned the lofty title of Highlands because it rose 3 feet higher than the commercial sector, which was located in a slough. When the first houses were built, only prairie grass covered the area, so young trees were brought up from along the James River and transplanted here to line the sedate streets. Many architectural styles have melded in the district over the years, and the result is a fascinating study in both modern and classical structures. Call (800) 645-3851 or go to visitaberdeensd.com for more information.

When you reach the dead end of 2nd Avenue Northwest, you have arrived at an isolated, strangely ominous home called *Easton Castle.* Drive by and inspect the Jacobean revival architecture that was popular in England in the 1830s. Multiple windows, peaked roofs, and gables distinguish this style. Samples of the home's French-made wallpaper, which remains intact, have been documented in the Cooper Hewitt Smithsonian Design Museum.

If you visit Aberdeen in the fall, you'll be in good company as pheasant hunters flood into eastern South Dakota and roam across its rich grasslands with bird dogs at their side. The Aberdeen area alone has more than 350,000 acres of public and private hunting lands with several counties that estimate more than 200 pheasants per square mile. Hunters who bag one of 100 specially banded birds can win prizes from $100 to $1 million—like a feathered lottery. If you're new to the sport, you can find many outfitters to ease you into it and find the best hunting locations. Call (605) 645-3851 or go to huntfishsd .com for more information.

While you're downtown, be sure to leave time to browse Aberdeen's Main Street, peppered with shops, restaurants, and the 1926 French art deco *Capitol Theatre,* which hosts new movies, Aberdeen Community Theatre productions, and the annual South Dakota Film Festival. The *Red Rooster Coffee House* at 218 South Main St. also provides night life by hosting local musicians playing everything from old-time jams and bluegrass to cover bands and rock. The coffee house also has an art gallery, hot sauce shop, and fair-trade gift store,

Aberdeen Railway Station Canteen

Aberdeen cemented its reputation as **Pheasant Capital of the World** and Home of the Pheasant Sandwich with a simple intention to support soldiers during World War II. The town set up a canteen in 1943 at the 1911 Milwaukee Depot (later renamed **Burlington Northern**) as thousands of troops flowed through it and arrived hungry. Red Cross and USO volunteers served what was available, and soon soldiers were raving about the pheasant sandwiches. Word spread quickly, demand skyrocketed, and the railroad fueled the fame by advertising these sought-after sandwiches in national magazines.

Aberdeen-area volunteers put in 24-hour shifts making and serving sandwiches, and locals gave up their own wartime rations for items such as butter to feed the troops. Others in the region and across the state helped with supplemental pheasant hunts, and a local meat locker kept up to 1,000 birds stashed and ready for soldiers. The canteen fed an average of 500 soldiers a day with a record number hitting 1,500 on its busiest day. The canteen operated through March 1946, serving an estimated 586,000 troops and forever linking pheasant to local hospitality.

You can view a documentary on the canteen at the Depot, which also houses the Aberdeen Area Convention and Visitors Bureau, at 10 Railroad Ave. SW, from 8 a.m. to 5 p.m. Mon through Fri.

Aberdeen's famous pheasant sandwiches:

Finely chop 3 cups cooked pheasant, 2 hard-boiled eggs, half a medium onion, and ½ cup celery. Add 2 grated carrots and 2 teaspoons pickle relish, plus salt and pepper to taste. Stir in enough mayonnaise or salad dressing to blend nicely and spread the mix onto bread.

—Courtesy of the WWII Pheasant Canteen

and serves croissant sandwiches, soup, bagels, hummus sandwiches, nachos, and baked goods. Visit redroostercoffeehouse.com for information or call (605) 225-6603.

As you head east or west of Aberdeen on US 12, take a little time to ponder this route's rich history as one of the country's first transcontinental highways, dubbed the **Yellowstone Trail.** J. W. Parmley, known as the "Father of the Yellowstone Trail," bought his first automobile in 1905 and spearheaded the idea of connecting rural communities from Minneapolis to Yellowstone National Park with "one main good road." That idea then expanded to one good road "from Plymouth Rock to Puget Sound."

Parmley lived just west of Aberdeen in the cozy burg of **Ipswich.** You can learn more about him and local history at the **J. W. Parmley Museum** at 319 4th St. Like other notable South Dakotans, he had a thing for geology and

airboatrides

You don't have to be in the Everglades to experience a unique way to zip across marshes and shallow ponds. **Ken's Airboat Service** at (605) 530-2430 can take up to six passengers into this area's remote and beautiful wetlands.

showcased his family's eccentric array of rocks, shells, and minerals collected during his family's travels when he built the two fireplaces in their home. An iron fence post, allegedly from a fence around Sitting Bull's grave when his remains were buried at Fort Yates, forms part of one fireplace. Another quirk of the 1919 home: Mr. Parmley considered himself a practical man (and lost his previous home to a prairie fire), so this one was built mostly from concrete, including floors and bathtubs. For more information call (605) 426-6580 or visit ipswich-sd.com. The home, along with *Parmley Western Land Office,* is open Memorial Day through Labor Day, Sun from 1 to 5 p.m.

Ipswich, platted in 1883, boasts some of South Dakota's finest fieldstone architecture. Check out its First Baptist Church, the community library (a charming Hansel-and-Gretel-like stone structure), and on its lawn the mysterious Prayer Rock, a giant boulder with handprints supposedly carved by a Native American medicine man. At the city park, you'll also find Memorial Arch that once arced over the Yellowstone Trail. It was reconstructed after a storm and like Parmley's fireplaces boasts an eclectic collection of stones from all 50 states, calcite crystals from the Badlands, fossils, and even stones brought back from World War II by soldiers stationed on Pacific Islands.

If traveling the Yellowstone Trail gets you in the mood to road-trip, take advantage of the Dakotas' excellent birding in the prairie pothole region.

South Dakota Hunting Seasons

Pheasant (traditional) mid-Oct to early Jan **(preserve)** Sept to Mar	**Waterfowl** Early Oct to late Dec (varies by type with non-residents having shorter seasons)
Prairie Chicken mid-Sept to early Jan	**East River deer (firearms)** mid-Nov to early Dec **(archery)** Sept to early Jan
Dove Sept to early Nov	**Turkey** Fall and Spring

BEST ANNUAL EVENTS IN NORTHEASTERN SOUTH DAKOTA

JUNE

Arts in the Park
Aberdeen
Aberdeenareaartscouncil.com/events/
arts-in-the-park/
(605) 226-1557

Laura Ingalls Wilder Pageant
De Smet
desmetpageant.org
(800) 776-3594

JULY

Storybook Land Festival
Aberdeen
aberdeen.sd.us/sblfestival
(605) 626-7015

SEPTEMBER

Northeast South Dakota Celtic Faire and Games
Aberdeen
nesdcelticfaire.com
(605) 228-1206

South Dakota Film Festival
Aberdeen
southdakotafilmfest.org
(605) 725-2697

South Dakota State Fair
Huron
(800) 529-0900
Sdstatefair.com

About 40 miles northeast of Aberdeen, ***Sand Lake National Wildlife Refuge*** boasts 21,498 acres of wildlife and waterfowl in grasslands, forest, lake, and marsh. The area surrounding the refuge was once vast, rolling grassland interrupted only by the slow-moving curves of the James River. Settlers arrived in 1887 and brought sweeping changes to the landscape. Farming and grazing depleted essential wildlife habitat, causing waterfowl to dwindle to alarmingly low numbers by the 1930s.

Congress established Sand Lake in 1935 to preserve critical habitat for nesting and migrating waterfowl, and it was also designated a Wetland of International Importance in 1971—one of only 39 such sites in the US. Today millions of ducks, geese, and other wildlife make Sand Lake their home. In fact, 266 species of birds have been recorded at the refuge since 1935, including white pelicans, snow geese, and western grebes, which are known for their almost comical mating dance that has them skittering upright across the water.

Most people choose to drive through the refuge. A nicely illustrated, self-guided auto-tour guide is available. Along the 15-mile route there are 12 numbered stations, which correspond to symbols and text in the brochure. Station Two, for instance, affords an overlook where two important duck-nesting habitats can be seen. Station Eight is perfect for birders. Great horned owls occasionally roost here, and mallards, pintails, and the smaller blue-winged and green-winged teal also can be seen. If you're craving more of a bird's-eye view, climb the 108-foot observation tower built by the Civilian Conservation Corps in 1936. Another good observation point is the Sand Lake Overlook in the Columbia Day Use Area.

To reach the refuge from Aberdeen, take US 12 east to CR 16 (Bath Corner, 7 miles east of Aberdeen). Drive 20 miles north, through Columbia, to the refuge entrance. You can tour the Wildlife Drive 7 days a week, from daylight to dark, between Apr 1 and mid-Oct. The visitor center and main office are open Mon through Fri, 8 a.m. to 4:30 p.m. and some additional weekends depending on the availability of volunteers. Visitor center restrooms have access 24 hours a day. For more information, call (605) 885-6320 or visit fws.gov/refuge/sand_lake/.

If you drive about 50 minutes west of the Sand Prairie National Wildlife Refuge, you'll find another excellent spot for birding at ***Samuel H. Ordway Jr. Memorial Preserve.*** At 7,800 acres, it's the Nature Conservancy's largest tract of preserved prairie in South Dakota. You can find it about 8 miles west of Leola, a small town that sits at the intersection of Highways 10 and 45. Look for a parking area just off Highway 10. Trails include a new self-guided lichen trail with more than 30 species identified, along with the chance to see spring and summer wildflowers, granite boulders and potholes left by glaciers, tipi rings, and a ruined homestead. You may also be able to see some of the conservancy's herd of 250 bison from the fence in the nature trail area. There are no facilities, so bring sunscreen, plenty of water, and bug repellent. Call

Let's Play Ball

If you continue east on US 12, you'll find the *birthplace of American Legion base-ball* in Milbank, home to 3,133 people on the South Dakota–Minnesota border (about 47 miles northeast of Watertown). American Legion baseball began at a 1925 convention of that organization in Milbank. A historical marker commemorating the birth of American Legion baseball is located near the community baseball field. Former American Legion players include Yogi Berra, Johnny Bench, Jim Palmer, Frank Robinson, Greg Gagne, and Jack Morris.

Baseball fans should also consider a trip to tiny *Lake Norden* (pop. 476) about 27 miles south of Watertown, following Highway 81 and heading east on Highway 28. It's home to the *South Dakota Amateur Baseball Hall of Fame*, 513 Main Ave. It chronicles 100 years of amateur baseball with photos and mementos of its best players. It's open 9 a.m. to 7 p.m. daily Apr through Oct. For more information, visit sdbaseballhalloffame.com or call (605) 785-3553.

(605) 439-3475 for more information or visit nature.org/en-us/get-involved/ how-to-help/places-we-protect/samuel-h-ordway-jr-memorial-preserve.

Only an hour's drive from Aberdeen (take SD 45 south from Ipswich, then go west on US 212) is the **Pickler Mansion** in **Faulkton,** a friendly town of 725 people. John A. Pickler served four terms as South Dakota's first US representative-at-large, and his wife, Alice W. Alt Pickler, campaigned for the suffrage cause. Fellow suffragette Susan B. Anthony was one of the more famous guests in the home, and some of her original letters found here are on display.

The home, a 20-room Victorian house on the prairie, is complete with a secret room and a 2,550-book library that features Civil War and congressional sections. Called the Pink Castle (its distinct pink color was chosen by pioneer artist· Charles T. Greener in 1894), the mansion is open daily from Memorial Day through Labor Day from 1 to 4 p.m. and at other times by appointment. Call (605) 598-4285 for a guide. Admission is $8 per person.

Faulkton is called the Carousel City because it is home to the state's only electrically operated permanent 1925 Parker carousel. The carousel features 19 original aluminum-cast horses. Located on 9th Avenue South, the **Happy Times Carousel** can be enjoyed for free Wed 7 to 9 p.m., and from 3 to 5 p.m. and 6:30 to 8 p.m. Sat and Sun during the summer season. Call (605) 598-6515 for more information.

One thing that visitors to Faulkton cannot miss seeing is a mural painted on three sides of the 110-foot-tall grain elevator that dominates the town and the surrounding plains. Said to be South Dakota's third largest public art project, following Mt. Rushmore and the Crazy Horse Memorial, the photo-realistic black and white image of a young boy and girl handing western hats to each other shows every fold in their clothing to every hair on their heads. The super-large art project got its start when David Hedt, an Australian transplant who manufactures farm equipment in Faulkton, arranged to have a fellow Aussie, muralist Guido van Helten, visit the town in 2016. Van Helten, who painted the mural in about a month after power-washing away the elevator's original paint, has painted large murals from Portugal and Wales to India and Iceland and places in between. To facilitate visitors, three viewing platforms have been built around the grain elevator complex.

Sisseton Lakes Area

If you travel 53 miles east of Aberdeen on US 12, you reach **Webster,** which sits on the cusp of an area dense with glacial lakes. Start with a visit to the **Day County Museum,** 214 Eighth Ave. West, in the basement of the Day

County Courthouse. Artifacts include Native American bow and arrows, spears, arrowheads, beautiful beaded items, stone tools, a drummer's stick, and three beaded war clubs. Among the farm equipment used by early-day settlers are cow and sheep bells, single and double oxen yokes, an iron hoe, and a hand corn planter. One of the more unusual items is a hair wreath made in 1865 from human hair, which was either crocheted, knitted, or wound around cardboard to make flower petals. The free museum is open 2 to 5 p.m. Mon, Wed, and Fri. For more information, call (605) 345-3765.

For an utterly eclectic museum experience, Webster also has the **Museum of Wildlife, Science & Industry.** The assortment of 23 buildings includes a shoe-shaped one housing a shoe collection, farmhouses, a jail, church, post office, and oddities such as the world's largest hairball. Open daily mid-May through mid-Oct. Call (605) 345-4751 or check sdmuseum.org for more details.

If you head 10 miles east on US 12 and turn north on 444th Avenue, you can find the **Blue Dog State Fish Hatchery** at 44437 139A St. in Waubay. Considered the largest hatchery in the state, the 53-acre facility produces 60 million fish a year. Stop at the visitor center and aquarium to learn how they harvest eggs, incubate them, and rear northern pike, walleye, yellow perch, large and smallmouth bass, bluegill, and crappie to stock the state's lakes. They also raise cold-water species, such as trout and Chinook salmon in the winter. Stop by between 8:30 a.m. and 4 p.m. Mon through Fri. Check gfp.sd.gov/bluedog/ for details.

If you head back to Webster and follow Highways 25 and 17 to the north for about 23 miles, you'll reach **Fort Sisseton State Park,** which is in the countryside southwest of Lake City. Here, you can step back into the western frontier at this 1864 site originally called Fort Wadsworth. To see it truly come to life with the bang of muzzleloaders, a whiff of black powder, and the clip-clop of cavalry horses, catch the annual Fort Sisseton Festival the first weekend in June. There also are a visitor center and museum, plus a self-guided tour of the buildings, open the weekend before Memorial Day through September. The park offers camping, cabins, boating, canoeing, hiking, and fishing. Call (605) 448-5474 for details on hours and other information or visit gfp.sd.gov/parks/detail/fort-sisseton-historic-state-park.

Two other notable state parks within 30 miles also are worth exploring. **Roy Lake State Park** at 11547 Northside Dr. in Lake City is only 20 minutes from Fort Sisseton State Park and offers a large, nicely shaded lakeside campground and camping cabins. With canoe and kayak rentals, hiking, a boat launch, beach, disc golf, and fishing, it's an ideal pick for a weekend of family camping. It is also a good option for skiing. For information, check gfp.sd.gov/parks/detail/roy-lake-state-park/ or call (605) 448-5701.

Worth noting: Families have been sharing meals along this shore since AD 1300 or earlier, according to burial mounds and artifacts found nearby. Call (800) 710-2267 or visit campSD.com for site reservations at either Fort Sisseton or Roy Lake.

If you follow winding CR 10 east of Highway 10 (a good map will help), you'll reach **Sica Hollow State Park.** Sica, a native word pronounced "she-cha," means evil or bad with Dakota lore telling of reddish bogs thought to be the blood of their ancestors and of other mysterious happenings. These days, the Trail of Spirits is a nationally designated trail and considered a scenic hike into the woods, along waterfalls and through patches of wildflowers. You can find campsites here as well, along with snowmobile trails and cross-country skiing in the winter. The 900-acre park has 8 miles of horse trails. Check gfp .sd.gov/parks/detail/sica-hollow-state-park or call (605) 448-5701 for more information.

One of the most pleasant ways to enjoy the gorgeous scenery of this region and its coteau topography is to take a trail ride with **Prairie Sky Ranch,** 44370 109th St., about 6 miles southwest of tiny Veblen. It's a gorgeous view and fantastic experience to spend a night in one of their cabins on the coteau—even with a storm rolling in and offering Mother Nature's sound-and-light show. Like most private South Dakota ranches or bed-and-breakfasts, hunters are their main customers. Your best bet is to make reservations before those seasons open. Call (605) 738-2411 or go to prairieskyranch.com for more information.

The Coteau des Prairies is the highest point between Winnipeg, Manitoba, Canada, and the Gulf of Mexico, and the Appalachians and the Black Hills. Lewis and Clark referred to it as the "mountain of the prairie" on their 1814 expedition maps. Today it's best known as an area where wind turbines spin

birdingtip

If you're going birding, bring binoculars, a good camera, and a helpful guide such as the *Northeastern South Dakota Glacial Lakes Birding Guide*. If you cannot find a copy at tourism offices, download one at gfp.sd.gov/userdocs/glacial-lakes-birding.pdf.

Coteau des Prairies

The often overlooked but beautiful National Natural Landmark known as Coteau des Prairies ("hills of the prairie") is a wedge-shaped plateau that rises more than 2,000 feet above the flat prairie of South Dakota, stretches 100 miles in width, and runs 200 miles, crossing into both southwestern Minnesota and Iowa.

Traverse Gap

From the Sisseton exit, 232, on I-29, head about ten miles to the east and south on South Dakota Hwy. 10 which leads toward Browns Valley, Minnesota, less than a half mile east of the border between the two states. In this area, a shallow valley links the south end of Lake Traverse, to the north, with Big Stone Lake, less than five miles to the south. Called the Traverse Gap, this valley is the southernmost point of the drainage basin that empties into Hudson's Bay more than 800 miles to the north in Canada, while conversely, the waters in the southern end of the valley usually go to the Gulf of Mexico, more than 1,100 miles to the south. However, with everything here at practically the same elevation–897 feet above sea level–the waters of the two lakes move between each other on windy days or during floods.

across the horizon and take advantage of coteau-influenced winds, especially in the southeast portion in Minnesota.

From Sica Hollow State Park, head back to Highway 10 and head east toward Sisseton. About 3.5 miles west of town you'll see the **Joseph N. Nicollet Tower and Interpretive Center,** which is dedicated to the French mapmaker who could very well be a sort of real-life Lieutenant Dunbar from the Academy Award–winning movie *Dances with Wolves.* (The Kevin Costner movie, by the way, was filmed in South Dakota.) Nicollet spent 1838 and 1839 creating the first accurate map of the vast area between the Mississippi and Missouri Rivers. He was trained as an astronomer in Paris, and he took highly accurate notes in his journals that recorded more than his precise mathematical calculations. Like those of the fictional Dunbar, Nicollet's journals also illuminated a love for the prairies and respect and understanding of native people. He wrote in 1839 of the Coteau des Prairies:

> May I not be permitted to introduce a few reflections of the prairies? . . . Their sight never wearies . . . to ascend one of its undulations, moving from wave to wave over alternate swells and depressions; and finally to reach the vast interminable low prairie, that extends itself in front, be it for hours, days or weeks, one never tires; pleasurable and exhilarating sensations are all the time felt. . . . I pity the man whose soul could remain unmoved under such a scene of excitement.

Today, the 75-foot observation tower with three floors affords a breathtaking view of the great valley carved by glaciers some 40,000 years ago. On clear days you should also see North Dakota and Minnesota. The "mother map" of the Midwest is displayed at the foot of the tower. Nicollet was the first person to create maps that showed elevations and topography changes. He also included many of the Native American names for rivers, lakes, and other natural features, many of which are still used today. He presented the map to the US Senate in 1841. Original artwork by nationally recognized wildlife artist John S. Wilson is displayed in the Interpretive Center, as are paintings depicting the Dakota people Nicollet described in his journals. The tower is open May through Oct, 10 a.m. to 5 p.m. Mon through Fri, and 1 to 4 p.m. Sun. Call (605) 698-7621 for more information.

While you're in the area, stop by the ***Stavig House Museum*** at 112 First Ave. W in Sisseton. The museum follows the lives of Norwegians in the area through many walks of life, from entrepreneur to humble fisherman. During the summer, the three-story 1916 Victorian home is open from 10 a.m. to 4 p.m. Thurs through Sat, 1 to 4 p.m. Sun. Open by appointment and for special events in the winter. A guided tour costs $5. Call (605) 698-4561 for more information and check sissetonmuseum.com/stavig-house.

From Sisseton take US 12 east to I-29 and go south until you reach the crossroads of I-29 and US 212. It is here that you will find ***Watertown.*** Known as the Lake City, Watertown quite naturally lives up to its name; the town is situated along the Big Sioux River and is bordered by Lake Kampeska and Lake Pelican. Originally called Kampeska, the settlement owed its initial boom to the railroads. These days it's a mostly agriculture-based community (population 21,995), diversified in small grains, row crops, and livestock.

No Watertown traveler can miss seeing its best-known attraction—the ***Redlin Art Center***—with its grandiose hilltop location and 24 massive granite columns that make it visible for miles. It may be tempting to skip if you think you've seen enough of artist Terry Redlin's work on Boy Scout tins, calendars, and puzzles, but the several floors inside tell a touching tale of a humble artist

The Legend of Sam Brown

The Dakotas are rich with legends great and small. One such hero is **Sam Brown,** who in 1866 was chief scout for Fort Wadsworth, now known as Fort Sisseton. He was told of an approaching Dakota war party, and Sam sent a warning message to a fort farther north. Sam mounted his horse and set off to scout a camp 60 miles west. When he arrived, he discovered that the war party was simply several Dakota delivering word of a new peace treaty. Sam knew that to prevent bloodshed, he must intercept his warning. Struggling through the freezing rain and snow of a ruthless spring blizzard, he managed to reach the fort by morning. But as he slipped from his horse, exhausted and half frozen, he was unable to stand. Sam Brown's heroic 150-mile ride cost him the use of his legs. He never walked again.

b&binthe country

The *Dakota Bed and Breakfast*, 45587 177th St., offers a pastoral country setting with grazing sheep and big-sky views that would fit right in with a Terry Redlin painting. The house built in 2008 includes four guest rooms and three bathrooms, six miles from Watertown. Call (605) 520-2521 or go to dakota-bed-breakfast.business .site.

from Watertown who poignantly captured scenes of everyday midwestern life that he called "romantic realism."

You can view Redlin's entire collection of more than 150 original paintings—from early sketches and wildlife scenes to the stirringly patriotic *America the Beautiful*. His "An American Portrait" series depicts a single home through several decades starting when the family's son was young and climbing trees to when a military officer arrives with news of the young man's death. There's a reason they keep a box of tissues near the video about those paintings. The center is also home to a collection of artifacts from **Langenfeld's Ice Cream and Dairy,** owned and operated by the family of Terry's wife, Helene. The center closes on major holidays, but its sprawling grounds make it a popular spot for watching Watertown's Fourth of July fireworks. The art center is open 9 a.m. to 5 p.m. Mon through Fri, 10 a.m. to 4 p.m. Sat, and noon to 4 p.m. Sun, with longer hours in the summer months. Admission is free. Call (877) 873-3546 or visit redlinart.com for more information.

Don't miss a trip into Watertown's sizable historic downtown. Besides numerous secondhand shops, there are several places worth checking out. The **Watertown Confectionery,** 116 E. Kemp Ave., features addictive chocolate-covered crushed jalapeño potato chips and other sweet treats, but it has

pheasantsgo wild

The Bramble Park Zoo was started in 1912 as a display of pheasants and waterfowl donated by Frank Bramble. Bramble also was instrumental in getting South Dakota to put 250 pairs of Chinese ringneck pheasants into the wild in 1911. They—obviously—thrived and have become a key part of South Dakota's culture.

become an even bigger draw for home brewers, winemakers, and even soda pop fans who come for classes, kits, and ingredients to make their own beverages, from a foamy stout and frothy root beer to special-occasion wines. For more information, call (605) 753-5249 or visit watertownconfectionery.com.

Across the street, **Birchtree Gallery and Framing** (605-881-0626; watertownartglass.com) offers stained glass, mosaic, and lapidary art classes, along with a nice variety of local artwork. You can also admire paintings and catch local musicians at the elegant **Goss Opera House** just down the block at 100 E. Kemp Ave. Lovingly restored, this historic building's main floor offers an elegant, eclectic spot for drinks, coffee, ice cream, and date-night dinners. Be sure to ask if you can take a peek at the 1889 opera house upstairs. It features lakeside murals and a Pied Piper leading a line of children. Call (605) 878-4677 or visit gossoperahouse.com for more information.

Pop into the **Codington County Heritage Museum** in a former Carnegie Library at 27 First Ave. SE, if you're interested in local history. Exhibits are heavy on war memorabilia, plus Native American, pioneer, and railroad artifacts. It's open 10 a.m. to 5 p.m. Mon through Fri in the summer and 1 to 5 p.m. in the off-season, along with 1 to 5 p.m. Sat. Admission is free; donations are accepted. Call (605) 886-7335 or visit cchsmuseum.org for more information.

If you meander into the residential area on the north side of town, you'll find more history at the **Mellette House,** 421 5th Ave. NW. Arthur C. Mellette, was appointed governor of the Dakota Territory by President Benjamin Harrison and later was elected governor of the new state of South Dakota. Free guided tours offer insight into South Dakota life in the 1880s as seen through one of its leading families. Artifacts in the Victorian-era rooms include Maggie Mellette china painting, crazy quilts made by the maid, and Native American beadwork and sashes. The home is open May 1 through Oct 1, Tues through Sun from 1 to 5 p.m. Call (605) 886-4730 or visit mellettehouse.org.

If you're traveling with children, don't miss **Bramble Park Zoo,** 800 10th St. NW, which brings you face-to-face with playful lemurs, a white Bengal tiger, and black bears among more than 500 mammals, reptiles, and birds from around the world as well as those native to the Great Plains. The zoo's small size keeps it relaxed and easy to get close to animals, especially free-roaming birds such as a scarlet ibis and peafowl that trail you like hungry

Buffalo Ridge

Buffalo Ridge Resort, 45 miles southeast of Watertown and near the Minnesota border, ranks among South Dakota's more intriguing places to stay. The centerpiece is the 19-room Herrick Hotel, a classy and art-filled transformation of the former South Dakota's first School for the Blind and Visually Impaired that opened in 1900. The resort opened in 2009 on the edge of Gary, population 225. The shaded, peaceful setting makes it a destination wedding spot and business retreat—especially for people in the wind industry that thrives in this region. The property includes more than 30 campsites and a tipi, walking trails, trout fishing at Lake Elsie, and the Rock Room Bar and Grill. Call (605) 272-7777 or go to buffaloridge.com for more information.

shadows. Indoors, the Terry Redlin Environmental Center includes dioramas with mounted animals and a variety of aquariums. On weekends in the summer, zookeepers offer special talks. The zoo is open year-round, weather permitting, from 10 a.m. to 7 p.m. in the summer, and from 10 a.m. to 4 p.m. in the winter. Admission ranges from free for ages 2 and under to $10 for adults. Call (605) 882-6269 or visit brambleparkzoo.com for general information and special events.

If you take I-29 south from Watertown for 44 miles, you'll reach the state's largest university, South Dakota State University, in **Brookings,** home to 23,938 people. The university enriches the community in many ways, from ice cream to an art museum, from gardens to college games that thrum with Jackrabbit pride.

It also boasts one of the state's best family attractions: **The Children's Museum of South Dakota** at 521 4th St. Even if you don't have kids or grandkids along or a few hours to explore its locally inspired exhibits, it's worth stopping by to see this inspirational and clever reuse of a historic school built in the 1920s. You can grab a hot or frozen coffee or a full meal (including a playful grilled cheese that looks like an owl) at the museum's **Coteau Cafe** in an open and airy atrium added onto the school in 2010. The many windows offer an entertaining view of the prairie-themed outdoor play area. Summer's definitely the best time to visit because you can watch kids fishing in a pond, splashing in a river, going through the prairie grass maze, and digging up dinosaur fossils. The big hit for most: a baby T-rex and his mama, who both pack a roar and move realistically enough to send some kids scurrying. The museum's open 10 a.m. to 5 p.m. Tues through Sat and noon to 5 p.m. Sun. Admission is $8 a person, but you can dine here without going into the museum. Call (605) 692-6700 or visit prairieplay.org for more information.

Across the street at 424 5th St. is another example of the town's creative architectural transformations. What was once a 1958 bank with drive-through lanes is now home to a boutique and the **Old Market Eatery and Bar.** The drive-through area was enclosed in glass to become a heated porch that's perfect for dining on balmy summer days when the breeze wafts through and the sun shines in. Try one of their citrusy salads, hand-cut market fries, fragrant hummus made with basil, and desserts such as tangy rhubarb upside-down cake. Open Mon through Sat 11 a.m. until bar closes; Sun closed. Call (605) 692-5757 or visit oldmarketeatery.com for more information.

While downtown, take a stroll to admire the colorful summer landscaping. The community's support of gardening shouldn't be a surprise when it's home to **McCrory Gardens and State Arboretum,** at 631 22nd Ave. With 20 acres of formal display gardens and 45 acres of arboretum, it's called the

Old-fashioned Hamburgers and Malts

For a blast from the past, don't miss **Nick's Hamburger Shop** at 427 Main, a local institution since 1929. Their burgers were priced at a nickel and haven't gone above $2.19. That means even money-strapped college students should be able to hop onto one of the red vinyl bar stools and splurge on fries, homemade pie, or a thick shake to go with it. They're open 11 a.m. to 7 p.m. Mon through Fri, 11 a.m. to 4 p.m. Sat. Call (605) 692-4324 or go to nickshamburgers.com to learn more.

prettiest quarter section in the state, and a visitor center built in 2012 makes an impressive entrance. No wonder that McCrory Gardens is among the top 10 small botanical gardens in the nation. Visitors can wander 14 formal theme gardens and a rose garden with more than 30 varieties, an herb garden, a sensory garden, a children's maze, a historic gas station renovated as a garden cottage, and a memorial to Governor George S. Mickelson. You can check out what's up and coming in the trial garden for All-America seed selections and explore a "green" building constructed with straw bales for insulation and crowned with sedum on the living roof. Admission is $6 ages 8 to 64; $4 ages 6 and 7, military personnel, and SDSU employees; free for children under 5 and SDSU students. Call (605) 688-6707 or visit mccrorygardens.com for more information.

You'll find several good stops at South Dakota State University's campus along Medary Avenue. The **South Dakota Art Museum,** at the intersection of Harvey Dunn and Medary Streets, features permanent galleries, changing exhibitions featuring national and international artists, lectures, workshops, guided tours, and a gift shop packed with artsy and regionally made gifts. The absolute must-see: Harvey Dunn's *The Prairie Is My Garden,* one of Dunn's most iconic paintings that took inspiration from his childhood as the son of South Dakota homesteaders. Dunn's painting *Something for Supper* was among 20 stamps that honored America's greatest illustrators in 2001. Dunn was one of eight artists chosen to document World War I as it was happening and was so prolific in later decades that he once produced more than 55 paintings in 11 weeks. The museum has more than 112 of Dunn's works, but also honors other notable South Dakota artists. Oscar Howe is among its featured Native American artists, and children's book illustrator Paul Goble is featured in a child-friendly exhibit and puppet theater. The museum is open from 10 a.m. to 5 p.m. Mon through Fri, from 10 a.m. to 4 p.m. Sat. It's also open noon to 4 p.m. Sun. Admission is free, although $2 to $3 donations are encouraged. For more information, call (605) 688-5423 or visit southdakotaartmuseum.com.

About a block away at the intersection of Medary Avenue and 11th Street you'll find the ***South Dakota Agricultural Heritage Museum.*** Giant harvesters, tractors, and displays of engines show the evolution of farming technology and South Dakota's influence on building and improving the machinery that gathers the state's crops. Among the engines is the Briggs and Stratton brand, founded and built by South Dakota State University graduates. The museum also includes a "Life on the Land" gallery with an original Dakota Territory claim shanty and replica of a 1915 farmhouse. Exhibits rotate, but all offer a slice of life on the farm. It's open 10 a.m. to 5 p.m. Mon through Fri, as well as 10 a.m. to 4 p.m. Sat; noon to 4 p.m. Sun. Closed Sun Jan through Mar, and state holidays. Admission is free, and you can call (605) 688-6226 or visit sdstate .edu/agmuseum for more information.

If you're looking for a tasty souvenir of Brookings's agricultural heritage, head to the second building to the north on the east side of Medary Ave. where the ***Dairy Bar*** is in Alfred Dairy Science Hall. Pride in SDSU ice cream can be felt throughout the region, and the campus claims to have invented cookies-and-cream ice cream in the 1970s. You can choose from several riffs on the standard cookies-and-cream, which may be minty or sweetened with extra caramel. The Dairy Bar, remodeled in 2011 to feel polished and welcoming, offers 60 rotating flavors of ice cream throughout the year, such as sweetly nutty butter almond, peanut butter revel, and tangerine sherbet. You can also find cheese varieties, butter, and milk. All products are made at the SDSU Davis Dairy Plant (also rebuilt in 2011), which involves students in processing 18,000 pounds of milk a week. The Dairy Bar is open 8:30 a.m. to 5:30 p.m. Mon through Fri. Call (605) 697-2585 or visit sdstate.edu/ds/plant for more information.

Ice-cream aficionados should also beeline to the ***Pheasant Restaurant and Lounge*** in the southwest section of Brookings at 726 Main Ave. South. It has been serving the area since 1949, but third-generation general manager Michael Johnson has transformed it into a chic eatery with an outdoor patio, frequent jazz and live music nights, local wines and microbrews, appetizers like pheasant lettuce wraps, fresh twists on juicy burgers (think crostini burger or bison burger with Thai seasoning), and wildly creative ice cream. The restaurant also has a classy Coteau des Prairies olive oil and vinegar bar in the lobby with exotic flavors that infuse the restaurant's menu with light, zingy salad dressings, zippy marinades, and even unusual desserts. Artisan ice cream maker Trevor Clements crafts out-of-the-box flavors such as 18-year-old balsamic, Swedish lingonberry, sweet corn, coffee ice cream with candied bacon, and a zippy cayenne ginger Fireworks ice cream with Pop Rocks for some pzazz. He also makes sorbets such as peach Riesling or watermelon basil. If you want a sweet way to enjoy a beer, try the dulce de leche ice cream in a Brau Brothers oatmeal stout. Plan on leaving absolutely stuffed and wanting to try more. For details on daily specials, scheduled musicians, or hours, call (605) 692-4723 or go to pheasantrestaurant.com.

South of Brookings and 30 miles north of Sioux Falls is the **Royal River Casino,** located in **Flandreau** off I-29 at exit 114. The casino, owned by the Santee Sioux tribe, has rejuvenated the community of 2,333 residents. The town, situated along the Big Sioux River, was settled in 1869 by 25 Christian Santee Sioux families who bravely gave up their tribal rights—and their surnames—so that they could homestead. For more information, call (877) 912-5825 or visit royalrivercasino.com.

Religious themes recur in Flandreau through several historic churches built in the 1800s. Most notable is the **First Presbyterian Church,** 1.4 miles north of town on SD 13, the oldest continuously operating church in South Dakota.

Local events include the **Good Old Summertime Festival** during the Fourth of July and the **Santee Sioux Powwow** during the third week of July when residents don their full regalia to perform traditional ceremonies.

Land of Laura Ingalls Wilder

Generations of Laura Ingalls Wilder fans from across the globe have found their way to tiny **De Smet** (population 1,067), the real setting for *Little House on the Prairie*, 42 miles west of Brookings at the intersection of SD 25 and US 14 (also part of the Laura Ingalls Wilder Historic Highway that runs from Wisconsin to South Dakota). Fresh-faced little girls and even grown-ups in crisp gingham bonnets evoke the stories of the town's most famous writer each summer during the **Laura Ingalls Wilder Pageant,** and the saplings that Pa Ingalls planted so long ago are now mature cottonwoods. Laura moved here as a child in 1879, and the prairie town figured prominently in six of her pioneer adventures books.

You can see many sites mentioned in the books. Start with the Laura Ingalls Wilder Historic Homes Tour where you can see the railroad surveyor's shanty where the family first lived in De Smet, the schoolhouse where Laura went to school, a replica of the Brewster school where she first taught, and the final house Pa built for his family in 1887 after giving up the homestead. It's filled with artifacts, exhibits on Laura's career and that of her journalist daughter, Rose, exhibits of the *Little House* books (including editions printed in other languages) and their illustrator Garth Williams, plus fascinating information on the real people who inspired these beloved stories. Admission is $14 for adults; $7 for children 5 and older. Call (605) 854-3383 or go to discoverlaura

.org for more information. De Smet also offers maps for visiting some sites on your own, including Silver Lake and the cemetery where Charles, Caroline, and Carrie Ingalls are buried.

Most visitors time a trip to De Smet to catch the July pageant, performed during three weekends on the open prairie a mile southeast of De Smet. Gates open at 6 p.m. when kids can take a ride in a horse-drawn wagon as they wait for the 8 p.m. show time. Guests find a seat on benches or in their own chairs as the sun is setting, and kids scramble up front with blankets and popcorn. Each year's script takes inspiration from different books with *The Long Winter* and *By the Shores of Silver Lake* being among the recent productions. Seating is general admission. Adults $12; ages 6 to 12 $8; 5 and under free. Visit desmet pageant.org or call (800) 880-3383 for advance tickets.

For kids, the best attraction is roaming the Ingalls' Homestead, a quarter section that Pa Ingalls claimed in 1880. Kids will love finding farm cats, seeing newborn foals or calves, ducking into a sod house, riding in a covered wagon, exploring barns, trying out pioneer chores like laundry, and driving a buggy to the one-room schoolhouse where the bell rings to announce classes. The homestead also offers a few tent and RV sites plus the chance to sleep in a bunkhouse or covered wagons (a fresh twist on a camping cabin). The open prairie can get hot by day, but it's also on a small rise, which helps cool it down by night and offers spectacular views of the sky. The homestead's open 9 a.m. to 7 p.m. daily Memorial Day weekend through Labor Day weekend with shorter hours throughout Sept and Oct. Admission is $15 per person over the age of 5. For details, call (800) 776-3594 or visit ingallshomestead.com.

To truly experience a place, you need to attend its state fair. Founded in 1885, the **South Dakota State Fair** claims to be one of the biggest ag-focused fairs in the nation. It's a true dose of Americana, a place where home-canned goods, roller coasters, livestock, machinery, race cars, rodeos, 4-H, and deep-fried foods all converge from the Thurs before Labor Day through Labor Day. Gates open 7 a.m. to 8 p.m. Daily admission is $6 for adults and $4 for kids ages 6 to 15. Visit sdstatefair.com or call (800) 529-0900 for more information.

The **Dakotaland Museum** is also located on the fairgrounds with more than 5,000 artifacts celebrating the heritage and history of Huron and Beadle County. It includes the entire Kouf family mammal and bird collections. Admission is free for 17 and younger; $5 for adults. The museum is open Memorial Day to Labor Day, from 10 a.m. to 6 p.m. Mon through Fri; 2:30 to 6:30 p.m. Sat; and 1 to 3 p.m. Sun. For more information, call (605) 352-4626 or visit thedakotalandmuseum.org.

Huron, population 13,118, and the Beadle County seat, also was home to the first elected female US senator, Gladys Pyle, who served in the Senate during the 1930s. This pioneering feminist's home, the **Pyle House Museum,** 376 Idaho Ave. SE, is open to the public. The 1894 Queen Anne–style building features stained glass, ornately carved golden oak woodwork, and Gladys's original furnishings. The home is open from 1 to 3:30 p.m. daily or by appointment. Call (605) 352-2528 or visit huronsd.com for more information.

Also in the annals of political and state history is Hubert H. Humphrey, the former senator and vice president of the US. He worked at his father's Huron drugstore during the Great Depression, and the still-operating **Humphrey Drugstore** retains some of that mid-1930s atmosphere and Humphrey family memorabilia at 233 Dakota Ave. South. Humphrey's nephew now runs the store, which is open from 8:30 a.m. to 6 p.m. daily. Call (605) 352-4064 for more information.

fishingformore

Walleye dominate the fishing scene in northeastern South Dakota, and most are caught trolling over hard gravel or sand bottoms. Other fish found in the area are smallmouth and largemouth bass, white bass, bullheads, yellow perch, and northern pike. More than 120 glacial lakes dot the northeastern landscape of the state. Anglers who travel to this rolling farm and ranch country will find that the lakes range in size from several acres to more than 16,000 acres. There are 16 state parks and recreation areas and several municipal and private campgrounds in the region. Resorts can be found at most of the larger lakes, but a few of the glacial lakes remain undeveloped and may be surrounded by private land.

Another way to learn the community's history is to check out its "Murals on the Town," a project that uses buildings as canvases with scenes from farming to the arrival of the railroad.

Located 15 miles northeast of Huron, **Lake Byron** has consistently been one of the top producers of trophy walleye. Expect to catch yellow perch, black crappie, carp, Northern pike, and black bullheads as well on this 1,805-acre lake. If you're not into dropping a line, try water-skiing, ski-boarding, camping, or picnicking.

Where to Stay in Northeastern South Dakota

ABERDEEN

AmericInn by Wyndham
310 Centennial St. S
(605) 225-4565
(800) 634-3444
Moderate

Best Western Ramkota Hotel
1400 8th Ave. NW
(605) 229-4040
Moderate

Foote Creek B&B
12841 383rd Ave.
(606) 225-1617
footecreek.com
Moderate

TownePlace Suites by Marriott
402 Norwood St. S
(605) 725-3500
marriott.com
Moderate

BROOKINGS

Country Inn & Suites
3000 Lefevre Dr.
(605) 692-3500
Moderate

Hampton Inn and Suites
3017 Lefevre Dr.
(605) 697-5232
brookingssuites
.hamptoninn.com
Moderate

Holiday Inn Express Hotel and Suites
3020 Lefevre Dr.
(605) 692-9060
hiexpress.com
Moderate

DE SMET

The Prairie House Manor Bed and Breakfast
209 Hwy. 25 S
(605) 854-9131or
(800) 297-2416
prairiehousemanor.com
Moderate

FLANDREAU

Royal River Casino and Hotel
607 Veterans St.
(877) 912-5825
Moderate

HURON

Best Western of Huron
2000 Dakota Ave. S
(605) 352-2000
Moderate

Crossroads Hotel at Huron Event Center
100 4th Ave. SW
(800) 876-5858
Moderate

Super 8 Motel
2189 Dakota Ave.
(605) 352-0740
Inexpensive

WATERTOWN

Dakota Sioux Casino
16415 Sioux Conifer Rd.
(800) 658-4717
Moderate

Days Inn
2900 9th Ave. SE
(605) 884-5067
daysinn.com
Moderate

Ramkota Hotel & Watertown Event Center
1901 9th Ave. SW
(605) 886-8011
ramkotawatertown.com
Moderate

Where to Eat in Northeastern South Dakota

ABERDEEN

Maverick Steaks and Cocktails
720 Lamont St. S
(605) 225-1314
maverickssteak.com
Moderate to expensive

Minervas Restaurant and Bar
1400 8th Ave. NW
(605) 226-2988
minervas.net
Moderate to expensive

Palm Garden Cafe
602 S. 3rd St.
(605) 725-4240
palmgardencafe.com
Inexpensive

Sammy's Restaurant & Omelette Shop
212 S. Main St.
(605) 229-4753
Inexpensive

SELECTED CHAMBERS OF COMMERCE

Aberdeen Convention & Visitors Bureau
10 Railroad Ave. SW
PO Box 78
Aberdeen 57402
(605) 225-2414 or
(800) 645-3851
visitaberdeensd.com

Brookings Area Chamber of Commerce and Convention Bureau
415 8th St. S
Brookings 57006
(605) 692-6125
brookingssd.com
brookingschamber.org

Huron Chamber & Visitors Bureau
1725 Dakota Ave. S
Huron 57350
(605) 352-0000 or
(800) 487-6673
huronsd.com

Sisseton Chamber of Commerce
406 2nd Ave. W
Sisseton 57262-0221
(605) 698-7261
sisseton.com

Watertown Area Chamber of Commerce and Convention and Visitors Bureau
1 E. Kemp Ave.
Watertown 57201
(605) 753-0282 or
(800) 658-4505
Visitwatertownsd.com

BROOKINGS

Cottonwood Bistro
1710 6th St.
(605) 692-8938
cottonwoodcoffee.com
Inexpensive

Sake Japanese Restaurant
724 22nd Ave. S
(605) 692-2888
Moderate

DE SMET

Ward's Store and Bakery
127 Calumet Ave. SE
(605) 854-3688
Inexpensive

HURON

Hangar Restaurant & Ace Lounge
1004th St. SW
(605) 352-1639
Moderate

La Hacienda
2933 Dakota Ave. S
(605) 352-3001
Inexpensive

Prime Time Tavern
2110 Dakota Ave. S
(605) 352-7631
Moderate

SISSETON

Crossroads Restaurant
Dakota Connection Casino
46102 Hwy. 10
(605) 698-4273
dakotaconnection.com
Moderate

Rosalie's Restaurant, Bakery and Lounge
9 8th Ave. E
(605) 698-7401
Inexpensive

WATERTOWN

Guadalajara
1509 9th Ave. SE
(605) 882-4548
Moderate to expensive

Dempsey's Brewery Pub
127 N. Broadway
(605) 882-9762
Inexpensive to moderate

Gather
122 E. Kemp Ave.
(605) 878-0177
Inexpensive to Moderate

WAVERLY

Waverly Steakhouse & Lounge
121 1st Ave.
(605) 882-8686
Moderate

Southeastern South Dakota

With more than 40 museums and galleries, countless parks, and the state's biggest metropolis, southeastern South Dakota easily claims to be the most cosmopolitan corner of the state. It deftly proves that life on the prairie can be chic. It can be pretty in pink, too. Look closely at the landscape—especially at Palisades State Park and at Sioux Falls' Falls Park—and you can see the rosy shades of pink quartzite. You might see that same rosy color glittering off the region's highways as you leave the city behind and head into the countryside to enjoy the parks, small towns, and great outdoors of southeastern South Dakota. The region is easily accessible via east–west I-90 or north–south I-29.

North of Sioux Falls

Tucked between Lake Madison and Lake Herman, the town of *Madison,* population 7,322, is a popular recreation spot. Formed by melting glacial ice thousands of years ago, the 1,350-acre Lake Herman was named for Herman Luce, who settled here in the 1870s with his son. The cabin they built, lived in, and used as a survey office is available for tour in *Lake Herman State Park.*

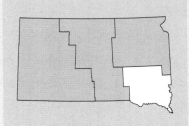

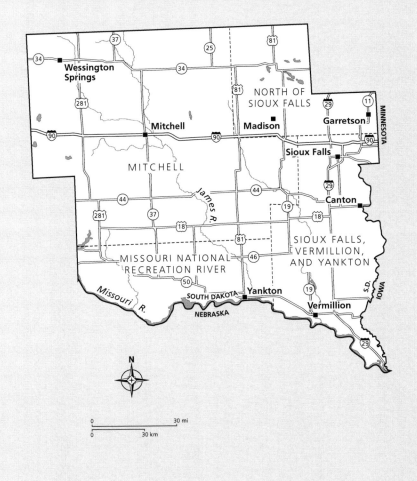

On Lake Madison the Chautauqua summer program was a pioneer's favorite pastime from 1891 to 1933. People gathered to hear lectures and concerts, watch plays, and engage in lively debates. The **Smith–Zimmermann Heritage Museum** on Madison's Dakota State University campus is home to the Chautauqua Collection, which is considered one of the most important in the Midwest. While you're here be sure to look at the Civil War memorabilia, the covered wagon, period clothing, and 1880s parlor. The museum, at 221 NE 8th St., is open from 9 a.m. to 3 p.m. Tues through Fri or by appointment. Admission is free. Call (605) 256-5308 or visit smith-zimmermann.dsu.edu.

Two miles west of Madison, **Prairie Village** is a living museum of an authentic pioneer town. Attractions include antique tractors, an 1893 steam-powered carousel, a sod house, and a log cabin. For more than 50 years, the annual Steam Threshing Jamboree in August has embraced an array of pioneer-worthy events that include horse-powered grain threshing, antique tractor pulling, weaving, and quilting. The village is open 10 a.m. to 5 p.m. Mon through Sat and 11 a.m. to 5 p.m. Sun from Mother's Day until Labor Day. Admission is $5 for adults; $2 for children ages 6 to 12; and free for children under 6. For an additional fee, the carousel is open daily, and train rides are offered on Saturday. Call (605) 256-3644 or (800) 693-3644 or visit prairievillage.org for more information.

The **Quarry Days** celebration is held the fourth weekend of every June in **Dell Rapids,** and the event shows the civic pride this small town has for its quartzite quarries 3 miles east of I-29 and only 15 miles north of the I-29 and I-90 intersection. The bounty of quartzite quarries is handsomely displayed as building stone in walls and foundations throughout the downtown district. Many of the buildings, which showcase Victorian, Romanesque revival, and

BEST ATTRACTIONS IN SOUTHEASTERN SOUTH DAKOTA

Corn Palace	National Music Museum
Dakota Discovery Museum	Old Courthouse Museum
Falls Park	Palisades State Park
Great Plains Zoo and Delbridge Museum	Prairie Village
	Sioux Falls downtown
Lewis and Clark Recreation Area	Washington Pavilion

neoclassical revival architectural styles, are listed on the National Register of Historic Places. The dells were formed more than 12,000 years ago by strong currents of water passing over exposed Sioux quartzite fissures. Native Americans called it *imnizeusteca,* or "canyon."

Winston Churchill once said, "We shape our buildings, and afterwards they shape us," and Dell Rapids' architecture has magnificently primed the community's cultural scene. You can pick up a Dell Rapids Walking Tour guide at the **Dell Rapids History Museum,** 407 E. 4th St., then hit the streets. First stop: Seeing the art deco glamour on the facade of the 1938 **Dells Theatre** at 511 E. 4th St. This restored art deco theater still has its original 1938 paint, seats, stage curtain, and light fixtures. Call (605) 428-4821 for more information.

Another glamorous building is the **Grand Opera House,** built in 1888. Located at 425 E. 4th St., it is where special occasions are celebrated in Dell Rapids. Check out the calendar of events online at dellrapidsgrandoperahouse .com or call (605) 321-9789.

Stay the night in the 1908 **Rose Stone Inn** (504 E. 4th St.; 605-428-3698; rosestoneinn.com) for another experience of small-town intimacy and the iridescence of quartzite, which is the inn's main building material. Originally built as an inn for traveling salesmen and now on the National Register of Historic Places, the B&B offers guest rooms furnished with fashionable pieces from the late-19th and early-20th centuries.

Drive southeast of Dell Rapids and walk in the footsteps of the legendary outlaw Jesse James near **Garretson.** At **Devil's Gulch,** a rocky chasm at least 20 feet across and 50 feet deep, the notorious outlaw stymied a posse trying to catch him after the infamous failed bank robbery in Northfield, Minnesota. The story goes like this: The James brothers were chased into eastern South Dakota. When Jesse reached Devil's Gulch, he reined in his horse and stared into the forbidding chasm. Jesse turned, retraced his steps to get a running start, let out a whooping battle cry, and dug his spurs into his horse. The horse bounded forward. Time stood still; then the bandit lurched forward as his mount landed. He had made it. The posse, too dumbfounded by Jesse's daring jump to follow, simply milled about as the outlaw rode off. Today you can stand on a footbridge that spans Devil's Gulch and picture yourself visiting the site in 1876, just like Jesse James.

Stop in the gift shop for a copy of the seven-point walking trail map that provides additional history and insight to the geography in the area. Call (605) 594-6721 for more information.

Each June, the escapades of the James brothers are celebrated during the **Jesse James Roundup Days** at Split Rock Park, just north of Garretson off SD

11. A Dutch oven cook-off, craft fair, chuck wagon feed, and theater production commemorate the nefarious, although exciting, James brothers' connection to South Dakota. The park is a perfect place for camping, hiking, and other outdoor sports.

To get onto the water, contact Jesse James Pontoon Rides at (605) 594-2225. Owner Bruce Rekstad narrates a pretty wild tale while the boat moves slowly up and down the creek. He grew up in the area and played in a cave that was apparently a hideout of Frank and Jesse James.

Spectacular quartzite chasms are a drawing card, too, in **Palisades State Park,** southwest of Garretson. The view is breathtaking, and the waters here are an inviting and dreamy blue. Colorful red quartzite pinnacles and formations with 50-foot vertical cliffs line Split Rock River, which winds through the park. Please take note of the many posted signs that say, "Don't jump off the cliffs," and then follow that advice, even if you see others doing it. Each summer, someone jumps into the water below onto a big rock under the water line, and the best you can hope for is a broken leg, a medical bill, and a $100 fine. Notice, too, the unique architecture of the WPA (Works Progress Administration) of the 1930s, which features a dam with a waterfall, a bathhouse, bridges, and a rock wall with a flower garden. You can camp at the park or stay in the camping cabins that overlook the river. At a minimum, plan on bringing a picnic lunch, taking a hike, and bringing a camera to capture the scenery. If you're more ambitious, the park's pinnacles—especially the King and Queen rocks—may be tempting to climb. For campsite or cabin reservations, call (605) 594-3824.

Near **Baltic** (10 miles north of exit 402 on I-90 and 15 miles north of Sioux Falls) is the **Earth Resources Observation Systems (EROS) Data Center,** which houses the US government's central archives for nonmilitary satellite images and aerial photography. The largest civilian collection of images of earth from space and high altitudes, EROS requires the largest mainframe computer in the state and one of the largest computer complexes in the US Department of the Interior. The center operates an archive with millions of photographs of the US taken from aircraft and millions more worldwide images acquired by sensors aboard several satellites. The complex reproduces and disseminates data to scientists throughout the world and assists users in the application of such photographs. It definitely offers a fresh way to admire the earth. One study surveys arctic lakes that emit greenhouse gasses; another monitors the movements of a 315-billion-ton iceberg that has split from the continent of Antarctica. Rising sea levels that threaten the existence of islands in Micronesia—eight have already been swallowed by the sea—are also observed. Also, the center's website has one part dedicated to wonderful artistic views of earth: eros.usgs.gov/image-gallery/earth-art. Exhibits in the lobby will take you on an engrossing 30- to 45-minute self-guided tour from 8 a.m. to 4 p.m. Mon through Fri. EROS is closed on federal holidays. Guided one-hour tours are offered at 10 a.m. and 2 p.m. Mon to Fri. Free admission. Visitors are required to show government-issued identification because vehicles will be screened before parking on the grounds; allow up to 15 minutes to enter the building or begin a tour. Some older state driver's licenses are not acceptable; they do not fit enhanced security standards. Bring a passport as backup ID, or call (605) 594-6511 or visit eros.usgs.gov for more details.

Sioux Falls

With a population of 176,888 and continually growing, *Sioux Falls* ranks as the largest city in the state. If you count its entire metropolitan area, it's close to 265,653 residents and has increased by 27 percent since 2000. For visitors, that means there are even more chic boutiques, funky restaurants, and artsy destinations to discover.

A good starting point is *Falls Park,* where the Big Sioux River rumbles across a series of picture-worthy waterfalls. About 7,400 gallons per second drop 100 feet over the falls through beautiful rosy quartzite formations that once drew hardworking pioneers and big dreamers. They were able to harness the river's power to start businesses and a fledgling community in 1865.

The former Sioux Falls Light and Power Company (built in 1908) provides a pretty setting for the *Falls Overlook Cafe,* a popular place to watch the falls while grabbing a light meal or Stensland Ice Cream, a popular cold delight made about 20 miles away. The *Falls Park Visitor Information Center* offers additional information on Falls Park and other Sioux Falls attractions, and includes a five-story observation tower and elevator. Don't miss that chance—it's the best way to see the remarkable path and iconic rocks of the Big Sioux River. Near the tower and center, a restored horse barn now houses the *Stockyards Ag Experience Barn and Plaza,* which explains the historical importance of agriculture to the city plus the "Pasture to Plate" concept of how much the world depends on agriculture for sustenance.

While at the falls, you can wander past the ruins of *Queen Bee Mill,* one of the first businesses to harvest the river's power and grind locally grown wheat.

Richard F. Pettigrew convinced an eastern investor to finance the construction of the huge, seven-story, 1,200-barrel-per-day Queen Bee flour mill. However, it closed only two years after it opened in 1881. Pettigrew also had an idea to use the river's power to slice petrified wood, which was briefly trendy at the turn of the 20th century as America's up-and-coming millionaires were building grand homes. The practice stopped when conservationists found a way to protect Arizona's petrified wood supply.

You can see the unique, colorful beauty of those petrified wood cross-sections on the exterior of the 1889 ***Pettigrew Home and Museum*** at 131 N. Duluth Ave., which is open for tours. Besides developing the mill, R.F. Pettigrew became South Dakota's first full-term US senator. He also was a sea-soned traveler who collected artifacts from across the world and left them for the community to see. They're shown in conjunction with natural history and cultural artifacts from the Siouxland area, such as Native American objects and the home's 5,000-volume research library that contains Pettigrew's personal papers. The site is open from 9 a.m. to 5 p.m. Mon through Sat, and from noon to 5 p.m. Sun, May 1 through Sept 30. After that, it's noon to 5 p.m. every day. Admission is free. Call (605) 367-7097; siouxlandmuseums.com.

Just next door you'll also find the ***Victorian House B&B***, (117 N. Duluth Ave.). After a day of exploring, leave time to also stroll the neighborhood and admire the grand homes built in the late 1800s and early 1900s within ***St. Joseph's Cathedral Historic District,*** stretching between 4th and 10th Streets and bordered by Prairie and Spring Streets. At the B&B, relax on the wrap-around porch or cozy up to the outdoor fireplace on the patio. The home has three second-floor guest rooms. Call (605) 799-1259 or go to thevictorianbedandbreakfast.com for more information.

Head east and downhill to reach downtown. Whet your appetite for his-tory and discover the heritage of the area in the ***Old Courthouse Museum,*** 200 W. 6th St., a restored three-story structure listed on the National Register of Historic Places.

The massive quartzite stone build-ing served as the county courthouse from 1890 to 1962. The first-floor exhib-its bring to life the history of early settlers and the Native Americans who lived on the plains, along with the art and cultural significance of Siouxland. A handsomely laid out building, the Old Courthouse is decorated with 16

didyouknow?

Chislic: Deep-fried cubes of beef or sheep is a specialty usually found in southeast South Dakota, occasionally on menus, at food stands or fairs.

Siouxland: Coined by author Frederick Manfred, Siouxland has become the nickname of a region centered around Sioux Falls and Sioux City, Iowa, that encompasses eastern South Dakota, southwest Minnesota, northwest Iowa, and northeast Nebraska. Manfred's most popular book, *Lord Grizzly,* was about the ordeals faced by plains explorer Hugh Glass in 1823 when he was mauled by a grizzly bear and left for dead by his comrades, after which he crawled more than 200 miles to a trading post.

Exploring Downtown

You could easily spend a weekend strolling, dining, and shopping your way through downtown *Sioux Falls.* The main downtown, anchored by Phillips Avenue, stretches for several blocks that are kept lively with artwork and the fair-weather energy of outdoor cafes. If you cross the **Big Sioux River** at E. 8th Street, you'll reach the up-and-coming, refreshingly hip **East Bank**, where boutiques, cafes, and restaurants infuse historic railroad buildings with great shopping and dining.

You can find public parking in ramps behind Shriver Square and across from the Washington Pavilion for downtown (free on evenings and weekends) and at the Eighth and Railroad Center for the East Bank, which has free parking.

Here's a look at our favorite stops, but you'll want to get a map and guide to decide for yourself given the wealth of choices. For more information, go to dtsf.com.

CH Patisserie
309 Phillips Ave.
(605) 275-0090
chpastries.com
Exquisite pastries, macaroons, and sweets, as well as pastry classes

Child's Play Toys
233 S. Phillips Ave.
(605) 274-8697
childsplaytoys.com
Creative toys, games, and upscale children's clothing and accessories

Great Outdoor Store
201 E. 10th St.
(605) 335-1132
greatoutdoorstoreonline.com
Moisture-wicking clothing and gear needed to enjoy outdoor recreation

Home Porch Gifts
217 Phillips Ave.
(605) 906-8914
homeporchgifts.com
A variety of keepsakes and gifts made in South Dakota

Mama's Ladas
116 W. 11th St.
(605) 332-2772
Mamasladas.com
Homey enchiladas in this small but appealing cafe that also serves cool sangrias

The Market on Phillips
196 E. 6th St.
(605) 275-9463
themarketsf.com
Fine wines, artisan cheeses, and other foodie finds for an upscale picnic

Mrs. Murphy's Irish Gifts
219 S. Phillips Ave.
(605) 333-9700
mrsmurphys.com
All things Celtic, from sweaters to Claddagh rings

murals of different sizes, created by the Norwegian artist Ole Running in 1915. You also can find the Queen City Mercantile at the museum, where local and regional books, crafts, old-fashioned toys, holiday collectibles, souvenirs, and exhibit-related items are for sale. The Old Courthouse Museum is open from

Phillips Avenue Diner

121 S. Phillips Ave.

phillipsavenuediner.com

(605) 335-4977

Hearty breakfasts, juicy burgers, or a Crazy Shake in a retro diner built around an upgraded Airstream trailer

Minervas

301 S. Phillips Ave.

(605) 334-0386

minervas.net

Long been considered one of the best restaurants in the city. A classy establishment, the restaurant is perfect for special occasions, dates, or any time you just want excellent food and impeccable service. Appetizers such as pheasant ravioli, almond duck strips, coconut shrimp, and crabmeat artichoke pique the taste buds. Main course options include Cajun chicken linguine, and Italian sausage and pepper pasta—musts for carb lovers. Meat-and-potato enthusiasts will find a mouthwatering selection of top sirloin, roast prime rib of beef, rib eye, filet mignon, and New York strip-sirloin steaks.

Its adjacent **Paramount Wine Bar** offers a more casual option for drinks and lighter plates. Don't miss trying a strawberry-basil martini dusted with black pepper. It's as fragrant as it is tasty. It also serves chislic, an eastern South Dakota specialty. Stop by between 8 and 11 p.m. Thurs and Fri for live music. Minervas is open from 11 a.m. to 2:30 p.m. and 5 to 10 p.m. Mon through Sat. Limited bar menu served 2:30 to 5 p.m. Mon through Sat. (Dinner reservations are suggested).

Minervas has a sister restaurant called **Spezia,** which is known for its Sunday brunch but also has great pizzas in a more casual setting. Spezia is located at 4801 S. Louise Ave.; (605) 334-7491.

Josiah's Coffeehouse, Cafe and Bakery

104 W. 12th St

(605) 659-8255

Breakfast and lunch with paninis, quinoa and black rice salad, pizzas, and coconut cupcakes

Queen City Bakery

324 E. 8th St.

(605) 274-6060

queencitybakery.com

Savory quiche, homemade granola, decadent cakes like Brooklyn Blackout (devil's food with sea-salt caramel), pies, and supersize cookies such as milk chocolate hazelnut praline

8th and Railroad Center

401 E. 8th St.

Packed with cool cafes and shops such as **Plum's Cooking Store,** which has whatever a kitchen needs from pots and glassware to sauces and spices; **Rug and Relic's** huge selection of exotic textiles and cool boots crafted with rugs; **K Restaurant** with modern American cuisine; and **Sanaa's** with its bright colors and a fragrant whiff of Middle Eastern spice from its fresh salads, savory meats, *fatayers* (flaky pita pockets), and sweet desserts.

8 a.m. to 5 p.m. Mon through Fri, from 9 a.m. to 5 p.m. Sat, and from noon to 5 p.m. on Sun. The museum also stays open until 9 p.m. on Thurs. Closed on major holidays. Free admission. Call (605) 367-4210 or visit siouxlandmuseums .com.

Native Art

If a visit to the Visual Arts Center stirs your interest in Native American art, plan a return visit for the annual **Northern Plains Indian Art Market,** organized by Sioux Falls' Sinte Gleska University on the Rosebud Sioux Reservation in late September. The country's largest art market devoted to Northern Plains tribes includes painting, sculpture, beadwork, jewelry, quillwork, and other unique styles such as ledger art, in which Native Americans would draw stories in old ledger books because they didn't have the luxury of blank art paper. For more information, go to npiam.org or call (605) 856-8100.

Three blocks from the museum, at the intersection of N. Phillips and 8th Street, you can get a brochure for downtown's beloved *SculptureWalk,* which has been bringing big, impressive, and conversation-sparking artworks to the city every year since 2004. Each year, a host of sculptures crafted by artists from across the world are erected in various places in downtown Sioux Falls, and the public votes on which are the best of each year's exhibit. Lately, on one corner, a grizzly bear high-fived passersby while a dancer with an overly stretched out body spun in a spiral, and an angel contemplated nearby. Topping all the sculptures on the walk is "Arc of Dreams," installed by Dale Lamphere in 2019. With two legs of an arch that don't quite touch, the sculpture spans the length of nearly a football field over the Big Sioux River between 6th and 8th Streets and represents the leap of faith that dreamers must make to see their dreams turn into reality. Also, the new SculptureWalk Visitor Center is in the second-floor lobby of the Washington Pavilion, at 301 S. Main Ave. You can also download information at sculpturewalksiouxfalls .com or call (605) 838-8102.

Nostalgic yet hip, funky yet classy, *Zandbroz Variety* (209 S. Phillips Ave.; 605-331-5137; zandbroz.com) offers a fresh blend of fine pens in antique cupboards, fine papers, books, cards, baskets, jewelry, gourmet foods, and other nifty things for giving (or keeping for yourself). Part of the charm is the way everything is displayed, often with vintage cabinetry from the drug-store days and a lot of color. The back room, once a popular soda fountain and coffee bar, now has a wealth of used books and carefully chosen vintage items—all keeping an emphasis on variety. This is eclecticism at its best.

The city is rightfully proud of its *Washington Pavilion of Arts and Science,* a creative transformation of the city's Washington High School at the corner of 11th and Main Streets. Its oldest section opened in 1908 and was expanded over the years, becoming a visually distinctive, 255,000-square-foot

Sioux Falls Parks

Sioux Falls has more than 80 parks in its 3,154-acre park system. There's also a 26-mile paved bike trail that wraps around the city and follows the Big Sioux River Greenway. You can get details by calling (605) 367-8222 or going to siouxfalls.org/parks.

Among the favorite parks is **Terrace Park** (1100 W. 4th St.). The Shoto–Teien Japanese Gardens are located here next to Covell Lake. Built from 1928 to 1936, the two-acre gardens feature a lush array of flowering trees and shrubs, a waterfall and stone pagodas, sculptures and lanterns. The Terrace Park Aquatic Center is a perfect jumping-off point, too, with swimming pools and water slides.

A full-scale cast of Michelangelo's *David* stands in the heart of Sioux Falls at **Fawick Park** (located on 2nd Avenue between 10th and 11th Streets). Thomas Fawick, a Sioux Falls philanthropist and industrialist who made a fortune as an inventor, gave the city the statue in 1972. The statue of *David,* fully in the buff, created enormous controversy when it first arrived. To mollify public opinion, the statue was placed facing away from traffic, and trees were planted to screen it from the street. (Fawick later gave the city the sculptor's statue of *Moses,* which was placed at the corner of 29th Street and Summit Avenue on the Augustana University campus.)

At 12th and Kiwanis Streets, the **USS South Dakota Battleship Memorial** in Sherman Park is a patriotic sample of World War II naval history. The battleship, which participated in every major battle in the Pacific from 1942 to 1945, was the most decorated of World War II. Parts of the actual battleship punctuate a concrete outline of the ship's width and length. Visitors can walk through the concrete configuration and learn about the military personnel who gave their lives while serving on this vessel. A gift shop is open daily 9:30 a.m. to 5:30 p.m. Memorial Day through Labor Day. Call (605) 367-7141 or visit usssouthdakota.com for more information.

building constructed of native Sioux quartzite. The roof balustrade and dentiled cornices are visible from many downtown Sioux Falls locations. The high school closed in 1992 until it was reopened with new purpose in 1999. It has since been a place where visitors can be touched by extraordinary artwork or dig in with interactive science displays.

The Pavilion's ***Visual Arts Center*** features 8 galleries of changing exhibits, including Native American artists, regional and national contemporary visual arts exhibitions, and a hands-on children's gallery. The Visual Arts Center has a collection of 1,600 works, including pieces by noted South Dakota artists Oscar Howe, Lova Jones, and Charles Greener. Other artists represented include Adolf Dehn, Richard Hunt, and Betty Woodman. The 300-seat Husby Performing Arts Center Theater is available for programs requiring more intimate space, such as musical ensembles, lectures, poetry readings, experimental theater, and

Best Sioux Falls Family Attractions

Butterfly House & Aquarium
4320 Oxbow Ave.
(605) 334-9466
butterflyhouseaquarium.org
You'll want to linger and enjoy the fluttering beauty here. Give yourself time to study vibrant corals, anemones, and tropical fish in the many aquariums, reach into the Midwest's only shark and stingray touch tank, and revel in the 80-degree warmth of the butterfly garden. There are more than 800 free-flying butterflies that flit among lush, lovely flowers, including the stunning blue morpho. Open 10 a.m. to 6 p.m. Mon through Sat, and 11 a.m. to 5 p.m. Sun, Memorial Day through Labor Day. The rest of the year, hours are 10 a.m. to 5 p.m. Mon through Sat, and 1 to 4 p.m. Sun. Admission is $9 for 3 to 12 years old; $12 for 13 to 59 years old; and $11 for seniors.

Country Apple Orchard
4 miles south of Sioux Falls on Minnesota Ave.
(605) 743-2424
countryappleorchard.com
Autumn enthusiasts can score their favorite sweet and crunchy apples or pick their own during one of the most treasured rites of the season. You can hop on a tractor-pulled wagon and jump off when you reach the spot where your favorite variety of apple is grown. Also look for pumpkins here each fall.

Great Bear Recreation Park
3 miles east of Sioux Falls on Rice St.
(605) 367-4309
greatbearpark.com
This is a must-visit for downhill skiing a la East River, with 12 runs nearly 1,500 feet long, a 250-foot vertical drop, chairlifts, and a chalet. A tubing hill, outdoor skating, and a terrain park for snowboarders are also offered at the resort. Ski instruction and rentals for

dance and piano recitals. The 1,800-seat Mary W. Sommervold is home to local community groups, as well as the South Dakota Symphony.

If science is more your style, check out the three-story, 21,300-square-foot *Kirby Science Discovery Center,* where you can fly a space shuttle, dig up a dinosaur, try to lift giant blocks of quartzite, watch bees that have a hive just outside the building or touch a tornado. Science adventure films are shown hourly on the four-story dome screen at the Wells Fargo CineDome Theater. For more information on current events, shows, and exhibits, call (877) 927-4728, or visit washingtonpavilion.org.

The *Sidewalk Arts Festival* entertains more than 65,000 visitors each year. The downtown festival along Main and 11th Streets showcases more than 250 artists and vendors from 15 states. The Paladino Hohm Sculpture Garden, both downhill and cross-country skiing are available. The park is also open for hiking during the summer.

Great Plains Zoo and Delbridge Museum
805 S. Kiwanis Ave.

(605) 367-7059

gpzoo.org

This zoo combines the rugged expanse of a North American plain, the wild recesses of an African veldt, and the quiet beauty of the Australian Outback. It is known for its big cat collection, which includes cheetahs and tigers, but there are also wallabies, flamingos, and bears that look cuddlier than they really are. This zoo is recognized nationally for its innovative partnership with the local children's hospital. Cameras in many of the animal habitats stream live video to the patient rooms, entertaining and educating children who otherwise might not visit the zoo for a long, long time. Open daily year-round. The zoo's hours vary with the seasons, and it is closed on New Year's Day, Thanksgiving, Christmas Eve Day, and Christmas. Tickets are $12.75 for adults; $11.75 for senior citizens; $9.25 for children ages 2 to 12; admission is free for children 2 years of age and younger. The Delbridge Museum of Natural History houses one of the largest collections of mounted animals in the world.

Sioux Falls Outdoor Campus
4500 S. Oxbow Ave.

(605) 362-2777

gfp.sd.gov/toc-east/

An initiative of the state Game, Fish, and Parks Department to help people get in touch with the outdoors through workshops and hands-on exhibits. Classes include everything for the outdoors from canoeing and kayaking to fishing, hiking, gardening, bird watching, rock climbing, cooking with Dutch ovens, and more. All classes are free, and most are just one or two sessions. This is also a place to come and enjoy without taking a class. There's a small museum with wildlife exhibits, camping information, and the like, and a butterfly garden, four picnic shelters, and a hiking trail.

on the north side of the Washington Pavilion, always has free entertainment. The festival, which is held the first Saturday after Labor Day, is the annual fund-raiser for the Visual Arts Center at the Washington Pavilion of Arts and Science. Call (605) 367-7397 ext. 2348 or visit washingtonpavilion.org/event/sidewalk-arts-festival.

Near the community of Brandon, just 5 miles east of Sioux Falls on I-90 at exit 406, you'll find ***Big Sioux Recreation Area*** (48351 264th St., Sioux Falls; 605-594-3824; gfp.sd.gov/parks/detail/beaver-creek-nature-area). One of the many treasures at Big Sioux Recreation Area is ***Bergeson's Homestead***—the park's very own little house on the prairie—which was built in 1869 by Ole and Soren Bergeson. Ole was one of the first settlers in Split Rock Township. The log frame, which is constructed of hand-hewn cottonwood, was

Southeastern Wineries

Like many states across the nation, South Dakota has seen a boom in wineries and microbreweries. Many rely on traditions passed down from their pioneer ancestors who brought recipes from the old country and would make wine with whatever fruit was available: rhubarb, chokecherries, raspberries, buffalo berries, juneberries/serviceberries, plums, currants, and dandelions. They've expanded to include the surge in northern-hardy varieties such as Frontenac, Le Crescent, and Valiant grapes that have been developed by Minnesota and South Dakota universities. In most cases, they offer a sweet and festive excuse to hit the road and find a rural winery.

You can download a *wine trail* brochure at southeastsouthdakota.com/what-to-do/winery-trail or call (888) 353-7382. More information also can be found through the South Dakota Wine Growers Association; (888) 353-7382; sdspecialtyproducers.org/producers/beverages/wineries.

Schadé Winery
Schadé Winery has a presence on both sides of the state. Here you can visit its original vineyard in the countryside at 21095 463rd St. in tiny Volga near Brookings; (605) 627-5545; schadewinery.com.

Strawbale Winery
With brightly colored Adirondack chairs, roving chickens, and farm cats, this winery at 47215 257th St. in Renner, offers country charm less than 4 miles from the I-29 and I-90 interchange. The wonderful laid-back atmosphere lends itself well to weekly concerts and an annual folk competition. Besides wine by the bottle, on a hot night you can also get frozen drinks made from their black currant wine and may find crisp stone-fired pizza from vendors. Watch for special wine tastings and appetizers during the holidays, followed by helicopter rides over Sioux Falls' Falls Park lit with Christmas lights; (605) 543-5071; strawbalewinery.com.

Tucker's Walk Vineyard
Look for cold-hardy grape, raspberry, wild plum, and rhubarb wines at this vineyard in the countryside at 48348 254th St., in Garretson (605) 594-6287.

Valiant Vineyards
The state's first winery opened in 1996 at 1500 W. Main St. in Vermillion on the western edge of town overlooking the Missouri River valley. They host the annual Great Dakota Wine Fest in the late summer and offer winery tours and tastings daily. You can even spend the night here at **Buffalo Run Resort,** which offers 5 elegant guest rooms. The Native American, the USD, the Frontier, the Queen Anne, and the Honeymoon Suite are all uniquely decorated. Call (605) 624-4500 or visit valiantvineyards.us.

Wilde Prairie Winery
This vineyard north of Brandon began in 1997. Today, Wilde Prairie Winery produces about five tons of grapes, which translates into about 2,000 gallons or 10,000 bottles of wine annually. They started out with tomato, rhubarb, and dandelion wine before moving toward northern-hardy varietals. The winery's 1911 barn serves as a tasting room or special event venue at 48052 259th St., Brandon; (605) 582-6471; wildeprairiewinery.com.

inadvertently discovered in the 20th century during the process of razing the entire old Bergeson homestead. Notice the fine dovetailed notchwork. If you want to spend the night, the park has campsites and cabins that come with heat, air conditioning, and electricity that would have looked luxurious to Ole and Soren Bergeson in the 1860s.

The **Valley of the Giants Trail** at Big Sioux is a 1.5-mile hiking trail that passes some of the oldest trees in the state. The cottonwood and ash trees provide a heavy cover, almost blocking out the sun. It's a pleasant hike around a little lake. There are 7 more miles of trails in the park, 1.5 miles of paved biking trails, a disc golf course, archery range, equestrian trails, and access to the Big Sioux River Canoe Trail. Call (605) 582-7243 or visit gfp.sd.gov/parks/detail/big-sioux-recreation-area.

Brandon's Hometown Days is an annual festival in McHardy Park each July. The three-day event attracts a wide variety of artists and food vendors. There are also games for the kids, musical entertainment, and a tractor pull.

The annual **Homesteader Day Harvest Festival** at **Beaver Creek Nature Area** (5 miles southeast of Brandon) offers a glimpse into what life on the prairie was like for the pioneers. First, turn back the clock to the year

Watch for Good Earth

South Dakota's newest park, **Good Earth State Park**, opened in 2012 and encompasses 588 acres about 8 miles southeast of Sioux Falls and along the Big Sioux River which forms the border with Iowa. It preserves one of the most significant archaeological sites in North America, spanning both sides of the river and known as Blood Run National Historic Landmark. It is one of the oldest sites of long-term human habitation in the country with more than 5,000 members of the Oneota culture residing here in the summer months. The river, fertile land, availability of pipestone, and protection from prairie winds made it an important gathering place for seasonal ceremonies and as a center of trade. Although the land may have been occupied as long ago as 6500 BC, its prime time as a trading center was from around AD 1300–1700. By the early 1700s, these occupants, who included Omaha, Ponca, Ioway, and Otto, were pushed out by other tribes, including the Lakota and Dakota who themselves had been pushed west by European settlers, or they were wiped out by the diseases Europeans brought. While the state park is still in its infancy and includes trails and guided hikes through the outdoor campus, it's considered a sacred place for Native Americans. An 11,000-square-foot visitor center opened in 2017 to showcase the natural and human histories of the park through a 20-minute, Emmy-nominated video, an 11-foot buffalo-skin lodge, and interactive exhibits. The park is at 26924 480th Ave., Sioux Falls. Call (605) 213-1036 or visit gfp.sd.gov/parks/detail/good-earth-state-park.gov for updates on the park's development.

Ethnic Festivals in Southeastern South Dakota

Schmeckfest started in Freeman in 1959 as a one-day event to celebrate the region's German heritage. It quickly became so popular that it has expanded to where it is now held over two weekends where more than 5,000 people show up. Schmeckfest, which means "tasting festival" in German, serves foods buffet style in one of the buildings on the grounds of Freeman Academy. Among the offerings are stewed beef, pork sausage, fried potatoes, cheese button, poppyseed rolls, and green bean soup. Kuchen (pronounced KOO-gan) pies, which are South Dakota's official dessert, are custard and fruit-filled sweets. Musicals are held in the nearby auditorium after the meals. For more information, visit schmeckfest.com.

Freeman is also the home of the relatively new **Chislic Festival** which proved so popular that 8,000 people showed up for the first one a few years ago, four times what the festival's organizers had expected. Chislic, which is hardly known outside of southeast South Dakota, began as cubed lamb that was deep-fried or grilled and served on skewers with sprinkles of garlic. Since it arrived with German-Russian immigrants in the latter part of the 19th century, the recipe has been altered to sometimes use beef, pork, and venison. For more information, visit sdchislicfestival.com.

To honor the Czechs who settled in southeast South Dakota in the 1860s, Tabor holds is **Czech Days** every June. Usually, more than 5,000 visitors attend the celebration which features a baseball game, Midwest and carnival on a Thursday. The Giant Parade begins at 1 p.m. on a Friday with floats and young and old participants riding them or walking the route. In mid-afternoon, candidates for the festival's queen lead the singing of the Czech national anthem. Competitions include Czech attire, polka dancing and the polka bands with their lively horns and heavy downbeats. Expect lots of roast pork, beef, potatoes, noodles, sauerkraut and, of course, those puffy pastries, kolaches, loaded with fruits and poppyseed.

Many of those in attendance wear clothing featuring red, black and white, and elaborate embroidery, and women embellish their national dress with lace. The Czech national folk dance, the *Beseda,* is put on Friday and Saturday evenings and Tabor prides itself on having the largest in the nation, featuring more than 230 dancers from ages 7 to at least 70 on the field at one time, creating swirls of color as they prance and dance. Remember, *Vitame Vas* means "We welcome you." For more information, visit taborczechdays.com.

The Swedish immigrants of Dalesburg celebrated their first **Midsommar Festival** when they founded the town in 1868, which makes it another of South Dakota's oldest ethnic festivals. While Dalesburg has never been a village or town but a region about 12 miles north of Vermillion, Midsommar has featured musicians from Scandinavian countries who perform in the Dalesburg Lutheran Church. Meals include potato sausage, fruit soup, herring, Swedish meatballs, and Scandinavian cookies. For information, visit dalesburg.org.

1869: John and Anna Samuelson, both Swedish immigrants, were newlyweds, and John bought his bride a 160-acre homestead east of present-day Sioux Falls. For the first three years, they made their home in a dugout carved from a nearby hill. They later moved to a log cabin, which is now the centerpiece of the Homesteader Day Harvest Festival every September. An interpretive shelter tells the story of the Samuelsons' cabin. As part of the festival, volunteers demonstrate candle making, sheep shearing, tatting, butter churning, wheat grinding, and more. Visitors can try their hand at rope making and can sample fresh-squeezed apple juice made in an antique apple press. The festival is held the first Sunday after Labor Day and is free. Call (605) 594-3824.

Vermillion

Vermillion, 56 miles south of Sioux Falls on I-29 and then a bit west on SD Hwy. 50, best fits the old description of a place where the college is the community. The economy of this town of 10,772 people thrives on the presence of the University of South Dakota (USD), the state's second-largest university, founded in 1862. Vermillion, the seat of Clay County, originally was settled below the bluffs of the Mighty Mo until the flood of 1881 changed the river's course, forcing residents to higher ground. Now it's located in a part of the state that was twice claimed by France and once by Spain before it was sold to the US. As in any college community, there is a vibrant, global energy that students and higher education bring—not to mention an impressive dose of culture.

Start a tour at the campus's ***W. H. Over Museum of Natural and Cultural History*** (1110 N. University St.), which lacks polish but has plenty to see, including oddities like the bones of an elephant that escaped from a circus visiting the small town of Elkton and went on a rampage before being killed, and a sarcophagus that's opened during special events to show its female mummy. Its strength are Native American exhibits (a life-size diorama of a Teton Dakota village, small replicas of Arikara farming, and intricate Lakota beadwork and art), pioneer artifacts, and the Lewis and Clark/Spirit Mound Learning Center that sheds light on the explorers' famous journey, especially through the region. Artifacts include a map drawn in 1806 from Lewis's notations and journal entries. The gift shop includes Dakota beading, pipestone carvings, and star quilts. The museum is free and open from 10 a.m. to 4 p.m. Mon through Sat. Call (605) 659-6151 or visit whovermuseum.org for more information.

The campus of the ***University of South Dakota*** (usd.edu) is a stately one, with historic buildings and grand shade trees. The Dakota Dome sports facility includes an indoor football stadium, where the USD Coyotes meet other colleges for competition. The school's strongest rival is the South Dakota State University

South Dakota's Musical Treasure

On the University of South Dakota campus, more than 15,000 musical instruments from across the globe are in the world-renowned **National Music Museum,** at the corner of E. Clark and N. Yale Streets. Opened in 1973 in a former Carnegie library that was built for the university, the NMM has grown from basically a private collection called "Shrine of Music" to an internationally-ranked museum with one of the largest and most ambitious collections of musical instruments, tracing the history, artistry, and science of those instruments.

In October 2018, the museum closed to begin a three-year, $15 million to $20 million expansion and renovation to add 16,000 square feet to the 22,000-square-foot complex by the time it re-opens in 2021. New features will include a special exhibits gallery, new concert hall, visitors atrium, more general display area, and more museum-operations space. Although the NMM collection may not be visited by the public during this time, some of it can be viewed on the "emuseum"—a collections portion of the NMM's website, nmmusd.org and via almost daily postings on the museum's Facebook page. The museum also continues to hold its popular *NMM Live!* concert series once a month in USD's Farber Hall (a listing of concerts is on the NMM website).

The museum preserves some of the most historic and important musical instruments. Among them is a stratospheric collection of four stringed instruments made by the incomparable Antonio Stradivari (Latinized as Stradivarius): violin, cello, mandolin, and guitar. The crown jewel is a priceless cello made by Andrea Amati in the mid-1500s. Made for the young French King Charles IX with an elaborate painting of an allegorical figure of sword-wielding "Justice" standing near symbols representing his reign, this earliest cello, appropriately nicknamed the "King," served as the template for the cello as we know it.

Jackrabbits. USD, whose alumni include former NBC news anchor Tom Brokaw, is considered one of the best liberal arts colleges in the state. Accordingly, there are fine productions to see on campus, including dance, theater, and fine arts. Slagle Auditorium is often home to concerts by the USD Chamber Singers and Chamber Orchestra and the USD Men's and Women's Chorus Concert. You also can see a play at the Fine Arts Building theater or enjoy a piano concert at the Colton Recital Hall. Events are listed at calendar.usd.edu.

Another worthy stop for history buffs is the **Austin–Whittemore House,** an impressive Italian villa–style structure that houses the **Clay County Historical Society Museum** (15 Austin St.). The museum, built in 1883 on a riverside bluff overlooking Vermillion, is best known for its Victorian furnishings and settings. Open 9 a.m. to noon and 1 p.m. to 3 p.m. Mon to Fri. Call (605) 624-8266 or visit cchssd.org.

If you work up an appetite, head to Vermillion's historic downtown to **Cafe Brule** (24 W. Main St.). It has built a huge fan base since it opened in

Also, the museum has extraordinary historic keyboards—among them the earliest-known, playable harpsichord, the "Neapolitan" (circa 1530), as well as instruments by Ruckers, Germain, Le Bas, Antunes, Chickering, and Steinway. Other impressive NMM offerings are the eye-dazzling saxophones created by Adolphe Sax (who, you will learn created other instruments as well), and guitars like the electric-acoustic made in 1937 by Gibson, the 1952 Les Paul model gold-body and a Martin D-28 used extensively by Johnny Cash when he wrote songs on his farm near Nashville.

The collection includes a 9-foot-tall slit drum from the South Pacific, Civil War instruments that led troops to battle, a crocodile-shaped zither from then-Burma, hundreds of ingeniously conceived "pop-culture" harmonics, sacred thighbone horns from Tibet, and a room-filling Javanese gamelan set teeming with brass "xylophones," gongs, drums, and more.

There are also electric theremins that produced eerie music used in mid-20th century science-fiction and horror film soundtracks and all manner of sweet-strumming ukuleles. Name it and it's possibly here—accordions, mouth harps, reed organs, a courting flute, drums made of rawhide—all in beautifully-made wood-and-glass display cases that allow visitors to walk around all sides of many instruments. Even the vintage New York workshop of renowned American arch-top guitar "Stradivari," John D'Angelica and James D'Aquisto, has been transplanted here along with several of their iconic guitars.

The museum's hours and admission rates are yet to be determined. Metered parking can be found in the lot adjacent to the museum campus. Free street parking can be found directly south of the museum. For more information, visit nmmusd.org, the Facebook page NationalMusicMuseum/USA, or call (605) 658-3450.

2011 with food such as a croque-monsieur with ham and gruyère on their own brioche bread, pot roast dip on a baguette, oriental chicken salad with mango vinaigrette, limoncello chicken, or smoked pork chops. Be sure to leave room for dessert with sumptuous choices such as vanilla champagne cake layered with raspberries or drunken berry compote, white chocolate mousse, ganache fondue cake, and buttercream frosting. They're open 7 a.m. to 8 p.m. Sun through Thurs, and 7 a.m. to 9 p.m. Fri and Sat. Call (605) 624-2945 or go to cafebrule.com for more details and a full menu.

Dakota Brickhouse (15 W. Main St.) is a family restaurant and a craft beer and whiskey bar features a rotating list of at least 20 craft beers. House favorites include lamb tacos and lamb kabobs, apple taco desserts, flavorful chili, and wood-fired pizza. Food hours are 5 a.m. to 11 p.m. Mon to Sat. Beer hours are 5 p.m. to midnight Mon through Thurs, and 5 p.m. to 2 a.m. Fri and Sat. For more information, visit dakotabrickhouse.com or call (605) 658-BEER.

Red Steakhouse (1 E. Main St.) is another popular restaurant in downtown Vermillion. Its menu has featured handmade tortellini filled with shiitake mushrooms, the Hellraiser Burger with peppers, pepper jack cheese, arugula, garlic aioli, and bacon, flatbread topped with pickled carrots and cabbage, unagi sauce, cilantro, Japanese mayo and pork, steaks of all types, braised short rib, pheasant and wild rice, salmon oscar, and fried meatloaf. Open 11 a.m. to 9 p.m. Tues through Thurs; 11 a.m. to 10 p.m. Fri; and 9 a.m. to 10 p.m. Sat. Closed Sun and Mon. For more information, visit theredsteakhouse.com or call (605) 624-0079.

Upon hearing how great a café and bakery *Mister Smith's* is, some visitors can't wait to go there, although they may be confused about its location—inside an Ace Hardware Store at 812 Cottage Ave. That's no joke. Mister Smith's started in a grocery store some years ago and when the Ace Hardware took over the building in 2014, Mister Smith's stayed, serving soups, salads, and sandwiches on, some say, the best breads in the world. The Sicilian salad, with spring mix greens accented with salami, prosciutto, provolone, olives, banana peppers and tomatoes is popular, as are the Smith Melts, grilled peasant bread with a choice of ham, turkey, or roast beef and cheese. Four types of vegetarian sandwiches are offered, too. You can design your own, too, with more than a dozen breads, meats, cheeses, sauces, and garnishes. Open 11 a.m. to 8 p.m. daily. Visit vermillionmenus.com/mister_smiths_menu.pdf or call (605) 624-2624.

To enjoy great views of the Missouri River while nibbling on your sandwiches, visit Clay County Park, about 4 miles west of Vermillion off SD 50. The park has 44 campsites, a boat ramp and dock and a 3-mile trail with a lookout across the valley. Another view requires you to cross the river into Nebraska. Once you're in Nebraska, take the first road to the east and that will lead up to a parking area. From there, a ¾-mile trail leads to two wonderful overlooks of the Missouri River 200 feet below.

About 8 miles north of Vermillion on Route 19, you can walk off the calories and walk in the footsteps of Lewis and Clark, who came through this area to the conical *Spirit Mound,* on August 25, 1804. The explorers were told native legends that claimed 18-inch devils with big heads and armed with arrows protected the mound, which also is one of the highest places in the county. However, the explorers were undaunted and claimed it to be a "most butifull landscape" with bison grazing there and flocks of birds in the sky. The bison aren't here anymore, but still, the mound is a wide-open prairie dotted with fragrant wild roses, deep-purple spiderwort, and lavender penstemon in early summer and swaying with native grasses later in the season. The reward for reaching the summit—about a three-quarter-mile hike from the parking lot—is a view that unfurls for miles and a peaceful silence occasionally

Southeastern South Dakota Parks and Birding

Union Grove State Park, located 11 miles south of Beresford off I-29, offers hiking and bridle trails, picnicking, camping, and a playground on 500 beautiful acres. Call (605) 987-2263.

Newton Hills State Park (28767 482nd St., Canton; 605-987-2263; gfp.sd.gov/parks/detail/newton-hills-state-park) just 6 miles south of Canton on CR 135, is a wooded oasis where plants and animals thrive. This southern tip of the Coteau des Prairies was spared the plow, and its grassy knolls and wooded ravines today shelter deer, wild turkey, and more than 200 species of birds. Explorers can make their way along several hiking trails, while horse riders and all-terrain bikers can enjoy a 6-mile multi-use trail. To add a little excitement, ride the hayracks, make crafts with the kids, watch pumpkins get catapulted high into the fall sky, and hike 2 miles of trails by candlelight during **FestiFall** the first Sat of Oct. The annual **Sioux River Folk Festival** (fotm.org) attracts music aficionados from all over and is held the first weekend in Aug.

Adams Homestead and Nature Preserve, located 2 miles southwest of McCook Lake (take exit 4 off I-29), includes 1,500 acres along the Missouri River, some of which encompass several restored buildings, including the Adams homestead, and 10 miles of hiking and biking trails. The town of McCook was the first homesteader settlement in the state, and the McCook Cemetery, plotted and registered in 1869, is regarded as the first homesteader cemetery. The visitor center is open from 9 a.m. to 4:30 p.m. Mon through Fri year-round; noon to 4 p.m. Sat and Sun from May through Oct. The visitor center is closed on weekends from Nov 1 through Apr.

The state park is open 6 a.m. to 11 p.m. May through Oct; 6 a.m. to 9 p.m. Nov 1 through Apr. Off exit 4, I-29. Free. Call (605) 232-0873 or visit gfp.sd.gov/parks/detail/adams-homestead-and-nature-preserve for more information.

interrupted by the honk of a pheasant or the trill of a meadowlark. For information about Spirit Mound Historic Prairie, visit gfp.sd.gov.

Like North Dakota, South Dakota takes great pride in its close relationship to Captains Meriwether Lewis and William Clark, who set out to explore America's newest land acquisition—the Louisiana Purchase—in 1804.

The Lewis and Clark National Historic Trail follows Highways 1804 and 1806, which hug the Missouri River and trace the route that Lewis and Clark traveled in the years 1804 and 1806. Indeed, some parts of the vast Missouri shoreline remain as wild and breathtaking as they were in the explorers' days. The South Dakota Tourism Department has a website about visiting places along the Lewis and Clark trail: travelsouthdakota.com/trip-ideas/article/lewis-clark-trail.

Missouri National Recreational River

Long before railways and interstates—and even the Dakota Territory—the fastest way to the Dakotas was along the Missouri River. The river enters the state at North Sioux City, winds its way past Vermillion, and then, less than 30 miles later, reaches *Yankton.* In this once-bustling capital of the Dakota Territory from the 1860s through 1889, you can see a *Dakota Territorial Capitol Replica,* a simple white structure in Yankton's Riverside Park, as a reminder of those ambitious beginnings before the title went to the more centrally located city of Pierre.

Yankton and its 14,700 residents are still closely tied to the river that constantly flows by, bringing boaters, paddlers, and migrating birds by the thousands and offering a serene view of the chalky white bluffs that rise from the Nebraska shoreline.

If you want to get a feel for the river's expanse without renting a boat or picking up a paddle, park near Walnut Street and take a stroll along Yankton's unique double-decker *Meridian Bridge.* Closed to vehicle traffic in 2008, the bridge reopened for foot and bike traffic in November 2011. It was originally built in 1924 and is considered the longest pedestrian bridge connecting two states. You can choose whether to walk on the top level or the lower level. It links to more than 30 miles of riding in the Meridian Trail System that connects Yankton and the Lewis and Clark Recreational Area.

If you want to learn about the area's history, check out the *Dakota Territorial Museum/Mead Cultural Education Center* (82 Mickelson Dr.). The Yankton County Historical Society has lovingly preserved and displayed rare memorabilia from early Yankton and Dakota Territory days, including a rural schoolhouse, a blacksmith shop, a Burlington Northern caboose, an American LaFrance fire engine, and artifacts such as vintage boat motors and fishing equipment and the musical instruments from General Custer's 7th Cavalry band. Free admission. Call (605) 665-3898 or go to meadbuilding.org.

Yankton boasts some of the finest historical homes in the Midwest. The Architectural Walking and Auto Tour of Historic Yankton Homes offers visitors at least a curbside glimpse at the exteriors of some homes, most of which are clustered on Douglas, Capital, Pine, and Mulberry Streets, between 5th and 6th Streets. Pick up brochures at the Yankton Chamber office (803 E. 4th St.; 605-665-3636) or at the Dakota Territorial Museum.

The *Cramer Kenyon Heritage Home* and *Dorothy Jencks Memorial Garden* at 509 Pine St. are an outstanding example of Queen Anne architecture. The home, erected in 1886, is open to the public from Memorial Day to Labor Day from 1 to 4 p.m. Wed through Sun and by appointment. Admission

Hickok's Killer Hanged

One of the most famous events to take place here was the trial of **Jack "Crooked Nose" McCall,** who shot and killed Wild Bill Hickok on August 2, 1876 in Deadwood. The trial was held in December 1876 in what is now the Charles Gurney Hotel (corner of 3rd and Capital Streets), and he was hanged on March 1, 1877—the first legal execution in the Dakota Territory. McCall is buried in the Yankton Cemetery. A historic marker in the parking lot at the corner of US 81 and SD 50 marks the spot of the hanging.

$7 for 12 and up; $3 for students under 12. Open year-round. Call (605) 665-7470 or go to cramer-kenyon.webs.com.

If you want to pick your own berries in this part of South Dakota, head for **Hebda Family Produce and Prairie Gardens** (30661 444th Ave., Mission Hill), an orchard and berry farm just 7.5 miles northeast of Yankton. Pluck strawberries or raspberries, pick apples or pumpkins, or buy fresh vegetables and jams, jellies, pies, and other South Dakota products. Fall visitors can take hayrack rides or challenge themselves with the corn maze. Call (605) 665-2806 or go to hebdaproduce.com.

Most visitors to Yankton head 4 miles west of downtown and settle into a spot along the river. There are two stretches of the 2,341-mile Missouri River that are protected as a National Recreational River, and Yankton sits ideally located on the upriver end of a 59-mile section that runs from the Gavins Point Dam east past Vermillion to Ponca State Park in Nebraska.

How beloved is this area? If you don't plan ahead on summer weekends (especially holidays), you'll find that the more than 400 campsites plus 19 camping cabins book quickly at the 31,400-acre **Lewis and Clark State Recreation Area** just west of Vermillion along SD Hwy. 52. You'll find all the amenities here—from hot showers and electric hookups to paved pads that stretch along Lewis and Clark Lake, created by Gavins Point Dam. For more information, call (605) 668-2985 or visit gfp.sd.gov/parks/detail/lewis-and-clark-recreation-area.

thelawrence welklegend

In 1928 a young accordionist and his novelty band from Strasburg, North Dakota, arrived in Yankton, South Dakota, and asked a new radio station, WNAX, if they could perform. Audience reaction was so tremendous that the manager offered to add the band to the station's roster of entertainers. That brief stop lasted almost nine years and began the career of the great Lawrence Welk.

If you want to be in a more tucked-away area, there are more than 200 additional campsites and cabins at *Chief White Crane Recreation Area* and *Pierson Ranch Recreation Area,* east of the dam and along the smaller Lake Yankton. Those campgrounds are accessed via Crest Road (or Toe Road), which crosses the dam and the Missouri River. Sites for all the campgrounds can be reserved by calling (800) 710-2267 or visiting gfp.sd.gov/camp.

calumetbluff

The Lewis and Clark Visitor Center sits on **Calumet Bluff** across the river from Yankton. It's where Lewis and Clark hosted a Grand Council with the Yankton Sioux in late August 1804. You can read a copy of Lewis's speech at the center.

While it's technically in Crofton, Nebraska, across the dam and on the opposite shore of the Missouri River, you'll want to check out the *Lewis and Clark Visitor Center* that overlooks the river. It tells a little about the famed Lewis and Clark expedition but is more focused on the area's geology and natural history, the river, and the landmark 1944 Pick-Sloan Plan Flood Control Act that sought to tame and control the country's biggest rivers after disastrous 1930s droughts and massive flooding in the early 1940s. For more information, call (402) 667-2546 or visit visityanktonsd.com/businesses/corps-discovery-welcome-center.

Gavins Point Dam, completed in 1957 at a cost of $51 million, created Lewis and Clark Lake, a reservoir that stretches for 30 miles upriver. It brims with large- and smallmouth bass and offers idyllic opportunities for sailing. If you like engineering and are intrigued by the colossal effort needed to build a dam, you can stop by the *Gavins Point Powerhouse.* Free tours are given Fri to Sun and holidays, Memorial Day through Labor Day. During the 45-minute tour, visitors can examine such areas as the control room, generator housing, and high-voltage cable areas. IDs are required for anyone 17 and older, and no cameras, phones, or bags are allowed. For more information call (402) 667-2546.

gavinspoint dam

Gavins Point Dam is one of 6 main dams and reservoirs along the Upper Missouri River Basin, stretching through both Dakotas. They were built between 1933 and 1964 to provide flood control and hydro-electric power.

If you have kids with you or are camping nearby, be sure to swing into the *Gavins Point National Fish Hatchery and Aquarium* (31227 436th Ave.), 3 miles west of Yankton on Highway 52. It's free and offers a quick introduction to what's beneath the water.

You can see fossils from when the area was a prehistoric inland sea, watch turtles, and see the bizarre contraband (think cowboy boots made from turtles) confiscated by the US Fish and Wildlife Service. You also can see the endangered paddlefish and pallid sturgeon. The hatchery harvests their eggs, nurtures the small fry, and releases these fish into the river. Open Apr through Sept, but call (605) 665-3352 or go to fws.gov/mountain-prairie/fisheries/gavinspoint .php to check for hours.

Anchoring the area's water sports is *Lewis and Clark Marina,* on the lake's northeast corner. The marina is home to more than 400 boats from Apr through Oct. Slips are available by the night, week, or season, and boats, pontoons, and personal watercraft can be rented. A boat-up gas dock, convenience store, and full-service dealer will keep you well provisioned. Call (605) 665-3111 or go to lewisandclarkmarina.com. You can also dine at *The Marina Grill* and enjoy some of the area's best views; for more information, call (605) 689-2111.

If you want to stay somewhere with a river view but prefer not to camp, you have a few options. *Lewis and Clark Resort,* located by the marina, offers 24 moderately priced motel rooms and 17 two- and three-bedroom cabins. There's an outdoor pool, along with easy river access. A six-bedroom lodge built in 2012 sleeps 28 people and can be ideal for special occasions and reunions. Call (605) 665-2680 or visit lewisandclarkpark.com.

Archery Central

Yankton is home to the **National Field Archery Association (NFAA) Headquarters and Museum**. The largest archery association in the world had been in Redland, California, for more than 60 years, but a combination of high real estate prices in California, the low cost of living in South Dakota, and the presence of the Easton Aluminum Company in Yankton, which makes arrows, resulted in the headquarters moving here in 2008. The property is 130 acres which cover three full-size field ranges, two Olympic archery fields, and a 90-meter indoor range.

You don't have to be a competitive archer to enjoy this center. For $10, you can come in, get equipped with all you need, and shoot at targets all day ($5 for NFAA members). There's also a museum on the history of archery, which is surprisingly interesting. It includes, among other items, artifacts from the Battle of the Little Big Horn and souvenirs from major movie sets. There also are classrooms, a fitness studio, and an art studio here, so you could find yourself taking classes in woodblock prints and Raku pottery or belly dancing and tae kwon do. The center is just east of town at 800 Archery Ln. Open 9 a.m. to 9 p.m. Mon through Fri; 10 a.m. to 7 p.m. Sat; noon to 7 p.m. Sun. Call (605) 260-9279 and check upcoming classes at yankton archerycomplex.org.

Take a Hike or Paddle

Stop at the interpretive center at the Lewis and Clark Recreational Area or the Yankton Visitor Center for a list of the many hiking trails along Lewis and Clark Lake. The 1.2-mile Gavins Point Nature Trail that loops through the west end of the park has about 10 interpretive stops with information on Native Americans' use of local plants, views of the Nebraska cliffs, a spot to look for some of the 414 species that migrate through the area, and how to identify animal tracks. If you're intrigued by the Nebraska cliffs, look at the interpretive center for examples of fossils found there. For more information about the Lewis and Clark Recreation Area's trails, visit: gfp.sd.gov/userdocs/lewis-and-clark-trails.pdf.

Leisurely paddlers can find kayaks and canoes to rent in the area, but for a true adventure, there's the 79-mile Missouri National Recreational Water Trail that runs from below Gavins Point dam to North Sioux City. For details, see mri.usd.edu/water trail and southdakota.com/yankton-trails.

About 21 miles west of Yankton near Springfield, there's another option for staying along the river at the **Cogan House Bed and Breakfast.** If you're not competing with sportsmen for prime hunting weekends, it's a peaceful place to soak up sweeping views of the river and an excellent spot for bird watching. The log home was built in 2009, but owners Greg and Diana and their son, Grant, are tapping some of South Dakota's deepest roots in hospitality. Their ancestors built the original Cogan House in 1869 and fed guests ranging from Sitting Bull to General Custer. If you're lucky, they might be serving pancakes with homemade chokecherry syrup for breakfast. Call (605) 464-0238 or go to thecoganhouse.com for more information.

Mitchell

Located 60 miles west of Sioux Falls on I-90, **Mitchell** (population 15,603) has been synonymous with its iconic **Corn Palace** since it was built in 1892. More than 750,000 people from around the world stop by each year to gawk at this "world's only" marvel at 604 N. Main St.

The effect is supersized seed art meets the Taj Mahal of the Great Plains with Russian onion-style domes. This ode to agriculture was dreamed up by city founders to debut with Mitchell's first Corn Belt Exposition. It was part of a big-wow trend in the late 1800s when farm communities were seeking to make a name for themselves. Aberdeen had the Grain Palace, and Rapid City had an Alfalfa Palace, and more than 20 other towns had palaces across the Midwest, but only Mitchell's has survived for more than 100 years. Work is under way on what's being called Next Generation Corn Palace with a walkout balcony, new lobby, illuminated exterior sign, larger murals, color-changing domes, and wind turbines.

The Corn Palace is open year-round with free tours from Memorial Day through Labor Day. Throughout the 3,200-seat building, you'll also find plenty of vintage photos showing past corn palace themes and designs and many fun, interactive exhibits about corn geared toward families. Performers who have played here include The Beach Boys, Pat Benatar, Chubby Checker, Clint Black, Blood Sweat & Tears, Charlie Daniels, Sammy Kershaw, Willie Nelson, and the Righteous Brothers. Hours are daily 8 a.m. to 9 p.m. Memorial Day through Labor Day.

Visit cornpalace.com or call (605) 995-8430 for more information including when the Corn Palace is open from Labor Day to Memorial Day. The Corn Palace also serves as a multi-use center for the community and region with stage shows as well as sports events in its arena. Every third weekend in July, thousands of people gather here to attend the nightly PRCA rodeo performances, as well as other activities throughout the ***Annual Corn Palace Stampede Rodeo.***

The corn craze peaks in late August with the ***Corn Palace Festival,*** a weeklong celebration with marching bands, country music concerts, a polka fest, and carnival rides. The highlight comes when the new mural is officially presented. Most years, themes are agricultural, or nature related, although previous designs have celebrated the space race, the youth of America, patriotism, nostalgia, and the internet.

Not surprisingly, the Corn Palace makes a mighty fine bird feeder. After Corn Palace Week ends and winter arrives, local pigeons and squirrels devour the murals. The area around the Corn Palace can be touristy, but don't brush off Mitchell as a one-attraction town. It's worth at least a full day of exploring.

Mitchell's ***Dakota Wesleyan University*** campus houses the ***Dakota Discovery Museum*** (1300 McGovern Ave.). More than 100,000 Native American and pioneer artifacts are displayed in the building complex. Sites include a

A Closer Look at the Corn Palace

Farmers plant 12 different colors of corn for the murals, which require about 275,000 ears that are sliced in half and nailed to the Corn Palace walls. Cherie Ramsdell creates the designs, which are accented with other locally grown grains and grasses that include: bundles of ryegrass and sour dock, bromegrass and bluegrass, wild oats, rye, straw, and wheat.

restored 1886 Victorian home, built for the cofounder of the Corn Palace; the 1909 Farwell Methodist Church; the Sheldon School, an 1885 one-room territorial school; and a 1914 railroad depot.

The *Middle Border Museum and Case Art Gallery* is best known for its display of the oil painting *Dakota Woman,* by Harvey Dunn. Over the years this classic of plains art, depicting a young woman basking in the sunshine in an open field while her baby rests under a parasol, has become synonymous with prairie life and prairie people.

Three other art galleries in the complex feature original works by Oscar Howe, Dunn, and Charles Hargens, James Earle Fraser, Gutzon Borglum (the sculptor of Mount Rushmore), and others. The changing exhibits gallery features one-person shows, emphasizing Native American artists of the Northern Plains.

Howe in particular was one of South Dakota's most revered artists and a graduate of Dakota Wesleyan University. Howe was born on the Crow Creek Indian Reservation in South Dakota. In 1940 the painter was commissioned to create the dome mural, *Sun and Rain Clouds Over Hills,* for the *Mitchell Public Library* as a WPA project. He also did many of the Corn Palace's early murals. In 1972 Howe was widely recognized as one of America's preeminent Native American artists. The Howe Gallery boasts a collection of drawings and paintings that traces the history of Howe's development as an artist from when he was a student of the Santa Fe Indian School. His later work reflects a highly stylized interpretation of his heritage, using the formal elements of line, color, and space to create vivid, abstract designs.

The *Hargens Gallery* includes an intriguing replica of his studio, which is packed with saddles, vintage furniture, pen nibs, easels, cowboy hats, and other props he used for painting characters and lively scenes that graced western novels and magazines for decades.

Kids will love *Dakota Discovery Museum,* an interactive center that allows children to experience life on the prairie from a number of different perspectives. They can grab a scavenger hunt list and feel a full sense of history with impressive exhibits and vivid murals. The gallery's gift shop features the work of area artists and artisans, including original works on canvas and paper, sculpture, pottery and ceramics, quilts, jewelry, and reproductions. Hours vary by season, and it may be closed one or two days a week. Admission is $7 for ages 18 to 63; $6 for 63 and over; $3 for ages 6 to 17; under 6 free. For more information, call (605) 996-2122 or visit dakotadiscovery.com

Other prominent alumni of Dakota Wesleyan University were 1972 presidential candidate George McGovern and his wife, Eleanor. The *McGovern Legacy Museum* at 1200 W. University Ave. tells the story of their years at the

Mitchell's Ancient History

A student from Dakota Wesleyan University first discovered evidence of ancient villages along the lake just north of Mitchell in 1910, and the **Mitchell Prehistoric Indian Village** has been an ongoing project since and the state's only National Archaeological Landmark. An estimated 200 people lived here about 1,100 years ago along the Firesteel Creek growing crops such as corn, beans, squash, sunflowers, and amaranth. A video and exhibits at the visitor center offer insight into this prehistoric community. You can then walk to the **Thomsen Center Archeodome,** where you can watch excavations in progress. College students from Exeter, England, and Sioux Falls' Augustana University come each summer to help with the work, and there are hands-on areas where you can see if you have an eye for significant fragments. Children also can dig for an arrowhead and try to throw an ancient weapon called an atlatl. The site, at 3200 Indian Village Rd., is open from 8 a.m. to 7 p.m. Mon through Sat and 10 a.m. to 6 p.m. Sun Memorial Day through Labor Day. It's also open 9 a.m. to 6 p.m. Mon through Sat and 10 a.m. to 6 p.m. Sun in Apr, May, and Sept and until Nov 15. Admission is $6 for adults; $5 for seniors; $4 for those between 6 and 18 years; free for those younger than 5. Call (605) 996-5473 or visit mitchellindianvillage.org.

university, followed by his service in World War II, the 22 years he represented South Dakota in Congress, and his work to end world hunger as an ambassador to the United Nations. Hours follow the campus schedule, so call ahead for details at (605) 995-2618 or go dwu.edu/about-dwu/centers-of-excellence/mcgovern-center. Free admission.

A drive through the hinterlands of South Dakota may seem lonely at first, but it can be the best way to see a generous slice of Americana. That's why it's worth a trek up SD 37 from Mitchell to find the epicenter of South Dakota's beloved ***Forestburg*** melons. Some people say it's the rich bottomlands of the James River Valley between Mitchell and Huron that makes these such stellar fruits, while others say sandy soil helps sweeten them. No matter what theory makes sense, you'll find a juicy bonanza from mid-August through the end of October, when old-fashioned produce stands overflow with watermelons, pumpkins, squash, Indian corn, sweet corn, and gourds. Apparently the local melon rage began in the grim 1930s, when Ernie Schwemle and Harold Smith planted a few seeds and sparked the tradition of an annual melon harvest.

From Forestburg, travel west on SD 34 to Wessington Springs and step back in time to the Renaissance and the enchanting ***Shakespeare Garden and Anne Hathaway Cottage*** in Wessington Springs. Shakespeare and Anne Hathaway in rural South Dakota? In 1926, Emma and Clark Shay, educators in Wessington Springs, borrowed $1,000 to travel throughout England. Her purpose was to increase her knowledge and ability to teach English literature. By the next year, on the April 23 birthday of England's most famous playwright, construction began for a Shakespeare Garden in an alfalfa patch on campus. The work was done by the Shays, other faculty, and students. Shrubs, trees, and flowers of all kinds were donated by the city, the May Seed Company, Henry Field Company, and private citizens. The summer house was built by the boys of the local school's English department, and the sophomore class of 1928 made the lily pond. A sundial and gazing globe were also donated. By the end of 1928, the Shakespeare Garden, South Dakota's first, was a noted attraction with many visitors. The Shays then built the Anne Hathaway Cottage when they retired in 1932 and were inspired by a postcard of the original at Stratford-on-Avon. In observance of the state's centennial in 1989, the Shakespeare Garden Society of Wessington Springs purchased the Shakespeare Garden and Anne Hathaway Cottage. Listed on the National Register of Historic Places, Anne Hathaway Cottage is the only thatched-roof building in South Dakota.

The cottage hosts teas, tours, Christmas events, and weddings. Live music serenades those who visit on Thursday evenings in July. Located at 501 Alene Ave. N, the garden is open during daylight hours and the cottage is open by appointment (or by calling one of the phone numbers posted on the front door or by asking around at the restaurants in town—someone there should know who to call for you—no joke, this is what being in a small town is like). Tea reservations and more information are at (605) 539-1999 and shakespeare -garden.com.

Wessington Springs also is fabled for its excellent pheasant hunting in the fall. The town is located in the draws of the Wessington Hills, surrounded by wooded gulches, fertile farmland, and rolling prairie. Two large springs that still provide water for the town first attracted native tribes, French fur traders, and settlers.

Where to Stay in Southeastern South Dakota

LENNOX

Steever House Bed and Breakfast
46850 276th St.
(605) 647-5055
steeverhouse.com
Inexpensive

SIOUX FALLS

ClubHouse Hotel and Suites
2320 S. Louise Ave.
(605) 361-8700
siouxfalls.clubhouseinn
.com
Moderate

Country Inn & Suites
200 E. 8th St.
(605) 373-0153
countryinn.com/
siouxfallssd_central
Moderate

Courtyard by Marriott
4300 Empire Place
(605) 444-4300
marriott.com/fsdcy
Moderate

Dakotah Lodge
3200 W. Russell St.
(605) 332-2000
dakotahlodge.reservations
.com
Inexpensive

Holiday Inn City Centre
100 W. 8th St.
(605) 339-2000
sfcchotel.com
Moderate

VERMILLION

Buffalo Run Resort
(at Valiant Vineyards)
1500 W. Main St.
(605) 624-4500
Moderate

Prairie Inn
916 N. Dakota St.
(605) 624-2824
prairieinnsd.com
Inexpensive

YANKTON

Best Western Kelly Inn
1607 E. Hwy. 50
(605) 665-2906
bestwesternyankton.com
Moderate

Riverfront Event Center
121 W. 3rd St.
(605) 760-6460
theriverfrontevent
center.com
Moderate

Where to Eat in Southeastern South Dakota

MITCHELL

Chef Louie's
601 E. Havens St.
(605) 996-7565
cheflouies.net
Moderate to expensive

SELECTED CHAMBERS OF COMMERCE

Southeast South Dakota Tourism
1101 Broadway St.
Yankton 57078
(605) 665-2435
SoutheastSouthDakota.com

Mitchell Convention and Visitors Bureau
601 N. Main St.
Mitchell 57301
(605) 996-6223
visitmitchell.com

Sioux Falls Convention and Visitors Bureau
200 N. Phillips Ave., Ste. 102
Sioux Falls 57104
(605) 275-6060
visitsiouxfalls.com

Vermillion Area Tourism
McVicker Plaza
2 E. Main St.
Vermillion 57069
(605) 624-5571
vermillioncvb.com

Yankton Convention and Visitors Bureau
803 E. 4th St.
Yankton 57078
(605) 665-3636
visityanktonsd.com

Crazy About Cupcakes
417 Main St., #102
(605) 990-9866
Inexpensive

The Depot Pub & Grill
210 S. Main St.
(605) 996-9417
mitchelldepot.com
Moderate

Elixir Roasterie
312 N. Main St.
(605) 990-2233
elixirroasterie.com
Inexpensive

SIOUX FALLS

Backyard Barbeque
323 S. Phillips Ave.
(605) 444-1800
bygrill.com
Inexpensive to moderate

**Cluckin' Good Chicken
& BBQ**
3607 E. 10th St.
(605) 336-7260
cluckingoodchicken.com
Inexpensive

Grille 26
1716 S. Western Ave.
(605) 444-1716
grille26.com
Moderate

Kaladi's Bistro
1716 S. Phillips Ave.
(605) 339-3322
kaladisbistro.com
Moderate

**Kathmandu Indian
Cuisine**
5310 Arrowhead Pkwy.
(605) 338-3003
Moderate

OG Greens
421 N. Phillips Ave., #111
(605) 271-2953
facebook.com/pg/
oggreens/menu
Moderate

Oh My Cupcakes!
5015 S. Western Ave., Ste.
290
(605) 310-6742
ohmycupcakes.com
Inexpensive

Pizza Di Paolo
2300 S. Minnesota Ave.,
Ste. B
(605) 271-3935
Moderate

VERMILLION

Red Steakhouse
1 E. Main St.
(605) 624-0079
theredsteakhouse.com
Moderate to expensive

Silk Road Cafe
12 W. Main St.
(605) 658-1923
Moderate

YANKTON

Ben's Brewing Company
222 W. 3rd St.
(605) 260-4844
bensbrewing.com
Inexpensive

Bur Oak Diner
304 W. 3rd
(605) 660-1031
facebook.com/buroakdiner
Moderate

Charlie's Pizza House
804 Summit St.
(605) 665-2212
Moderate

River's Edge
104 Capitol St.
(605) 664-2779
facebook.com/
riversedgeyankton
Moderate to expensive

Tastee Treet Drive-In
413 W. 4th St.
(605) 665-7512
Inexpensive

Tokyo Japanese Cuisine
2007 Broadway Ave.
(605) 260-3388
Inexpensive to moderate

Along the Missouri River

For sheer wanderlust and a love of the outdoors, travel the **Missouri River** section of South Dakota. It's a hunting and fishing paradise, rich in water, wildlife refuges, and parks. Beyond the capital, there are few communities along this central strip—except those of Old World and Native American heritage that proudly share their culture. The Missouri River winds through central South Dakota for 453 miles, offering not only a spectacular ribbon of blue water but also shore land rich in history, mystery, and adventure. Sliding past forts, monuments, ruins, reservations, and pioneer towns in South Dakota, the Missouri River ultimately flows into the Mississippi River and then to the Gulf of Mexico.

The powerful Missouri neatly divides the state into two dissimilar geographic and cultural regions. Along the west side of the river, wide stretches of prairie are broken by low hills and cut by ravines. Trees are sparse, and great cattle ranches fill the expanse of land. In the extreme west rise the forested Black Hills, one of the primary sources of the nation's gold. Fertile farmlands stretch out east of the Missouri River. Culturally speaking, East River is the well-heeled cousin who needs to be sent away to the spirited West River once in a while to

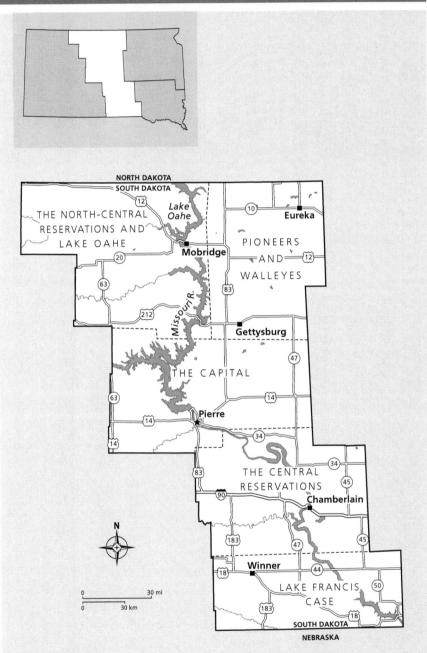

THE NORTH-CENTRAL
RESERVATIONS AND
LAKE OAHE

Lake
Oahe

Mobridge

Eureka

PIONEERS
AND
WALLEYES

Gettysburg

THE CAPITAL

Pierre

THE CENTRAL
RESERVATIONS

Chamberlain

Winner

LAKE FRANCIS
CASE

NORTH DAKOTA
SOUTH DAKOTA

MISSOURI R.

SOUTH DAKOTA
NEBRASKA

N

0   30 mi

0   30 km

The Oyate Trail

The concept of a scenic route to the Black Hills of South Dakota has been around since before the Missouri River was dammed and before Mount Rushmore was even finished. Since the day the state could boast of having a "fully improved road" along its southern border, South Dakotans have been promoting this 388-mile stretch of highway as an educational alternative to the interstate. Travelers will discover diverse geography, as well as the cultural and historical contributions of both the Dakota Nation and European immigrants along this trail, pronounced oh-YAH-tay.

The *Oyate Trail* of today turns off I-29 near Vermillion and heads west on SD 50 and US 18 to Edgemont near the Wyoming border. For local attractions along the way and suggested itineraries, call the Southeast Tourism Association, (888) 353-7382, or visit southeastsouthdakota.com/journey/oyate-trail.

get a good grasp of terra firma in his hand and in his soul. Likewise, West River could head east to mellow out the wildness and soak up some culture.

The Mighty Mo, or the Big Muddy, as some residents call the river, served as the first highway into the region at a time when fur trappers pulled keelboats up the river by hand. Later, fur traders arrived in steamboats, beginning with the arrival of the *Yellowstone* in 1831. They sang the now-familiar folk song "Oh, Shenandoah," and you can almost hear the strain of ". . . across the wide Missouri."

River traffic became a thing of the past as the railroad reached the area at the turn of the 20th century, and the number of settlements increased rapidly thereafter. The river in those days was also known as the Muddy Mo, and the standard joke was that a person didn't know whether to plow it or drink it. Jokers had their last laugh when the construction of four dams across the Missouri River created Lewis and Clark Lake, Lake Francis Case, Lake Sharpe, and Lake Oahe. These reservoirs have transformed Old Muddy into a series of crystalline blue lakes that have become popular recreation areas for South Dakotans and nonresidents alike.

Today life along the Missouri River isn't as bustling as life in East River or as animated as that in West River, but the beauty of wildlife, the grandeur of the bluffs, and the peaceful flow of the river make the Mighty Mo a magical place to be.

Lake Francis Case

The first lake you'll reach after exploring southeastern South Dakota and heading west is 120-mile-long *Lake Francis Case.* While it feels more open and remote than the Lewis and Clark Recreational Area, this lake, **Pickstown** (population 227), and the Fort Randall Dam have their share of boating, fishing (catfish, walleye, bass, and pike), camping, and birding.

Start at the **Fort Randall Dam Visitor Center** for an overview of the area's history, including its time as a frontier fort and the creation of the 165-foot-high dam that was begun in 1946. Tours of the dam are offered three times a day Memorial Day through Labor Day. Call (605) 487-7845 for details.

You also can get directions and a self-guided tour for exploring the fort's cemetery, the original site of the 1856 **Fort Randall Military Post** with remaining building foundations and salvaged ruins of the fort's church. Wooden grave markers in the fort's cemetery, dating back to the 19th century, give an idea of how life could end on the prairie, sometimes as a result of a disease that swept through the area, laying low several within days of each other. The fort's visitors list reads like a Who's Who in Great Plains history: George Custer, Philip Sheridan, and Hunkpapa leader Sitting Bull (who was held prisoner at the fort for two years). Call (605) 487-7847 for more information.

Birders should also check out the area's national wildlife refuges. **Lake Andes National Wildlife Refuge Complex** includes **Karl E. Mundt National Wildlife Refuge** near **Randall Creek Recreation Area** on the south side of the river. The 1,085-acre refuge Mundt NWR is one of the country's most important habitats for bald eagles. Although it is closed to the public year-round, it's still possible to approach the edges of the refuge and see some of the 300 or so eagles that roost here in the winter months. Some nest in cottonwoods along the shore. Call (605) 487-7603 for more information or go to fws.gov/refuge/karl_e_mundt.

If you continue traveling west, crossing the Missouri River and staying on Highway 18, you'll reach **Gregory County** and the town of Gregory, where a large artificial pheasant greets visitors arriving from the west. Thousands of hunters flock to this area every year, making hunting the second-largest industry in the county, behind agriculture.

lewisandclark

Near Greenwood in the south-central part of the state, Lewis and Clark wrapped a newborn Yankton in a US flag and predicted the babe would always be a friend of the whites. The child grew up to become Struck by the Ree, chief of the Yankton, a subgroup of the Dakota. In 1865, he testified at a Congressional hearing how bad things were in Yankton: "Before the soldiers came along, we had good health, but, the soldiers go to my women, and they want to sleep with them, and the women being hungry will sleep with them in order to get something to eat, and will get a bad disease, and then the women go to their husbands and give them the bad disease."

Circle H Ranch (605-731-5050; circlehranch.com), located a bit more than 9 miles south and east of Gregory, is a working ranch known throughout the region for its fine crops, superb grassland, and excellent natural game habitat. In 1992, the ranch was opened as a private retreat to accommodate pheasant hunters and guests for business retreats and vacations. The quiet serenity, along with the breathtaking natural beauty of the land, makes a visit to the Circle H Ranch a perfect getaway. Accommodations include the main lodge with 5 guest rooms, dining facilities for 42 guests, a guest house with 5 rooms, or a renovated pioneer church with 5 bedrooms.

Ten miles straight south of Gregory is *Carlock*. Once it was a small community, but that has faded away except for one building, one of the few extant dancehalls in the state, and that's simply called Carlock now. Begun as a grocery with a small dance floor in the 1940s, it has grown into a family-style dance hall that opens at 8 p.m. on Sat from Apr through Oct. Live music, which spans from county and rock to two-step and polka, propels the dancers on the 40-by-100-foot hardware floor. Those dancing range from small-uns riding on the toes of their parents' boots to their grandparents. Admission is $10 per person, although sometimes for big acts such as Molli B, the price is a touch higher. About three to four dances a year are free, and admission is always free for those under 16 and older than 90 (although the older folks are never carded). The bar serves beer and snack foods.

If you want to travel across South Dakota's longest bridge, connect to east-bound SD 44 and cross the Missouri River on the *Platte-Winner Bridge* which is 5,655 feet long. A note about the Platte-Winner Bridge: The state has plans to modify or replace it during the 2020 decade, so be aware that construction will probably take place there for a few years. About 2.5 miles beyond the west end of the bridge is the entrance to *Buryanek State Recreation Area*. The year-round park has a beach, campsites, two cabins, picnic areas, boat ramp, fishing, hiking, and water sports including water skiing, sailing, and windsurfing. For more information, call (605) 337-2587 or visit gfp.sd.gov/parks/detail/buryanek-recreation-area.

Off the east end of the bridge is *Snake Creek Recreation Area* which has 115 campsites, ten cabins, a picnic area, a boat ramp, sandy beach and, on the north side of the highway, *Dock 44*—a restaurant with some tasty specials, a gift shop, and a marina in a sheltered cove. A turnout, just east of the park entrance, leads to a hilltop with a wonderful overlook of the area.

Continue traveling north along SD 50 (the Lewis and Clark Trail) until you reach I-90. Go one exit west, and you'll reach the Chamberlain-Oacoma (pronounced oh-ah-KOE-mah) community. The beautiful, undulating bluffs that flank the Missouri River make quite a statement and create what feels like a gateway to the Old West.

Chamberlain, population 2,389, was named for Selah Chamberlain, who was director of the Milwaukee Railroad in 1880, when the town was started. Rumor has it that, before 1880, natives called Chamberlain *Makah Tepee,* or "mud house," because a hermit had a dugout there.

The rest stop on the south side of I-90 from Chamberlain is dominated by a 50-foot-tall, stainless-steel statue of a Native American woman wearing a two-hide Native dress of the mid-19th century. Called *Dignity,* the statue honoring the Lakota and Dakota was constructed over three years by Dale Lamphere, South Dakota's Artist Laureate (he also created the *Arc of Dreams* in Sioux Falls), and placed atop a bluff overlooking the Missouri River. He fashioned the statue after using three Native American women as models. Overall, the statue is made of more than 1,000 pieces including 128 colored diamond shapes that highlight the star quilt. Erected in 2016, *Dignity* is now seen on several South Dakota license plates.

When traveling between the Black Hills and Sioux Falls, one of the most popular stops is **Al's Oasis,** off exit 260 on I-90. A great almost-halfway-there point (or over-halfway-there, depending on which way you're traveling), the restaurant has been a respite for weary travelers for more than 80 years. They come for the homemade pie, buffalo burgers, and 5-cent coffee. Owners Albert and Veda Mueller moved the Oasis to its present location in the 1950s when it was a grocery store and 10-stool lunch counter. Since then Al's Oasis has expanded into a full-menu, 325-seat restaurant and lounge with moderate prices. The Oasis Trading Post and General Store has anything and everything you forgot or need on your trip—from food and toiletries to men's, women's, and children's clothing, and cowboy boots—as well as a campground and an 86-room inn if you need to crash for the night. Call (605) 234-6051 or visit alsoasis.com for more information.

The **Arrowwood Cedar Shore Resort** (1500 Shoreline Dr.) is the first resort erected on the shores of the Missouri River. Formerly Cedar Shore Resort, the 80,000-square-foot facility on 164 acres features a full-service hotel, cottages, campground, day spa, convention center, and a 200-seat restaurant with lounge, art gallery, and more. The interior design centers on themes indigenous to the area such as buckskin, the pasqueflower, yucca, coyotes, horses, and the prairie wind. The marina facility is one of a kind on the river, with 100 boat slips and a floating concession. For more information, call (888) 697-6363 or visit arrowwoodcedarshore.com.

Driving north on SD 50, you'll reach both the **Crow Creek and Lower Brule Indian Reservations,** which flank both sides of the Missouri between

Chamberlain and Pierre. This is **Lake Sharpe** country as well, a looping reservoir created by the Big Bend Dam in the early 1960s.

With the side-by-side reservations, this area also is a handy place to test your luck at casinos. The **Lode Star Casino** (605-245-6000; lodestarcasino .com) in **Fort Thompson** is accessible from the Native American Loop just north of Chamberlain. Owned by the Crow Creek Sioux tribe, the Lode Star boasts 250 slot machines, 6 game tables, and bingo. A 50-room hotel and restaurant also are on-site. To reach the **Golden Buffalo Casino,** cross the river at Fort Thompson and head northwest on Highway 10/1806 until you reach **Lower Brule.** Slot machines and live blackjack and poker in the 9,000-square-foot casino keep the adrenaline flowing. The 38-room resort motel and convention center, restaurant, lounge, and gift shop overlook Lake Sharpe. Call (605) 473-5577 or go to thegoldenbuffalocasino.com for more information.

While driving in the area, keep an eye out for the **Lower Brule buffalo herd** of about 300 spread across 6,200 acres. If you're yearning to learn more about South Dakota's most iconic mammal and to get a closer look, stop in at the Buffalo Interpretive Center, 29349 Hwy. 1806, 7 miles east of Fort Pierre. The center includes videos and hands-on exhibits about the importance of buffalo to the plains culture. For more information, call (605) 223-2260.

The Capital

The easiest way South Dakotans can spot a newcomer is by how he or she pronounces **Pierre,** the state capital. French class will be no help. Here, they say *pier.* The ruggedly autonomous forefathers were perhaps trying to downplay the *très français* beginnings of the state, but it was indeed a Frenchman who started South Dakota's first permanent white settlement in 1832. American Fur Company agent Pierre Chouteau Jr. piloted his steamboat, the *Yellowstone,* to the mouth of the Bad River and established Fort Pierre Chouteau. Representatives from nine Native American tribes brought their furs to trade, principally buffalo, which were valued at the time from $3 to $4 per hide. An average of 17,000 buffalo robes were traded each year. The site of the settlement is now a designated landmark on the National Register of Historic Places. Pierre is the nation's second-smallest capital, with a population of 14,004, but its central location in the middle of the state makes it neutral when it comes to East River–West River favoritism.

The **Oahe Dam,** 4 miles north of Pierre on SD 1806, is a rolled-earth dam that creates the fourth-largest man-made reservoir in the US, running 231 miles from Pierre to Bismarck. With 2,250 miles of shoreline, it claims a longer coast than the state of California and boasts 51 recreational areas. The power plant produces more power than any other in the state—781 MW. Dedicated by President John F. Kennedy in 1962, it houses seven of the world's largest generators. If you want to tour the plant, go to the Oahe Visitor Center at 20207 SD 1804 to sign up and show your ID. Tours are offered three times a day Memorial Day through Labor Day. Call (605) 224-4617 or go to sdmissouririver .com/calendar-event-details/10.

Overlooking the Oahe Reservoir, the **Oahe** (pronounced Oh-ah-ee) **Visitor Center** offers information on anything from recreation to local hotels and restaurants. The center has numerous informational displays, which include Lewis and Clark, the Oahe Chapel, Oahe intake structures, and a Kid's Korner. The center is open from Memorial Day through Labor Day.

The lake takes its name from the Oahe Mission, started in 1874 by the Reverend Thomas L. Riggs, a Congregational minister, and his wife, Cornelia Margaret Foster, to serve the Dakota. The mission was originally located on the site of an old Arikara village, about 5 miles from the location of the modern-day chapel. In Lakota, *Oahe* means "a place to stand on," or "foundation."

In the 1950s, when it became evident that the completion of the Oahe Dam would flood the mission location, the chapel was given to the South Dakota Historical Society. In 1964 it was relocated at the eastern end of Oahe Dam, where it stands today. Nondenominational Sunday services start at 8 a.m. Memorial Day through Labor Day. The chapel is also a popular wedding location.

Fishing on Lake Oahe or Lake Sharpe is legendary. The Walleye Capital of the World also is known for its trophy northern pike, Chinook salmon, white and smallmouth bass, brown and rainbow trout, and catfish also are caught here. Eminent filmmaker Ken Burns, creator of the popular PBS documentaries *Baseball* and *The Civil War,* made a documentary of the Lewis and Clark expedition along the Missouri River system. His crews visited Pierre in the summer of 1995 to capture sections of the river and to film buffalo near the Lower Brule Indian Reservation. "We're looking for stretches of river that represent how it really was," Burns told the *Lincoln* (Nebraska) *Star Journal.* "We want to see it as [Lewis and Clark] might have seen it."

The French connection is underscored at the **Vérendrye Monument** in Fort Pierre, just off US 83 across the Missouri River. The two French brothers Vérendrye were the first white people to set foot in South Dakota in 1743. They buried a lead plate on a bluff that overlooks Fort Pierre to claim the area for King Louis XV of France. A monument in Fort Pierre marks the spot where the plate was discovered after being covered by dirt for generations. Schoolchildren accidentally unearthed it in February 1913. Now the artifact is on display at the ***South Dakota Cultural Heritage Center,*** 900 Governors Dr., a must-see during a visit to Pierre. The free museum uses award-winning displays and hands-on activities to explain the state's heritage of northern plains tribes, trappers, soldiers, pioneers, ruthless gold-diggers, and Old West scoundrels. *Oyate Tawicoh'an* ("The Ways of the People"), a permanent exhibit, showcases Native American history with more than 300 Native American artifacts, including an eagle feather headdress, a full-size tipi, and a mounted buffalo. It's open from 9 a.m. to 4:30 p.m. Mon through Sat, and 1 to 4:30 p.m. Sun year-round. Hours extend until 6:30 p.m. Mon through Sat from Memorial Day through Labor Day. Admission is $4 for adults; $3 for seniors; free for children under 17. All visitors can get in free on the first Sunday of every month. Call (605) 773-3458 or go to history.sd.gov for more details.

During the Thanksgiving and Christmas seasons, the ***Capitol Rotunda*** at 500 E. Capitol Ave. is awash in the lights and color of beautifully hand-decorated trees. The annual ***Christmas at the Capitol*** event began in 1981 after Dottie Howe and her friends couldn't find a perfect tree to display in the rotunda. The group took a dozen or so and bunched them together—kind of like an exaggerated version of Charlie Brown's Christmas tree. Now the display has grown to include close to 100 trees—Black Hills spruce, pine, and other evergreens—that are decorated with holiday themes. See a teddy bear tree, a Victorian Christmas tree, one that's sponsored by the South Dakota China Painters, another fashioned by 5th grade students from Vandenberg Elementary School in Box Elder, the governor's office, members of an appaloosa horse club, a music tree, and even a pheasant tree. More than 50,000 people visit the striking display each year. ***Capitol Christmas Trees*** is open 8 a.m. to 10 p.m. daily the week of Thanksgiving until just after Christmas. For more details, call (605) 773-3178.

South Dakota's State Capitol, which more than casually resembles the Capitol in Washington, DC, looks dazzling. You can see for yourself by scheduling tours with volunteer guides or taking your own self-guided tour between 8 a.m. and 7 p.m. Mon through Fri or 8 a.m. to 5 p.m. weekends and holidays. Call (605) 773-3688 or stop by the Capitol Lake Visitor Center for more information.

Built on a foundation of South Dakota granite, the graceful building features terrazzo floors, coolly elegant marble staircases, stained-glass skylights, and a solid copper dome. This striking limestone structure, which looks much as it did when it was completed in 1910, is one of the most fully restored capitols in the US. The state seal, which bears the motto "Under God the People Rule," symbolizes the way of life in South Dakota and the resources that keep it vital: farming, ranching, industries, tourism, lumbering, manufacturing, and mining, seen in many places in the capitol. The seal was adopted in 1885, four years before the state was admitted to the union, and it appears on the state flag. A blazing sun encircles the seal, which contains the state motto.

Fed by a warm artesian well, *Capitol Lake* never entirely freezes. It has become a winter haven for Canada geese, mallards, wood ducks, and many other varieties of migratory waterfowl. The *Flaming Fountain* perpetually glows as a memorial to all veterans while the *South Dakota Korean & Vietnam War Memorial* stands as a tribute to the valiant South Dakotans who lost their lives in these wars. The names of these slain veterans are carved in granite next to the Flaming Fountain.

didyouknow?

A reproduction of Korczak Ziolkowski's *Fighting Stallions* also stands on the capitol grounds. It was erected in remembrance of the late governor George S. Mickelson and seven staff members and state leaders who died in a plane crash in 1993.

Pierre also has a long military history from the Civil War to the Iraq War. You can learn more about it and get up close to a Sherman tank, General Custer's sword, a Civil War horse-drawn gun, and an A-7D jet fighter at the *South Dakota National Guard Museum* (301 E. Dakota St.). It's open 9 a.m. to 4 p.m. Mon through Fri. Tours can be arranged by calling (605) 773-2475 or visiting sdnationalguardmuseum.sd.gov.

While the goings-on of state government present a busy and intriguing scene in Pierre, this town has more to offer than politics. Another popular Pierre stop is the *South Dakota Discovery Center and Aquarium* (805 W. Sioux Ave.), a former Pierre power plant that now houses hands-on science and technology exhibits and much more. Three aquariums feature native

Pierre Celebrations

In June, visitors can take in the sights and sounds of the city's *Oahe Days*, a three-day celebration of the arts and music. Fun events include paddle board races; a volleyball tournament; children's theater; pony rides; carnival rides; art vendors showing their wares such as rock art, jewelry, soaps, and wood carving. If you're feeling hungry, there's a beer garden, Cuban food, funnel cakes, tacos, pizza, and Greek foods. Stay around in the late afternoons and evenings for events like a pie eating contest, a car show, a rodeo, and main stage entertainment. Check oahedays.com for more information.

species of fish. Visitors can experience the universe through astronomy in the Sky Lab planetarium or test their reflex skills in the reactionary car. The center is open Sun through Fri 1 to 5 p.m. and Sat 10 a.m. to 5 p.m. Summer hours are from 10 a.m. to 5 p.m. Mon through Sat, 1 to 5 p.m. Sun. Admission is $4 for adults and $3 for children 3 and older. For more information, call (605) 224-8295 or visit sd-discovery.com.

If you've worked up an appetite, settle into **La Minestra,** in a restored 1886 tavern at 106 E. Dakota, with wainscoting and original pressed metal walls and ceiling. You might wish the walls could talk—the building has been a funeral parlor, a pool hall and card room, and a country-western bar. As a popular Italian restaurant, it's now known for freshly made pasta dishes and hand-cut steaks. Call (605) 224-8090 or visit laminestra.com.

Fort Pierre was the stomping ground of rodeo legend **Casey Tibbs,** who was born in a log cabin on the family homestead outside Fort Pierre in 1929. A life-size statue of Casey, riding the famous bronc "Necktie," is on display at the Fort Pierre community park and historical turnout. By 15, he was in nationwide competitions, and in 1949, at age 19, Casey became the youngest man ever to win the national saddle bronc-riding crown. Between 1949 and 1955, he won a total of six PRCA saddle bronc-riding championships, a record still unchallenged, plus two all-around cowboy championships and one bareback-riding championship. You can learn more about his colorful, spirited life (including a couple of movies and stunt work) and celebrate South Dakota's rich rodeo history at the **Casey Tibbs Rodeo Center** (210 Verendrye Dr.) overlooking Pierre and Fort Pierre. Exhibits spotlight the work of Mattie Goff Newcombe, a spectacular trick rider of the 1920s, and the work of rodeo clowns, cowboys, entertainers, and rodeo queens. Ride a simulated bronc to see how long 8 seconds really feels, practice throwing a western hat, and marvel at the five large bronze statues. Hours are 9 a.m. to 5 p.m. Mon through Fri; 10 a.m. to 5 p.m. Sat; and noon to 5 p.m. Sun, June through Aug. The rest of the year, hours are 10 a.m. to 5 p.m. Tues through Fri; 10 a.m. to 3 p.m. Sat. Admission is $6 adults, $5 seniors, $4 veterans and kids 6 to 18. Call (605) 494-1094 or visit caseytibbs.com to learn more.

About 8 miles south of Pierre is the **Fort Pierre National Grassland**, 200 undulating square miles of grasslands bisected by US 83. It's a hotspot for birders who come to see the greater prairie chicken, burrowing owls, and raptors, which are especially easy to see during the winter months. This is part of the national grassland that ranges across Nebraska and central and western South Dakota. Open year-round, admission is free. Call (605) 224-5517 for more information.

On Lake Oahe

South Dakota's most northern stretch of the Missouri River snakes its way from North Dakota to Pierre, much of it a lonely stretch with few towns and Standing Rock and Cheyenne River Reservations expanding west from the river. The largest city, **Mobridge** (population 3,520), enjoys the prosperity that the river has afforded. Mobridge calls itself the Walleye Capital of the World, and no one is likely to dispute that moniker, since both the Missouri and the Oahe Reservoir envelop this town. In 1906 the Milwaukee Railroad built the first bridge to cross the Missouri River in South Dakota, at what was formerly the site of an Arikara and Dakota village. A telegraph operator used the contraction *Mobridge* to indicate his location, and the name has stuck.

Lake Oahe, with a shoreline of more than 2,250 miles, is the longest lake on the mainstream of the Missouri River, stretching 231 miles from Pierre to Bismarck, North Dakota. Begun in 1948, it is the largest of the four impoundments. The shoreline is virtually devoid of trees, making it a curious earthbound moonscape. The lake's azure waters and native stands of grass on the bluff, however, make it appealingly endless and warm.

The genuinely down-to-earth people of Mobridge are eager to accommodate the visitors who flock to the town during hunting, fishing, and boating seasons. The choices in lodging are appropriate for both the serious-minded and casual sportsperson.

The sparsely furnished but clean rooms of the **Mo-Rest Motel** on US 12 are perfect for no-frills fishermen who appreciate special amenities for anglers such as aerial river maps. The motel is across the street from two bait shops with boat repair, and you can easily find a guide for on-the-water instruction using the latest fishing techniques and boat control. Call the motel at (605) 845-3668.

Site Selection

Founded in 1901, **Pollock,** northeast of Mobridge in Campbell County, thrived until the early 1950s, when construction of the Oahe Dam threatened to leave the town underwater. For several years the people of Pollock struggled with whether to move, abandon their town, or consolidate with nearby Herreid. After much consideration the town decided to move. But in what direction? A vote was held, and ballots cast, some with a touch of humor. One vote called for Pollock to be put even deeper under the waters of Lake Oahe. Groundbreaking ceremonies for the "new" town were held on June 4, 1955. Today Pollock is surrounded on three sides by water and enjoys its reputation as one of South Dakota's most mobile cities.

History buffs will find a profusion of items to marvel at in the 1930s-era, art-deco **Scherr Howe Arena,** or the city auditorium, on Main Street. Colorful murals by the late Oscar Howe, a highly esteemed Dakota and art professor at the University of South Dakota, depict the history and ceremonies of Native Americans. Each mural measures about 16 feet high by 20 feet wide. For instance, one mural depicts the Social Dance, a prenuptial ceremony common among the Dakota. Custom prescribed a well-established routine for courtship and marriage, but the marital relationship was mostly the result of an agreement between the parties. Since marriage involved being taken into the families of the contracting parties, there were usually group meetings of the relatives with feasting, dancing, and ceremonies that sometimes lasted four or five days. Members of the family wishing to pay tribute to the bride and groom brought appropriate gifts. The bride was suitably honored, her hair combed and braided, and she was given face paints and beautiful garments. Earthenware vessels and other household goods also were common wedding presents.

The groom's father also brought gifts that he bestowed upon his son. Spirited horses and weapons used in the chase and in battle were among the gifts given to honor the new union. Songs of praise about the newlyweds were sung, and small gifts were distributed to the elderly and needy people of the camp. Admission to the center is free. Call (605) 845-3700 for more information.

For more history on the Arikara and Dakota, head 2 miles west on US 12 to the **Klein Museum** at 1820 W. Grand Crossing. Arikara and Dakota artifacts share space with relics of the pioneer past, such as old farm machinery and a restored schoolhouse. This museum was the dream of an early homesteader, Jake Klein, long before the building was ever designed. His goal was to have a top-notch museum that would represent the counties of Campbell, Corson, Dewey, and Walworth, where he traded, homesteaded, and finally retired.

The museum building, with its native stone front, was Klein's gift to Mobridge and the surrounding area with the help of a $15,000 grant from the South Dakota Bicentennial Commission. The museum displays focus on prairie and Native American artifacts. More than 20 pictures of Sitting Bull are featured, along with stone and bone artifacts. The culture of the Dakota and Arikara is reflected in the many articles of clothing, beadwork, pottery, tools, and implements that are on display. The daily tasks of the early pioneers also come alive through the room scenes. For instance, the 1900s pre-electric kitchen features a wood/coal stove, large doughmaker, berry press, kraut cutter, and wooden icebox. A one-room schoolhouse and the original Glencross post office are also located on the museum grounds.

Mobridge's Mystical Stones

One of the biggest mysteries in Mobridge can be found in City Park on N. Main Street. It's here that what was called the **Conqueror's Stones** were discovered. No one knows why or when they were put here on the north side of the park, platted in 1910. The original inscription once said:

Note the grooves
According to tradition, defeated Indian warriors were required to place their hands in these grooves as a sign of submission

Shetak captives rescued here
November 1862
by fool soldier band

Continued research revealed a more hopeful meaning. The stones were commonly referred to as prayer rocks. Native Americans would place their hands in the grooves in the rocks when taking an oath as part of initiation ceremonies. Some believe the grooves are the handprints of the Thunderheads, the powerful gods displayed on totem poles. According to this belief, by putting their hands in the prints before they died, the Native Americans would be taken to the Sky World, or heaven.

The museum is open 9 a.m. to noon and 1 to 5 p.m. Mon through Fri; 1 to 5 p.m. Sat and Sun, Apr 15 through Oct 15. It's closed Tues in Apr, May, and Oct. Admission is $3 for adults, $2 for students. For more information, call (605) 845-7243.

The *Fool Soldier Band Monument* is located at the Klein Museum. On August 20–22, 1862, a group of Santee, a subgroup of the Dakota, fled west with a group of white captives as part of the US-Dakota War that started in August 1862 in the southwest Minnesota. A group of young Teton, also called Lakota, negotiated for the release of the white captives and returned them to their families in Minnesota. They expected no rewards or reimbursement, and their actions seemed to be motivated by purely humanitarian concerns. This act of heroism took place in what is now Walworth County.

In Mobridge the Missouri River and Lake Oahe are the center of outdoor leisure. Fishing isn't the only sport in town; the Mobridge area is also a hunter's paradise, with open seasons on pheasant, grouse, turkey, deer, and antelope. Water-skiing, swimming, boating, or just soaking up the brilliant South Dakota sun can easily fill an afternoon.

Indian Creek Recreation Area (located 2 miles east on US 12, then 1 mile south) on the Oahe Reservoir offers fishing and water sports, along with picnicking, playgrounds, tent, and trailer sites and 2.5 miles of trails. For more information call (605) 845-7112. **Bridge City Marina** (605-845-9129; bridgecity marina.com) is also located here.

Sitting Bull Monument, in Dakota Memorial Park, west of Mobridge on US 12, marks the burial site of the famous Hunkpapa medicine man. Like many chapters in the collective story of Native Americans living on the plains, Sitting Bull's is one of a fascinating, enigmatic man who met an untimely death. Sitting Bull was born in 1834 on the Grand River, a few miles west of Mobridge, and his tragic demise years later occurred in the same place. The last known leader of the *Cante Tizna*, an elite warrior society, Sitting Bull helped to defeat General George Custer's troops in 1876 at the Battle of the Little Big Horn. Sitting Bull met his own death, however, after he was arrested and then shot at his camp on the Standing Rock agency near Fort Yates in North Dakota.

The bodies of Sitting Bull and his men were buried in the corner of a post cemetery at Fort Yates. On April 8, 1953, descendants, with the help of the Dakota Memorial Association, moved Sitting Bull's remains to the present location and dedicated the memorial.

The giant granite bust of Sitting Bull was carved by Korczak Ziolkowski, who also started the Crazy Horse Memorial in the Black Hills. The marker today

didyouknow?

Some 135 million years ago, the area around Mobridge was covered by a great shallow sea, teeming with marine mollusks and shellfish. Clues to their prehistoric existence have turned up along the shores of Lake Oahe in the form of fossil ammonites, baculites, and belemnites that range from 1 to 6 inches long. If you look hard enough, you might find one of the ancient treasures.

Native South Dakota

After the US-Dakota War in 1862, most of Minnesota's Dakota tribes were banished west by the US government to reservations in South Dakota. Today, South Dakota has nine tribes, representing about 62,000 residents and operating as sovereign nations. They speak three dialects: Dakota, Lakota, and Nakota. They include:

Cheyenne River Sioux

Crow Creek Sioux

Flandreau Santee Sioux

Lower Brule Sioux

Oglala Sioux

Rosebud Sioux

Sisseton-Wahpeton Sioux

Standing Rock Sioux

Yankton Sioux

Powwow Etiquette

With numerous tribes throughout South Dakota, you can find *wacipis* (powwows) throughout the year. These celebratory, spiritual, and often public events offer non–Native Americans a chance to learn about the culture. They can last anywhere from a few hours to several days and frequently include craft displays, rodeos, ethnic foods, cultural exhibits, and the marvelous drumming, singing, dancing, and vibrant regalia.

To be a courteous guest at a powwow, here are a few tips:

- It's generally acceptable to take photos or videos, but check beforehand.
- Ask permission before taking someone's photo outside of the dance circle.
- Stand at the "Grand Entry" to pay respect to the dancers. Remain standing for the Great Sioux Nation's national anthem.
- The dance area is considered sacred; don't enter it unless invited.
- Many powwows lack seating, so bring along a lawn chair or blanket and make yourself comfortable.
- To find out about upcoming powwows, check with sites such as sdtribalrelations .com or drumhop.com.

seems desolate and rather forgotten. Sitting Bull's remains, encased in a steel vault, are embedded in a 20-ton block of concrete on which the monument stands. The grave site is open to the public free of charge.

Adjacent to the Sitting Bull Monument on the west bank of the Missouri River is the ***Cheyenne River Tribe's Grand River Casino & Resort,*** with more than 15,000 square feet of gambling fun, as well as a lounge, an outdoor amphitheater, and a restaurant, perched high on a bluff overlooking Lake Oahe. The Grand River casino, owned by the Standing Rock Sioux tribe, features slots, blackjack, and poker. The casino walls are decorated with the artwork of Del Iron Cloud. The casino is located 2.5 miles west of Mobridge on US 12. For more information call (605) 845-7104 or go to grandrivercasino.com.

It is also fitting that a memorial to Sakakawea (an alternate spelling of Sacagawea), the indomitable guide of Lewis and Clark, is located near the Sitting Bull Monument. Sakakawea, or Bird Woman, was a 12-year-old Shoshone living in the Big Horn Mountains of Montana when she was captured by raiding Hidatsu. They later sold or traded her to a French fur trapper, and she lived with him as his wife in what is now central North Dakota. Four years later, she and her husband were hired by explorers Lewis and Clark to accompany their expedition on their trip west in 1804.

BEST ATTRACTIONS ALONG THE MISSOURI RIVER

Grand River Casino & Resort	Sitting Bull Monument
Karl E. Mundt National Wildlife Refuge	South Dakota Cultural Heritage Center
Oahe Dam	South Dakota Discovery Center and Aquarium
Scherr Howe Arena	
	West Whitlock Recreation Area

Sakakawea guided the expedition over seemingly insurmountable obstacles. Much of the credit for the venture's success is given to her. She died later of "putrid fever" in 1812, at the age of 25, at Fort Manuel, a short distance north of Mobridge. In 1929, Mobridge schoolchildren donated pennies to erect a monument to honor this illustrious Shoshone. On September 27, 1929, a graceful cement shaft with a bronze plaque was erected at the Dakota Memorial Park in her memory.

Two of the state's more sparsely populated Indian reservations abut Mobridge to the west. The **Standing Rock Indian Reservation** covers 562,366 acres in South Dakota (it extends into south-central North Dakota). The **Cheyenne River Indian Reservation** covers 1.4 million acres, making it the second-largest reservation in the state.

In Eagle Butte southwest of Mobridge, the **H. V. Johnston Cultural Center** (605-964-2542) displays traditional beadwork and murals that depict the Lakota way of life. You also can buy beadwork and paintings by contemporary artists here. The center is located on US 212 near SD 63 on the Cheyenne River Indian Reservation. Free admission.

One of the area's more famous residents is Arvol Looking Horse, a 19th-generation keeper of the Sacred Pipe of the Great Sioux Nation. In this position he cares for the Sacred Pipe, presented by the White Buffalo Calf Woman many years ago. Born in 1954, Looking Horse leads the annual Sacred Pipestone Run, which was formed to stop the sale of sacred pipestone. He holds an honorary degree from the University of South Dakota and has been profiled many times by local and national media. Looking Horse also is featured in the book of portraiture, *Visions Quest,* the photographic story of contemporary Lakotas, Dakotas, and Nakotas who have chosen to carry on the traditions and culture of their people.

South Dakota Mixtape

Liven up a long road trip with downloads, audio books, and compact discs from South Dakota authors and artists:

Dakota: A Spiritual Geography by Kathleen Norris

Little House on the Prairie by Laura Ingalls Wilder

A Long Way from Home: Growing up in the American Heartland, The Greatest Generation, An Album of Memories from longtime NBC Nightly News anchor Tom Brokaw

Seth Bullock: Black Hills Lawman by David A. Wolff, a factual account of the lawman portrayed on the TV series, *Deadwood*

"A Few Small Repairs" or "Fat City" from singer/songwriter Shawn Colvin

"We the People" or other recordings by Brule, one of the nation's best-known and most award-winning Native American musical groups

Pioneers and Walleyes

While Native American history swells from the central plains of the state, the tiny town of *Eureka,* northeast of Mobridge on SD 10, shows the Old World's contribution to America's melting pot. For more than 100 years, beginning in the late 1700s, German colonists had been permitted to live in Russia and retain their culture, customs, and language; then, in 1871, Czar Alexander II revoked the agreement, which spurred a mass exodus. Thousands of German-Russian immigrants made their way to Dakota Territory, and eventually to Eureka. You can find German influences throughout Eureka. Many of the 840 residents still speak German, often slipping between English and German without a thought. The Lutheran church had two pastors—one English-speaking and one German-speaking—well into the 1960s. Appropriately, the town celebrates its heritage with the annual *German-Russian Schmeckfest* during the third weekend in September. It's an ideal opportunity to enjoy the local cuisine, from savory sausages to the famed state dessert—*kuchen.* The town even has a kuchen factory, so you're sure to find a wide variety of the sweet, custardy dessert. For more information, see eurekasd.com.

You can learn more about the area's German-Russian roots and its frontier past at *the Eureka Pioneer Museum of McPherson County* on SD 10 at the west edge of town. Open Wed through Sun, Apr 15 to Nov 1, its exhibits encompass military memorabilia, furniture, household items, and antique farm machinery. There is no admission charge, but donations are always appreciated. Call (605) 284-2711 or visit eurekasd.com/Unique/museum.htm for hours.

Neuharth is a common name in this part of the country, and it's also the last name of Al Neuharth, one of its most famous natives. Founder of Gannett Newspapers, Al Neuharth recalls his impoverished youth in his book, *Confessions of an S.O.B.* The town's information booth on the west edge of town is dedicated to Al Neuharth's father, Daniel J. Neuharth.

To see one of South Dakota's more intriguing pieces of history, take US 212 east for just a few miles to ***Gettysburg*** (population 1,116), located in the Whitlock Bay area on the eastern shore of Lake Oahe. Gettysburg was settled in 1883 by 211 veterans of the famous Civil War battle after which the town was named. Many of the streets, townships, and communities in the area share names intrinsically associated with the Civil War. The town's most popular historic exhibit is the mysterious 40-ton Medicine Rock on display at the ***Dakota Sunset Museum*** (205 W. Commercial St.). The rock—considered sacred by local Native Americans—is embedded with footprints believed to have been made by the Great Spirit. The limestone rock measures 10 by 20 feet and doesn't sit all that high. The museum also includes a Civil War exhibit, big game exhibition, and a painting of the Battle of Shiloh. The local historical society also takes care of the ***G. L. Stocker Blacksmith Shop,*** which served as the Grand Army of the Republic Hall during the post–Civil War years and later became a blacksmith shop. Renovated to its original condition from the early part of the 20th century, it includes an interpretive center. Dakota Sunset museum is open 1 to 5 p.m. daily during summer months, and Tues through Sat the rest of the year. For more information call (605) 765-9480 or visit dakota sunsetmuseum.com.

If you like camping, Gettysburg offers free sites in its city park, and you'll find both state-run and privately operated camping facilities nearby. One of the most popular destinations for campers, boaters, and anglers is ***West Whitlock Recreation Area*** with its 105 sites and 2 camping cabins (800-710-2267; gfp .sd.gov/parks/). Just 15 minutes west of Gettysburg on US 212, its beautiful setting on giant Lake Oahe began as a campsite for the Arikara and Mandan people. The replica of an Arikara earth lodge found in the park is a reminder of the many lodges that the Lewis and Clark expedition saw as they traveled

wheatkings

From 1887 to 1902, Eureka was known as the greatest primary wheat market in the world. As many as 32 grain buyers worked day and night, storing and shipping wheat brought in by horses and oxen. In 1892, 3,330 freight-car loads of wheat were shipped from the town.

fishingrules

You can request a copy of the current *South Dakota Fishing Handbook* by visiting flipsnack.com/SDGamefishparks/gfp-fishing-handbook-2019.html.

this area. Each lodge, made of cottonwood logs, willow branches, and grass, could house up to 20 people. The Arikara people were farmers and grew crops such as corn, beans, squash, sunflowers, and tobacco.

When the area became a park, it was named for Mrs. J. F. Whitlock, whose pioneering family once owned the land. Whitlock Crossing was the name given to a small settlement that operated a ferry across the river near the area. Although a 36-pound northern pike was caught from shore in 1993, the main sport fish here is walleye. The annual *Whitlock Bay Walleye Tournament,* which is held each summer, offers competitors big prizes and lots of action. For more information, call (605) 769-4148 or visit northernoaheseries.com/whitlock-bay.php.

The reservoir's newest sport fish is the Chinook salmon. Each year up to a million eggs are taken from adult salmon at *Whitlock Bay Salmon Spawning Station*; after hatching, fingerling salmon are returned to the lake. When adult salmon return in the fall, these fast and furious swimmers will test the skills of even the most avid fishermen. The salmon station at Whitlock Bay is open on spawn days during October. Call (605) 223-7681 or go to gfp.sd.gov/whitlock/ for more information.

Hunters will feel right at home on the 10,000-acre *Paul Nelson Farm.* Half the acreage is dedicated to pheasant hunting. They offer different hunting packages, corporate retreats, shooting schools, fly-fishing schools, and more. For more information, call (605) 765-2469 or visit paulnelsonfarm.com.

SELECTED CHAMBERS OF COMMERCE

Chamberlain–Oacoma Area Chamber of Commerce
112 N. Main St.
Chamberlain 57325
(605) 234-4416
chamberlainsd.org

Mobridge Chamber of Commerce
212 N. Main St.
Mobridge 57601
(605) 845-2387
mobridge.org

Pierre Convention and Visitors Bureau
800 W. Dakota Ave.
Pierre 57501
(605) 224-7361
pierre.org

South Dakota Missouri River Tourism
(888) 386-4617
sdmissouririver.com

Where to Stay Along the Missouri River

CHAMBERLAIN-OACOMA

Howard Johnson Inn and Suites
203 East W. Hwy.
(605) 679-6367
wyndhamhotels.com/hojo
Moderate

Quality Inn
100 Hwy. 16
(605) 734-5593
choicehotels.com
Moderate

EUREKA

Lakeview Motel
1307 J Ave., Hwy. 10
(605) 284-2400
Inexpensive

MOBRIDGE

Wrangler Inn
820 W. Grand Crossing
(605) 845-3641
wranglerinn.com
Inexpensive

PIERRE/FT. PIERRE

Eagle's View Bed & Breakfast
710 Verendrye Dr.
(605) 224-4053
eaglesview.org
Inexpensive to moderate

Governor's Inn
700 W. Sioux Ave.
(605) 224-4200
govinn.com
Moderate

Hitching Horse Inn
635 N. Euclid Ave.
(605) 494-9550
Moderate

Quality Inn
410 W. Sioux Ave.
(605) 609-0325
choicehotels.com
Moderate

Ramkota Hotel
920 W. Sioux Ave.
(605) 224-6877
ramkotapierre.com
Moderate

Where to Eat Along the Missouri River

CHAMBERLAIN/OACOMA

Anchor Grille
117 S. Main St.
(605) 234-5481
Inexpensive to moderate

Bridges Restaurant & Lounge
(at Cedar Shore Resort)
1500 Shoreline Dr.
(605) 734-6376
arrowwoodcedarshore.com
Moderate

Charlys Restaurant & Lounge
606 E. King St.
(605) 234-6238
Moderate

The Smoking Mule
309 E. N St.
(605) 234-6853
Moderate

GREGORY

The Homesteader
119 Main St.
(605) 835-8881
Moderate

MOBRIDGE

Great Plains Family Restaurant
906 W. Great Plains Crossing
(605) 845-7495
facebook.com/GreatPlains FamilyRestaurant
Inexpensive to moderate

PIERRE

Big Tom's Diner
1415 E. Wells Ave.
(605) 224-7600
Inexpensive

Cattleman's Club Steakhouse
29608 Hwy. 34
(605) 224-9774
cattlemansclublodge.com
Moderate to expensive

RedRossa Italian Grill
1859 W. Sioux Ave. #200
(605) 494-2599
redrossa.com
Moderate

Zesto Shop
213 W. Capitol
(605) 224-4681
Moderate

Western South Dakota

While glaciers flattened the eastern half of South Dakota, the west kept its ruggedness in more than just geography. Strength and a sense of individualism thrive in the lifestyles of its residents, from its early visionaries, explorers, and miners to modern cowboys and Native Americans who also embrace centuries-old traditions. This is a land so rich in natural wonders, you'll find something fresh to experience no matter how many times you visit. There are few other places where you can go deep into a jeweled cave and enjoy top-of-the-world views in the same day. No wonder there's a tangible spirit here in this often sacred landscape that the Lakota call Paha Sapa, or Black Hills.

That diverse topography and spirit also make a trip here one of America's most beloved road trips, from wide-open grasslands and the eerie moonscape of the Badlands to the patriotic pride of Mount Rushmore and fragrant, thick pine forests. The Black Hills in particular buzz with activity from Memorial Day to Labor Day as seasonal shops and attractions hit full swing. Visitors stream in from across the globe, especially for the famed Sturgis bike rally. It's surprisingly easy, though, to dodge crowds and find overlooked places or fresh

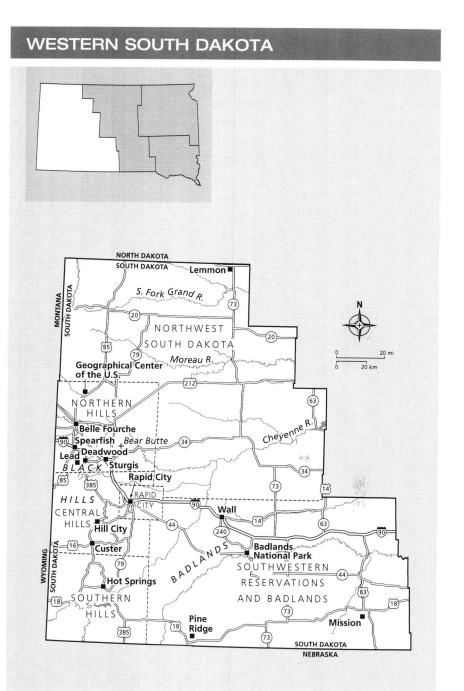

ways to experience favorite attractions. Give yourself time for quiet hikes along the Black Hills' glittering trails where you can hear the wind singing through the pines. Or walk across wide-open prairies to imagine the lives of Native Americans more than a century ago.

Southwestern Reservations

To truly get off the beaten path, explore some of South Dakota's reservations where towns are few and far between, but history and tradition remain deeply rooted in the rolling hills and grasslands. Nine federally recognized tribes call South Dakota home. Rosebud Reservation, home of the Rosebud Sioux, and Pine Ridge Reservation, home of the Oglala, are among the largest. Far away from the noise of more prominent attractions, their towns and other Dakota reservations offer an authentic glimpse at the state's Native American culture, both its past and its present.

Start at *Rosebud Indian Reservation* in south-central South Dakota. The state's most populated reservation, with 11,354 residents, covers 992,759 acres with headquarters in Rosebud. Most visitors head to St. Francis, home of the *Buechel Memorial Lakota Museum* (350 S. Oak St.). The museum displays many Lakota items, ranging from traditional dress to hunting tools, as well as historic photographs of Sicangu Brulé Lakota Chief Spotted Tail, who strove for peace between his people and the white settlers during the turbulent 1800s. Spotted Tail selected this land for his followers in 1877.

The museum was named for another spiritual leader of the times, although he was not a Native American. Father Eugene Buechel was a Jesuit priest assigned to the St. Francis Mission. Intrigued by the native culture, he collected photographs and artifacts and wrote several books in Lakota. His collection is the heart of the museum. Located on the grounds of the St. Francis Mission (which was built in 1916), the museum is open 8 a.m. to 5 p.m. Mon through Sat, and 9 a.m. to 4 p.m. Sun, Memorial Day through Labor Day. Admission is free although a $5 donation is suggested. You may be able to visit in the off-season by making an appointment. Call (605) 747-2361 for more information or visit sfmission.org.

If you drive about two hours west of the Rosebud Reservation, following US 18, you'll reach the heart of *Pine Ridge Indian Reservation*, the second-largest reservation in the country.

Pine Ridge is most famous for the tragedy of *Wounded Knee,* a massacre of innocents in the winter of 1890. Chief Big Foot and his Minniconjou band had set out for Pine Ridge following the death of spiritual leader Sitting Bull on December 15. They were intercepted by the 7th Cavalry and were brought,

Famous Sons

The late **Ben Reifel,** a five-term US congressman, was born near Parmelee on the Rosebud Reservation in 1906. During his lifetime he worked for the Bureau of Indian Affairs, served in the US Army, and received a doctoral degree from Harvard University. Reifel ran for office in 1960 and served until his retirement in 1971. He died in 1990. The Badlands Visitors Center is named for him.

White Eagle, a member of the Rosebud Sioux tribe, was the first Native American to sing leading tenor roles in American musical theater and opera. He graduated from the prestigious Merola Opera program at the San Francisco Opera and performed with the Pennsylvania Opera Theatre, Florentine Opera, and Cleveland Opera, among others.

Tim Giago is a journalist and publisher of the *Lakota Times*, the first independent Native American newspaper in the nation. In 2009, he founded the *Native Sun News,* and is a columnist for the *Huffington Post*. He also started the Native American Journalists Association which has 500 members across the US.

Among the most famous members of the Pine Ridge Indian Reservation is runner **Billy Mills,** who won the 1964 Olympic gold for the 10,000-meter race, becoming the first American to win it.

under a white flag of truce, to Wounded Knee. On the morning of December 29, soldiers prepared to search the band for weapons. A rifle was fired, setting off intense shooting that killed more than 250 natives, most of them unarmed. Bodies of women and children were found as far as 3 miles from the site, apparently shot as they fled into the plains.

If you know the story and don't mind the extra driving, you can visit the **Wounded Knee National Historic Landmark,** which is 8 miles east of the town of Pine Ridge on US 18, then 7 miles north on an unnumbered paved road. While bits of prayer fabric tied to the chain-link fence riffle in the wind, it's a sad site that doesn't seem to have the care and dignity you'd expect for a national historic landmark and tragedy of this size. A solitary stone monument stands on the mass grave site.

Residents of Pine Ridge Reservation struggle with the highest level of poverty in the US with up to 80 percent unemployment. The culture and traditions are rich, though, and you can learn more about the tribe by heading north toward Kyle, where you'll find a visitor center at 7900 Lakota Prairie Dr. and **Oglala Lakota College Historical Center** about 7 miles southwest of Kyle. The historical center depicts their story from the early 1800s through the Wounded Knee Massacre. Call (605) 455-6000 for details or go to olc.edu.

BEST ANNUAL EVENTS IN WESTERN SOUTH DAKOTA

JULY

Days of '76 (Rodeo and Parade)
Deadwood
daysof76.com

Gold Discovery Days
Custer
(605) 673-2244

AUGUST

Central States Fair
Rapid City
centralstatesfair.com

SEPTEMBER

Buffalo Roundup and Arts Festival
Custer State Park
gfp.sd.gov/buffalo-roundup/

OCTOBER

Black Hills Powwow and Art Expo
Rapid City
blackhillspowwow.com

Native American Day
Crazy Horse Memorial

The *Heritage Center at Red Cloud Indian School* (100 Mission Dr.) features a Native American art collection that is considered one of the finest in the Northern Plains. It includes more than 2,000 graphics, paintings, and sculptures from the annual Red Cloud Indian Arts show, a large national competition for native artists from all over North America. The show runs from June through mid-Aug and attracts more than 11,000 visitors who enjoy discovering up-and-coming Native American artists. Leave time to browse the gift shop with its locally crafted star quilts, bead and quill work, Dakota dictionaries, pottery, and music recordings. Purchases help support the community. The Heritage Center is open year-round from 8 a.m. to 5 p.m. Mon through Fri; open weekends and holidays by appointment. Call (605) 867-1105 or visit redcloudschool.org for more information.

For more information on the Pine Ridge community and its attractions, including tours, horseback rides, and events, check with the Pine Ridge Area Chamber of Commerce at (605) 455-2685 or pineridgechamber.com.

About 120,000 acres of the Pine Ridge Indian Reservation lie within *Badlands National Park.* Farther from the interstate, this less-crowded South Unit was added to the park in 1976. Oglala Sioux Parks and Recreation Authority runs the White River Visitor Center here, open 9 a.m. to 5 p.m. daily (summer only). It includes cultural exhibits and a videotape program on Oglala history. Call (605) 455-2878 for more information.

Heading into the Badlands

If you're approaching the **Badlands** from the east, take exit 131 off I-90 and look for the new visitor center at the **Minuteman Missile National Historic Site** that opened on the north side of the exit in November 2014. The historic site itself opened to the public in 2004, and a 12-minute video will get you oriented to South Dakota's Minuteman Missile Field that included 150 silos and cost $56 million to build in the early 1960s. By today's dollars, the Cold War national defense would be well over $9 billion. These missiles, which were part of the Minuteman Missile force located in other parts of the US, were operational from 1961 to 1994. Two officers were on duty at all times to launch the ten missiles under their control if ordered by the president of the US.

Visitors can look through a glass enclosure atop the Delta-09 missile silo, catch a ranger talk, or choose a cell-phone or self-guided brochure tour. This site is located just south of exit 116. The National Park Service advises visitors coming here not to use GPS devices because of unreliable signals. This site is open daily, 9 a.m. to 3 p.m. Free.

The best option, though, is to plan ahead and get a coveted spot on the in-depth 30-minute tours that visit the underground Delta-01 launch control site. South Dakota's missiles were operational from 1961 to 1994. Admission

AUTHOR'S FAVORITES IN WESTERN SOUTH DAKOTA

Badlands National Park
(605) 433-5361
nps.gov/badl

Black Hills National Forest
(605) 673-9200
fs.usda.gov/blackhills

Crazy Horse Memorial
(605) 673-4681
crazyhorsememorial.org

Custer State Park
(605) 255-4515
gfp.sd.gov/parks/detail/custer-state-park

Jewel Cave National Monument
(605) 673-8300
nps.gov/jeca

Mammoth Site
Hot Springs
(605) 745-6017
mammothsite.org

Mount Rushmore National Memorial
(605) 574-2523
nps.gov/moru

Rapid City Downtown
(800) 487-3223
downtownrapidcity.com

for the Delta-01 Launch Control Facility is $12 for adults and $8 for ages 6 to 16. The visitor center is free.

Due to confines within Delta-01, only six spots are available per tour and can be reserved up to three months in advance. The site is now open year-round, with spring and fall the ideal times to secure a tour. Call (605) 433-5552 or go to nps.gov/mimi for more information.

From the missile site exit, head south on SD 240 toward Badlands National Park and its east entrance. On the way you'll pass **Prairie Homestead Historic Site,** with one of the original sod buildings on public display in South Dakota. It is furnished in the style of the original homesteaders, and letters and photographs of the original homesteader's family and neighbors offer riveting insight into the hardships they endured. Many of the early homes on the plains and prairies of the Dakotas were built of sod. The homes were efficient—cool in the summer and warm in the winter—but also dark, dirty, and often infested with mice, bedbugs, and other unsavory houseguests. It is open daily, sunrise to sunset, from May through Sept. For more information call (605) 433-5400 or go to prairiehomestead.com.

Badlands National Park is as otherworldly as land can be; soft clays and sandstones were deposited as sediments 26 million to 37 million years ago by streams from the Black Hills that left vast plains. This once rich landscape attracted a community of ancient creatures. Remains of three-toed horses, dog-size camels, and saber-toothed cats have been discovered here in the Oligocene beds. They're considered some of the world's richest vertebrate fossil sites. More than 250,000 of the discovered fossils have been collected by the Museum of Geology in Rapid City while others have gone on to museums such as the Smithsonian. Protecting these fossils from the golden age of mammals was one reason the park expanded to include the White River unit that's part of the Pine Ridge Indian Reservation.

Eventually humans stumbled upon this seemingly hostile land. Upon arriving in the Badlands, native tribes called it *mako sica,* meaning "land bad." French Canadian trappers who traveled through its rugged terrain in the early 1800s dubbed it *les mauvaises terres à traverser,* or "bad lands to travel across." But that doesn't mean they're barren. Keep your eyes peeled and binoculars

fifteenminutes offame

Scenes from *Starship Troopers,* the Paul Verhoeven movie based on Robert A. Heinlein's classic 1959 science-fiction novel, were filmed in the Badlands. Although the movie didn't win an Oscar for best acting or script writing, it gets two thumbs-up for best natural location that is as otherworldly as it gets.

handy, and you may spot Rocky Mountain bighorn sheep, antelope, mule deer, prairie dogs, bison, and the reintroduced black-footed ferret and swift fox living among the Badlands. At a minimum, most visitors drive the stunning 32-mile **Badlands Loop,** which begins at exit 131 off I-90. Leave plenty of time to stop at numerous scenic points for photos and hikes. The Badlands may look stark from the highway, but a closer look lets you see some of the 200 kinds of wildflowers and 50 grasses.

As you wind down the road, you'll pass the **Ben Reifel Visitor Center,** which offers the best all-around introduction to the park from 7 a.m. to as late as 7 p.m. in peak season. Check out the exhibits and cool off in the air-conditioned theater that shows "Land of Stone and Light."

Even if you've seen the Badlands once or several times, they're always worth another look. Like a fine wine, they improve with time as every rainstorm and windstorm gnaws at the sediments and accentuates each ravine and ragged pinnacle. Shifting light constantly repaints the landscape in new colors. If you're lucky enough to see the Badlands when heat lightning crackles up from the horizon or when a rainbow follows a sultry storm, it's a sight you'll never forget. The same goes for staying in the park and enjoying the sunset and moonrise. You'll see rabbits emerging at twilight and hear nocturnal birds and insects cue their evening song. Sunrise, too, can be spectacular with its extra dose of golden light blanketing the buttes and peaks. Favorite hikes include the Fossil Trail, Castle Trail, Door Trail, and Notch Trail.

You can camp in the park's Cedar Pass Campground or the primitive Sage Creek Campground or check into the nearby four-season **Cedar Pass Lodge** cabins. With porches facing the Badlands, small refrigerators, microwaves, and hand-built log beds as part of a major renovation and rebuild, they offer a good reason to stay for a night or more. Call (605) 433-5460 or visit cedarpasslodge .com for more information.

You can also head to the **Badlands Inn** a few miles away near the small town of Interior. If you need a place to dine, stop at the Cedar Pass Lodge restaurant, which includes Indian fry bread buffalo tacos as its signature item, along with lovely views and a gift shop with handmade Oglala Dakota jewelry and crafts, benches made from wagon wheels, local wine, and some groceries.

Because the park's location is far from large urban areas and their lights, it is perfect for gazing at the night heavens. Each year the park takes advantage of its darkness and hosts the annual **Badlands Astronomy Festival.** The dates for the three-day festival change every year based on when the moon is not in the sky, making this one of the darkest places in the country to spot all those glistening, glittering stars. The Black Hills Astronomical Society, Dark Ranger

Telescope Tours, and the national park provide telescopes for those wanting a closer look at faraway galaxies, the moons of Jupiter, Saturn's rings, the Martian polar caps, double stars that look like single ones to the naked eye, and star clusters. During the day, some telescopes are set to safely observe the sun, its spots, and solar flares. For more information, call the park at (605) 433-5361 or watch its website, nps.gov/badl.

As you leave the Badlands at exit 110, you might be parched. The Hustead family built its iconic, campy *Wall Drug* complex banking on that theory and first luring Depression-era travelers with free ice water. Curiosity is the other draw after seeing countless hyped-up billboards spool past on the interstate. It's the kind of place where people playfully pose with statues of cowboys and showgirls perched on benches or sitting atop the famous and fabled 6-foot jackalope. My kids barely give it any notice—not with a snarling, roaring, smoke-snorting animatronic T-Rex that comes to life about every 15 minutes. There's also a water show with jumping jets of water that tempt kids to get playfully soaked. Beyond the gimmicks and souvenirs, the tale of this sprawling 72,000-square-foot emporium and how it became famous is in itself interesting. You also can enjoy displays with more than 600 cattle brands, hundreds of historical pictures, and a collection of Native American artifacts. The cafe still serves 5-cent coffee. You might want a homemade donut or hot beef sandwich

A Rock Hound's Paradise

South Dakota's Badlands and Black Hills region ranks among the top five places in the US for its variety of minerals and rocks. The Black Hills are obviously famous for gold, but also copper, silver, iron, lead, tin, zinc, feldspar, spodumene, and more than 140 other minerals. Expansive surface outcroppings of all three major rock types—igneous, metamorphic, and sedimentary—yield not only rock specimens, but embedded crystals, ores, and fossils. Beds of alluvial outwash on the perimeter of the Black Hills offer a colorful mix of all kinds of stones.

While it's a no-no for rock hounds to go collecting in Badlands National Park, the surrounding public lands—*Buffalo Gap National Grasslands*—hold some fine rock beds that produce Fairburn agates, funny eye, gay prairie, and bubblegum agates, red jasper, blue chalcedony, and petrified wood.

You can stop by the *National Grasslands Visitor Center* at 708 Main St. in Wall to learn more about four main ecosystems of the High Plains and learn more about one of the country's largest protected mixed-grass prairies. Kids can earn one of the national park service's junior ranger badges, and you can get maps and advice for the best areas to find rocks. Call (605) 279-2125 or visit fs.usda.gov/nebraska for more information.

to eat with it. Wall Drug Store is open year-round. Call or go online for current hours; (605) 279-2175; walldrug.com.

Just a minute away from Wall Drug Store at 600 Main St., **Wounded Knee Museum** shares harrowing and heartbreaking details of the Wounded Knee Massacre through vivid graphics and photographs. Native American gifts, jewelry, books, and T-shirts are also sold here. For more information, call (605) 279-2573 or visit woundedkneemuseum.org.

As the Badlands disappear into the rearview mirror, it's just an hour to Rapid City and the foothills of the Black Hills National Forest. About 7 miles before you reach the city, you'll hit exit 66 and Ellsworth Air Force Base. Besides being an active base, it's home to the **South Dakota Air & Space Museum** (2890 Rushmore Rd.). The free museum includes historic bombers, fighters, missiles, and utility aircraft, as well as many indoor exhibits of aviation memorabilia June 1 through early Sept. Here you can see a three-fifths-scale model of the Honda Stealth bomber and General Eisenhower's personal Mitchell B-25 bomber. Ellsworth is home to the 28th Bomb Wing and B-1B bombers—one is displayed at the museum—and it's not uncommon to see the sleek, low-level bomber graze the skyline. Visitors can also take a 60- to 90-minute bus tour of the base and a Minuteman Missile silo for $5 to $10 per person mid-May through mid-Sept. Identification is required for anyone over 18. The museum's hours vary seasonally. For more information call (605) 385-5189 or visit sdairandspacemuseum.com.

Once you hit the Hills, the number of places to go and things to do can be overwhelming. Head to the **Black Hills Visitor Information Center** to get oriented to the vast region and to get help with must-have maps, on-site trip counseling, free Wi-Fi, and brochures galore. Exhibits and displays preview national parks, state parks, and every community in the Black Hills and Badlands region. To reach the center at 1851 Discovery Circle in Rapid City, take exit 61 (Elk Vale Road) north off I-90 to E. Mall Dr. Open year-round from 8 a.m. to 6 p.m. daily, with extended hours from May through Sept. Call (605) 355-3700 for more information or go to blackhillsbadlands.com.

Rapid City

To "lay out a Denver" was what the city founders—a group of unlucky miners—had in mind for **Rapid City** when they established it in 1876. With a population of 74,421, South Dakota's second-largest city didn't reach the same size as Colorado's capital, but you won't hear anyone complaining. Growth has been steady, downtown is thriving, and Rapid City is large enough to lure a variety of cultural attractions while remaining laid-back and welcoming.

Dinos, Fossils, and Rocks

Head to the **Museum of Geology** at the **South Dakota School of Mines and Technology** (501 E. St. Joseph St.) on the third floor of the O'Harra Building, and you'll understand why folks from Rapid City are so crazy about dinosaurs. This gem of a museum exhibits some of the best local fossils, giant fish, prehistoric mammals, and dinosaurs, including the state's official dinosaur, a triceratops skeleton found in Harding County in 1927. The school boasts the largest paleontology program in the country. It's no wonder with major digs and discoveries in western South Dakota and eastern Wyoming.

Dioramas tell the story of the Badlands and the strange and wild creatures that once lived there. Rock hounds can find a collection of minerals, ores, and local agates, including the state gemstone: the beautiful Fairburn agate. Hours are 9 a.m. to 5 p.m. Mon through Fri; until 6 p.m. on Sat; and noon to 5 p.m. Sun during the summer. From Labor Day through Memorial Day it's open 9 a.m. to 4 p.m. Mon through Fri, and 10 a.m. to 4 p.m. Sat. Call (605) 394-2467 or go to museum.sdsmt.edu for details and special programs, including hands-on paleo trips for families or adults during the summer. Admission is free, but donations are appreciated.

Rapid City's most remarkable museum, *The Journey* (222 New York St.) blends local history with the nature of the universe. Its excursion through time unifies collections from five sources: the Museum of Geology, the South Dakota State Archaeological Research Center, the Sioux Indian Museum, the Minnilusa Pioneer Museum Collection, and the Duhamel Collection. The museum tour begins with a 20-minute video, which details pioneer and Native American history. The self-guided tour begins with 1,000 points of light that represent the immense nature of a universe deep in space and time. The time line takes you from the formation of the Black Hills billions of years ago to the present day. Visitors are given sound sticks so they can listen to historical stories and descriptions at each exhibit. Open Mon through Sat from 9 a.m. to 6 p.m., Sun 11 a.m. to 5 p.m. during the summer. Winter hours are Mon through Sat 10 a.m. to 5 p.m., and Sun 1 to 5 p.m. Admission is $12 for adults, $10 for seniors, $7 for children ages 6 to 17. Call (605) 394-6923 or go to journeymuseum.org for information about special events that bring to life the colorful and sometimes infamous characters of the Dakota past.

Don't miss **Rapid City's historic downtown** district, especially if you haven't seen it in a few years. With the **Main Street Square** project that creates a lively gathering place, fountains, and events, there's new energy humming along its pretty blocks, and you'll want at least a few hours to explore and enjoy it. What else will you need? Bring an appetite for the tasty temptations down every block, tucked between galleries and boutiques and offering date-night dinners, kick-back lunches, and cold beers. At a minimum, grab an ice-cream cone or frothy coffee and take a seat at Main Street Square to watch kids playing in the fountains on sunny summer days or skating in the winter.

If it's summer, grab a seat in the shady courtyard outside **Firehouse Brewing Co.** (610 Main St.; 605-348-1915; firehousebrewing.com). If you traveled from the east, you probably saw their red attention-grabbing fire engines along the interstate, because, yes, this is in an honest-to-goodness 1915 firehouse, complete with historic photos and memorabilia. It was the first brew-pub in the state and now makes 40 beers a year with 9 always on tap, including seasonal brews. They expanded in 2014 to include the **Firehouse Wine Cellars** with more than 30 wines. The restaurant is popular for English pub foods such as beer-battered fish and chips and bangers, gorgonzola ale soup and beer bread, gumbo, and ribs. Call (605) 716-9463 or go to firehousewinecellars.com.

> ## didyouknow?
>
> You can see more than 700 dancers in full regalia, hear the jingle of skirts, and feel the drums each October at the **Black Hills Powwow**. Plains Indians from nearly 60 tribes attend this annual event at the Rushmore Plaza Civic Center. Call (605) 341-0925 or visit blackhillspowwow.com for more information.

At the sleek **Tally's Silver Spoon** (530 6th St.; 605-342-7621; tallyssilver spoon.com), chef and owner Benjamin Klinkel's focus is on food, from regular pancakes to "Really French Toast" with foie gras, berries, granola, and maple cream. Choose buffalo hanger steak on a baguette or pulled pork with a pickled beet slaw for lunch. Try the Paha Sapa bison with spaghetti squash, kale, and wojape or an autumn oak pheasant with chestnut stuffing for supper. Leave room for desserts like crepes or "S'morea Indoors" made with buttermilk cake and smoked chocolate.

Enigma also has drawn praise. While it's located in the Rushmore Hotel and Suites (445 Mount Rushmore Rd.), it doesn't feel anything like a typical hotel restaurant. Diners slide into dark-wood booths beneath blue pendant lights and choose from menu items that may include steak and potato Caesar salad, Moroccan lamb, pan-seared duck, parm panini, and cedar plank salmon. Desserts might include sweet potato cheesecake and almond tiramisu. If you're in the mood for a drink, its **445 Martini Lounge** serves more than 50 types of martinis plus specialty drinks. Call (605) 716-0600 or visit enigmarestaurant .com for details.

Looming over downtown, you'll see the stately **Hotel Alex Johnson** (523 6th St.). Built in 1925 and on the National Register of Historic Places, the

Art Alley

If you prefer wilder art than you'll find at galleries, check out the vibrant, often-surprising street art that covers Rapid City's *Art Alley*. The alley, which runs behind the buildings that border Main and St. Joseph Streets between 6th and 7th Streets, is packed with cultural icons from Homer Simpson to Bob Marley, thought-provoking statements, and deep thoughts. The visual jungle of color covers everything, even electrical transformers and Dumpsters. Our kids were so wowed by it and willing to pose near their favorite graphics that this graffiti-filled alley provided a memorable and fun backdrop for one of our all-time favorite (and unexpected) family photo shoots.

impressive yet manly lobby has hosted countless celebrities and politicians over the years. It's also one of the city's grandest places to stay, after extensive renovations in the late 2000s. If you need an excuse to wander the lobby, head to its *Chubby Chipmunk* shop for a taste of hand-dipped chocolates and fancy truffles. To learn more, call (605) 342-1210 or visit alexjohnson.com.

Less than a block away you'll find downtown's No. 1 don't-miss destination: *Prairie Edge & Sioux Trading Post* (606 Main St.; 800-541-2388; prairie edge.com). It's jaw-dropping to see the vast arrangement of Native American art, much of it Smithsonian quality. You might be lucky enough to catch a demonstration of native flute playing, see an astonishingly detailed wall-size homemade paper casting of a powwow or buffalo hunt scene, admire handmade beaded cradleboards and drums, and wander through an airy, high-ceilinged room full of Native American work. The multilevel store continues upstairs and sideways, with new rooms and collections around every corner: modern paintings and a music collection with more than 500 Native American titles, an impressive bookstore, wool and buffalo leather clothing and accessories, a glass bead museum in the loft, and even a Native American trading post with bundles of sage and every adornment used to make powwow regalia. Think of this store as more like a museum than an art gallery and give yourself the luxury of time to savor what it offers. You're sure to leave impressed.

You'll spot a few sculptures, such as the Dakota woman and child, in front of the Prairie's Edge Gallery, but Rapid City is first and foremost the *City of Presidents.* Ronald Reagan in his cowboy hat beams from one street corner while Jimmy Carter waves a big hello from another. John F. Kennedy smiles down at his young son, and polio survivor Franklin D. Roosevelt stands tall with the help of a podium. Every president is represented through Barack Obama. All the presidents were cast in bronze and designed to be life-size, which can be a fun lesson for kids by pointing out eras when people were smaller but could still have a supersize impact on America for generations to come. For more details and to find out where specific presidents are located, go to cityofpresidents.com.

At 512 6th St., the 1911 Elks Lodge and opera house—now the **Elks Theatre**—offers the grandest, cushiest spot to nuzzle next to a date over a bucket of popcorn, especially if you're in the balcony with the most sweeping view of the state's largest movie screen. Movies start at just $5. To learn more, call (605) 343-7888 or visit elkstheatre.com.

A few blocks away, at the corner of 7th and Quincy Streets, the **Dahl Fine Arts Center** is another great place to admire local talent and art. It houses 3 galleries, including one that brings in world-class artists; the Cyclorama Gallery, a unique 180-foot oil-on-canvas panorama spanning 200 years of US history; and an interactive children's area. In the Dahl's 170-seat theater, the Black Hills Community Theatre stages five productions during the fall and winter. The Dahl is open 10 a.m. to 6 p.m. Mon through Fri, and 10 a.m. to 5 p.m. Sat. Free music every Fri 5:30 to 7 p.m. Admission is free although donations are welcomed. To learn more, call (605) 394-4101 or visit thedahl.org.

If you travel south on **West Boulevard,** you'll see the grand homes of this residential historic district with turn-of-the-20th-century grandeur. Tudor revival, neoclassical, Queen Anne, federal revival, and many more styles are represented on this street. Residents take great pride in their homes, and it shows through their vigilant upkeep of the properties and some fantastic flower gardens. If you're here in wintertime, take a slow drive up and down

Rapid City Park Sampler

Memorial Park & Garden, north of downtown along Omaha Street, is dedicated to the 238 people who died in the devastating flood of 1972. Stroll fragrant rose gardens, catch a concert at the band shell, and see one of America's largest sections of the Berlin Wall.

Dinosaur Park, along Skyline Drive, geographically divides the town in half and offers some of the city's finest scenic views. Let yours kids loose among 7 life-size replicas of dinosaurs, including a triceratops and a Tyrannosaurus rex, all on the National Register of Historic Places.

Storybook Island (1301 Sheridan Lake Rd.) is another nostalgic (and free) family favorite.

The **Rapid City Urban Mountain Park** encompasses 390 acres of land, including Hanson-Larsen Memorial Park with 12 miles of mountain biking, hiking, and running trails and the Skyline Drive Wilderness Area with fantastic views.

Take a Spin Through the Hills

Biking has soared in popularity in the Black Hills. Rapid City has a 13.5-mile bikeway along Rapid Creek, but most riding is done on the area's wide-shouldered highways. Some of the favorite routes are Rapid City to Mount Rushmore, the Needles Highway, Iron Mountain Road, Spearfish Canyon, and the Badlands Loop Road. All feature some steep grades and long climbs, but the spectacular scenery along the way makes the effort worth it.

Mountain bikers can explore nearly 6,000 miles of fire trails, logging roads, and abandoned railroad grades that crisscross the backcountry ridges, wind down canyons, and climb to mountaintops. Or they can join the fun at the annual *Black Hills Mountain Fest* (formerly known as the Black Hills Fat Tire Festival). For more information, visit bhmtfest.com.

the boulevard to see some ornate Christmas light displays that make the area shine like an enchanted village.

Chocoholics can't miss *Mostly Chocolates* at 1919 Mount Rushmore Rd. The charming store features more than 23 kinds of truffles. The fudge is equally tempting, especially in such seasonal themes as pumpkin pie and fresh strawberry. To keep the sugar buzz going on steamy summer days, you can also try the frozen yogurt bar. For more information call (605) 341-2264 or go to bhchocolates.com.

Located 5 miles west of the downtown district at 3788 Chapel Ln. is *Chapel in the Hills.* Stavkirke, as it also is known, is an exact replica of the famous 12th-century Borgund Church in Norway. Wood carvings, Christian symbols, and Norse dragon heads adorn the building, which features pegged construction. It's a favorite and most romantic place for couples to exchange their wedding vows. Services start at 7:30 p.m. daily during the summer and last about 30 minutes. The chapel itself is open 8 a.m. to 8 p.m. May 1 to Sept 30. While you're there, check out the nearby *Norwegian Log Cabin Museum.* Admission is free; donations are welcome. Call (605) 342-8281 or visit chapel-in-the-hills.org to learn more.

For the most part, western South Dakota has taken advantage of its handsome surroundings, and tourism is vital. The tourist trappings are evident in Rapid City—sometimes upscale, sometimes cheesy—but to get a true snapshot of what makes this part of the country so magical, just get in the car, drive, and go wherever the wind takes you.

If you take US 16 west, you'll find tourist attractions and small towns threaded throughout the *Black Hills National Forest.* Actually a domed mountain region, the **Black Hills** cover about 8,426 square miles. They often are described as intimate because they don't loom above you like the Rockies and other mountain ranges. Ingenious scenic roads and hiking and biking trails all tug you into the landscape, threading through thick pine forests, tunneling through rocks, ambling along cold, clear streams or through prairie wildflowers. Round out your adventures with fishing, camping, skiing, mountain climbing, rock hunting, and daydreaming, and you have an outdoors-lover's menu for magic. Where else can you hike across trails where mica sparkles like glitter beneath your feet and hillsides are studded with pink quartz?

Mount Rushmore and Keystone Area

Making their way from Rapid City toward Mount Rushmore on US 16, families may find themselves happily distracted by two of the area's venerable attractions. **Reptile Gardens** has been fascinating visitors since it was started in 1937, and one of its stars is Maniac, a 16-foot-long, 1,250-pound saltwater crocodile. Even if you aren't a fan of creatures that slither, there's a two-level botanical garden, called the Sky Dome, with exotic birds and blooms. Nearby, you can stroll through a meditative garden where waters drop over Tortuga Falls to run into a turtle and koi pond that's watched over by Darwin, a kookaburra with a raspy laugh.

Look closely at exhibits, which show off founder Earl Brockelsby's museum-worthy collection of rocks and crystals. You may see a 12-foot-long, 150-pound albino Burmese python that's named Marilyn. Blue arrow frogs from the Amazon perch on the lip of a water bowl made from beautifully polished agate. Outdoor exhibits let kids pet giant land tortoises. The vast gift shop, which can be visited without purchasing admission to the park, features plenty for rock and fossil fans, and a large collection of tribal crafts from Papau New Guinea. Admission is $14 for adults; $13 for seniors; $12 for youths 11 to 15; and $10 for children ages 4 to 10. The park is closed from Dec through Feb. Call (605) 342-5873 or go to reptilegardens.com for more information.

Eight miles from Rapid City and just down the road from Reptile Gardens, you can watch bear, elk, wolves, bighorns, and other North American wildlife from the safety and comfort of your car during a two-mile drive through **Bear Country USA.** You'll do the most dawdling at the end, where you can watch bear cubs, wolf pups, and other park offspring along the Wildlife Walkway at the end of the driving tour. Bear Country is open daily from 8 a.m. to 6 p.m. in the summer months; 9 a.m. to 4 p.m. in May, Sept, and Oct; and 9 a.m. to 3 p.m. in Nov. Tickets are $12 for children 5 to 12, $16 for seniors, and $18 for adults. Call (605) 343-2290 or visit bearcountryusa.com for more information.

Most travelers beeline from Rapid City to the most famous rock of all: the carved-granite faces upon **Mount Rushmore National Monument.** In this one parking lot, you'll likely see license plates from almost all 50 states—testimony this truly is an all-American road trip. The monument's located 25 miles southwest of Rapid City. If you follow Mount Rushmore Road in Rapid City to the south, you'll be on US 16 and on your way to Mount Rushmore. Many signs point the way.

You'll hit **Keystone** (population 339) on your way to Mount Rushmore. Its carnival atmosphere will stand out as one of the most raucous and cluttered displays of tourism in the Hills. You either embrace the fudge shops, gem panning, gold-mine tour, old-time photos, ziplines, and other diversions, or you keep driving. Breathing room is just minutes away.

Here's a little secret: Get up and get going at the crack of dawn, and you'll not only skip the crowds and the parking fee as you enter Mount Rushmore National Monument, but you'll be able to get stunning photos of the presidents in the rosy glow as the sun rises. The softer morning light shows more details in the carvings and a few sparkles of quartz you might miss in the full light of midday. The downside of an early arrival is needing to kill time before the museum opens, but it's a good opportunity to take the mile-long **Presidential Trail** that loops closer to the presidents and past the sculptor's studio. If you start getting winded climbing all the steps on the way back up to the terrace and museum, imagine the daily commute of the carvers who had to get all the way up the mountain.

Gutzon Borglum designed and led the carving on the 60-foot granite heads of George Washington, Thomas Jefferson, Abraham Lincoln, and Theodore Roosevelt. Mount Rushmore was commissioned as a national memorial by Congress in 1929, although work actually began in 1927. The project was not always looked at favorably. Back east, a newspaper blasted: "Borglum is about to destroy another monument. Thank God it is in South Dakota, where no one will ever see it." Fortunately, Borglum and others had more foresight. When President Calvin Coolidge dedicated the project in 1927, he proclaimed that Mount Rushmore was "decidedly American in its conception, magnitude, and meaning. It is altogether worthy of our country."

Over the next 12 years, Borglum and his crews, using pneumatic drills and dynamite, carved four massive heads out of the mountaintop. Although the sculptor died before the project was finished, his son, Lincoln, made sure his father's vision continued. At present, more than 2 million visitors each year see the Borglums' legacy to America and the four men who inspired it.

A walk down the **Avenue of the Flags** with all 50 states plus territories colorfully frames Mount Rushmore as you approach Grandview Terrace and the amphitheater. Go below ground to the **Lincoln Borglum Museum** and see what the mountain would have looked like if the sculptors had finished the project down to the presidents' waistlines. Kids and adults love pushing a mock detonator and seeing a virtual blast. Two videos tell tales of the monuments, but you can go even more in-depth with the award-winning audio tour that's considered one of the best in the national parks system. It blends narration, music, sound effects, and historic recordings and runs 30 to 120 minutes. It comes in multiple languages, including Lakota.

One of the park's newer attractions is a **Lakota, Nakota, and Dakota Heritage Village** on the first section of the half-mile Presidential Trail loop. Preserving the history of these Native Americans who have been here for centuries, the village is open and staffed daily from 10 a.m. to 2 p.m. mid-June through mid-Aug. It's also a good place to look for mountain goats. They're not native to the area, but they have thrived here since 1924 when Canada gave six of them to Custer State Park as a gift. You might even spot one on the presidents' heads if you have binoculars handy.

In the **Sculptor's Studio**, built in 1939, you'll find winches, jackhammers, and pneumatic drills that date from the time of construction. Borglum's original model of Mount Rushmore also can be viewed here. During summer months, there's also a sculptor-in-residence nearby, creating works using many of the techniques that created Mount Rushmore. You can catch 15-minute ranger talks at the studio or 30-minute talks at Grandview Terrace throughout the day. Check times when you arrive. If you're traveling with children, have them get a junior ranger workbook to make the most of their visit and earn a cool badge before leaving.

Carver's Cafe serves food and drinks with great views of the mountain, plus the chance to cool off or warm up, depending on the weather. One of the newest treats is ice cream made using a recipe of Thomas Jefferson.

A patriotically fitting end to a day at Mount Rushmore is watching the 45-minute evening lighting ceremony from the outdoor amphitheater. Evenings can be downright chilly, so bring a light jacket. The ceremony is held daily at 9 p.m. late May through mid-Aug, and at 8 p.m. through the end of Sept. Mount Rushmore National Memorial is open year-round, and while admission is free, plan on purchasing a private vehicle parking pass for $10 that's good for a year. Call (605) 574-2523 or see nps.gov/moru for more information.

Hill City and the Black Hills

Hill City, population 1,008, has a touristy streak but feels far more genuine and laid-back as a base for Black Hills exploring. It also makes for a great day trip if you're staying elsewhere. As Pennington County's oldest town, Hill City was a bustling region when gold first was discovered in the Palmer Gulch area. Bigger strikes in the Deadwood area left the town almost deserted, but when the Burlington Railroad ran its Hot Springs–Deadwood line through Hill City in 1892, the town reclaimed its place as a gateway to the central Black Hills. It's hard to imagine that the town had a population of 3,000 in the 1890s, but you can close your eyes and imagine that era when the historic *1880 Train* chugs from Keystone to Hill City's depot, wailing its welcome whistle. Round trips that last 2.5 hours run early May through mid-Oct. Passengers ride in restored coaches, some of which date back to 1913, and are pulled by diesel or steam locomotives. Look for special events, such as the Oktoberfest Express with German food, beer, and polka music or the family-oriented Holiday Express. For more information call (605) 574-2222 or go to 1880train.com.

Modern Hill City boasts an artsy flair with a number of great galleries, a trio of wineries, shops, and cafes. You can't miss its standout sculpture of a horse created by John Lopez, of Lemmon. He uses found objects such as gears,

Black Hills Wine and Beer Trail

As in eastern South Dakota, wines and microbrews are booming in the Black Hills. There's even an official *Black Hills and Badlands Tasting Trail* (blackhillsbadlands.com/maps/tasting-trail). Here's a look at some of the standouts:

Wine lovers will enjoy sipping samples at the stylish, multistory *Prairie Berry Winery,* just 3 miles northeast of Hill City on US 16. The patio offers fabulous views of Black Elk Peak, making it easy to linger and savor the flavors. Among their 19 wines are Wild Bill, a semi-sweet Catawba grape wine with strawberry and sweet grape; Buffaloberry Fusion made of buffaloberries with hints of grapefruit, honeysuckle, and sweet lemon peel; and a semi-sweet sassily named Red-Ass Rhubarb wine with raspberries that has earned its share of awards. It's also a good and family-friendly lunch stop with flat-grill sandwiches and soups. Prairie Berry also has a microbrewery, *Miner Brewing Company,* down the hill. One of the most popular ways to visit the winery is by boarding the 1880 Train for fall's Wine Express weekend. Call (877) 226-9453 or visit prairieberry.com for details.

Tapping the bawdy side of Black Hills visitors, *Naked Winery* offers tasting rooms in Hill City, Deadwood, and Custer, along with light meals that include pizza, soft pretzels, and sandwiches. Tastings include their wines with names like Vixen Sarah and Booty Call Sweet Blush, their Sick-n-Twisted microbrews—more than 100 made with 34 on tap—and even ice cream. Call (605) 574-9200 or visit nakedwinerysd.com.

Eastern South Dakota's wineries also have Black Hills' outposts. *Stone Faces Winery* is part of Vermillion's Valiant Vineyards and runs a tasting room at 12670 Robins Roost Rd. just off Hwy. 385 a few miles north of Hill City. It offers a nice variety of whites and reds, silverware, farm tools, and other castoff objects to create incredible details despite using an "I Spy" range of materials.

The statue stands in front of the 200 block of Main Street where you can find *Jewels of the West* with jewelry, western art, pottery, and more, along with Dakota Nature and Art Gallery. More art can be found at Warrior's Work Studio and Ben West Gallery, Jon Crane Gallery, Sandy Swallow Gallery, and ArtForms Gallery, which is a member-owned gallery of regional artists.

One of the better-kept secrets in the Black Hills is the *Museum @ Black Hills Institute* (117 Main St.). These are the folks who discovered the famous Tyrannosaurus rex named Sue in Faith, South Dakota, but lost the lengthy court battle to keep her when the Field Museum of Chicago bought her for millions. This museum does, however, have Stan, another stellar South Dakota T-rex find. The original bones are on display in Hill City, but he's been reproduced for the Smithsonian, Oxford University, and 28 other museums worldwide. You'll get a great cross-section of dinosaurs, mammals, birds, minerals, and other fossils here. Their Everything Prehistoric shop is a great place to buy native fossils and minerals, plus resin and bronze casts of dinosaur teeth. Admission is $4 for kids

but also some dessert wines including a dry Rushmore Red and Wild Grape Port, the only port in the world made of wild grapes and aged 14 years. Call (605) 574-3600 or go to stonefaceswinery.com for more information.

Volga-based *Schadé Winery* has a tasting room at 250 US 14A in Deadwood. It specializes in wines packaged as Black Hills and South Dakota souvenirs with scenic labels and names. Call (605) 627-5545 or go to schadevineyard.com.

Twisted Pine Winery, 124 Main St., Hill City, has a collection of wines from across South Dakota and beyond. This tasting room also includes a variety of gourmet olive oils and vinegars. Call (605) 574-2023 or visit twistedpinewinery.com to learn more.

Belle Joli Winery has a tasting room for its sparkling wines, traditional wines, and fruit dessert wines at 594 Main St. in Deadwood, but you'll find a more scenic place to try them on the patio overlooking a five-acre vineyard at 3951 Vanocker Canyon Rd. in Sturgis. Call (605) 571-1006 or go to bellejoli.com.

Crow Peak Brewing Co. at 125 W. Hwy. 14 in Spearfish has built a big following with its brews, including the English pale ale, Spearbeer; Bambino's Bar Crawl; Pile O' Dirt Porter; and seasonal brews such as a fall chili ale. The top sellers come in cans, making them easier than a growler to take home. Call (605) 717-0006 or go to crowpeakbrewing .com.

For more information on regional wineries and breweries, along with tours that provide designated drivers (and unique vehicles that include a stretched Volkswagen limousine bus), check with the Black Hills and Badlands Tourism Association at (605) 355-3700 or blackhillsbadlands.com.

ages 6 to 15, $6 for seniors and military folks, and $7.50 for adults. Call (605) 574-3919 or visit bhigr.com/museum for more information.

If you've worked up an appetite, check out the ***Alpine Inn Restaurant*** (133 Main St.), located in a classic 1886 hotel. The lunch menu has German entrees and American sandwiches, whereas filet mignon dinners with salad, baked potato, and Texas toast rule the dinner menu, along with German dumpling, Swiss cheese, vegetables, and Texas toast. The homemade dessert menu is famous with more than 30 treats to choose from—including grasshopper ice cream pie. Open Mon through Sat. Moderately priced bed-and-breakfast arrangements also are available. Call (605) 519-9163 or visit alpineinnhillcity .com for more information.

About two blocks away, at 301 Main St., you can settle in for a meal with charming Old West ambience at ***Desperados Cowboy Restaurant*** which was built around South Dakota's oldest commercial log building dating back to 1885. The food's hearty, too, with big lunches such as muleskinner chili, and baked bean skillets with corn bread. Try the bread pudding with caramel sauce for dessert. Call (605) 574-2959 for more information.

If you like entertainment with your meal and enjoy the sweet harmonizing of cowboy crooners, head to the ***Circle B Chuckwagon,*** a Black Hills attraction that opened in 1945 and has since relocated to High Country Guest Ranch a few miles out of Hill City. The pre-dinner theatrics—the arrest of the Biscuit Bandit—get schmaltzy, but you can wander about and watch woodcarving, too. Dinners of hot dogs, chicken, brisket, or buffalo served with beans, biscuits, potatoes, and desserts are eaten indoors where the musicians perform after the meal is cleared. (Tip: If you're bringing kids, it helps to watch *Toy Story 2* to get them into the cowboy mood and to have something they can fidget with if they don't sit still for long.) Tickets are $33–$34 per adult; $14–$16 for kids ages 5 to 12; and children under 4 are free. Reservations strongly suggested so call (605) 574-2129 or go to circle-b-ranch.com for more information.

High Country Guest Ranch offers 45-minute trail rides with about a dozen horses that head into the surrounding Black Hills National Forest. Groups are small, so reserve early to get your pick of days and times. The wranglers welcome kids as young as 6 to participate, and the ride is gentle enough for first-timers. $35 for children ages 6 to 12, and $38 for teens 13 and up. Call (605) 574-9003 or visit highcountryranch.com/trail-rides to learn more.

Twelve miles north of Hill City off US 385 and on Horseman's Ranch Road, you can taste a little bit of Europe while nestled into the forest. Swiss-born Hanspeter and Christine Streich run ***Coyote Blues Village Bed and Breakfast,*** a cedar-lodge haven they built more than a decade ago. Guests pick from themed rooms: Barcelona, Mediterranean, Turkish, Swiss, Lakota, Safari, or Celtic. Each is equipped with a deck, hot tub, and private bath. There are three smaller rooms as well. Call (605) 574-4477 or go to coyotebluesvillage .com for details on seasonal rates.

Not far from Hill City on US 16A, you can better appreciate the accomplishment of Mount Rushmore by seeing an even larger undertaking—***Crazy Horse Memorial***—painstakingly progressing, blast by blast. The late Korczak Ziolkowski began the project more than 60 years ago when several chiefs asked him to create a sculpture of the famous Oglala Lakota leader. Chief Henry Standing Bear's invitation said, "My fellow chiefs and I would like the white man to know the red man has great heroes, too." Although Ziolkowski died in 1982, and his wife, Ruth, in 2014, their 10 children continue the sculptor's dream, guided by his scale models and detailed plans. The process has been slow but steady and precise; Ziolkowski insisted that no federal or state monies be used to fund the project. The nine-story-high face of Crazy Horse was completed in 1998. The horse's head, which measures 219 feet (or 22 stories), is the focus of current work on the mountain. You can get the most amazing (and rare) up-close view of Crazy Horse by joining in the annual 10K ***Volksmarch*** in June and Sept. The strenuous two- to four-hour hike up the mountain has drawn up to 15,000 people eager to see the carving face-to-face.

Stay after dark (or return later in the day) to see the evening ***Legends in Light Laser Show*** May through late Sept. They use some of the world's largest lasers and projectors for a multimedia blend of Native American music and stories with the mountain providing a 500-foot backdrop.

Beyond the fascinating story of the monument and the work that will be under way for generations to come, the site also is noteworthy for its ***Indian Museum of North America*** and ***Native American Educational and Cultural Center,*** the sculptor's studio; and a 40,000-square-foot Orientation Center and theaters. Many Native American artists and craftspeople create their artwork and visit with guests at the memorial during the summer season.

There are two dramatic night blasts, featuring pyrotechnical works, scheduled: one to commemorate Ruth's birthday and the Battle of the Little Bighorn in late June, and one to celebrate the death of Crazy Horse and Korczak's birthday over Labor Day weekend. There also is one during early October's Native Americans' Day, a celebration of art, music, dancing, and storytelling, plus free buffalo stew. Crazy Horse is open year-round; admission is $30 for 3 or more people in a vehicle; $24 for 2 people; $12 for 1 person; $7 for a person on a bike or motorcycle or walking. For more information, call (605) 673-4681 or visit crazyhorsememorial.org.

Heading south on US 16/385, drive west at **Custer** and the intersection of US 16A. It's a 13-mile trip to **Jewel Cave National Monument,** the third-longest cave in the world. As of 2019, explorers had mapped 208 miles of passages—many of them beneath just 3 square miles of land. Jewel Cave also is considered one of the country's prettiest caves with calcite crystals glittering along the walls. Guides will point out other formations such as moonmilk, scintillites, and hydromagnesite balloons. Prospectors discovered the cave around 1900 when they heard wind rushing through a hole in the rocks in Hell Canyon. It became part of the National Park System by 1908.

Visitors have a choice of tours to experience this wonder of nature, and all tours require tickets. The least strenuous way to see the cave is the 20-minute Discovery Talk with a look at one of the larger caverns. Admission for this talk is $4 for ages 16 and over and tickets are sold on a first-come, first-served basis on the day of the tour. The talk is great for children and can be negotiated by people who have difficulty with stairs or require wheelchair accessibility.

The very popular 80-minute **Scenic Tour** is moderately strenuous, requiring visitors to go up and down 723 stairs on its half-mile route. This tour requires reservations to be made through Black Hills Vacations so call (866) 601-5103 or visit its website, blackhillsvacations.com, and then click on "Things to Do," "National and State Parks," "National Parks," and finally "Jewel Cave." Tickets are $12 for ages 17 and older, and $8 for ages 6 to 16.

Tickets for the 105-minute **Historic Lantern Tour** are sold on a first-come, first-served basis on the day of the tour. Tickets for this tour are also $12 for ages 17 and older, and $8 for ages 6 to 16.

If you don't mind belly crawling through a few tight spaces while wearing a hard hat and headlamp, the **Wild Caving/Spelunking Tour** provides a 3- to 4-hour adventure that's essentially an underground obstacle course with climbing, sliding, and wriggling through some tight spaces. Still, it's a chance to experience rarer parts of the cave, such as feeling the wind at Hurricane Corner and squeezing into the Brain Drain. The rangers consider this tour extremely strenuous. Reservations are required and dates are limited for the Wild Caving Tour. Tickets are $31 per person, and no one younger than 16 is permitted on this tour. Call (605) 673-8300 to make reservations for the Scenic Tour or explore more details at nps.gov/jeca.

Returning to Custer, breathe in the local history at the **1881 Custer County Courthouse Museum** (411 Mount Rushmore Rd.). Residents and businesses have lovingly contributed pieces of the past to fill this commanding brick Italianate building. Visitors see slices of early Custer life, from artifacts of the timber and farming industries, which made the town prosper, to Victorian

Bike Trails Through the Black Hills

One of the best ways to see the spectacular scenery of the Black Hills is pedaling along the 114-mile *George S. Mickelson Trail*. It follows the historic Burlington Railroad line from Deadwood to Edgemont, putting bicyclists right in the heart of the Hills. It's easily accessed in Hill City and Custer. It's $3/day to use the trail, payable at self-service stations.

If you prefer a more rugged journey, the *Centennial Trail* spans 111 miles from Bear Butte State Park to Wind Cave National Park. For information on either trail, call (605) 584-3896 or go to gfp.sd.gov.

If you need to rent a bike, including electronic bicycles that can take you up to 28 mph, or to hire a shuttle service, or need parts or repairs, contact *Rabbit Bicycles and Repair* in Hill City. Call (605) 574-4302 or visit rabbitbike.com to learn more.

apparel and furnishings. On the museum grounds, printing equipment from Custer's 1879 first continuously operated newspaper and blacksmith forge and tools are on display. The Custer room depicts photographs of the 1874 Custer expedition when General George A. Custer entered the Black Hills and one of his men, Horatio Ross, discovered gold at Frenchman's Creek. Custer's epaulets and a first edition of his book, *My Life on the Plains,* are also displayed. Upstairs is the courtroom with the original cherry furniture and judge's chamber. There's plenty to see here so put aside a couple hours. Admission is $6 for adults, $5 for seniors, $1 for 12 to 18, and free for children under 11. The museum is open May through Sept, 10 a.m. to 7 p.m. Mon through Sat; 1 to 7 p.m. Sun. For more information, call (605) 673-2443 or visit 1881courthouse museum.com.

Custer State Park and Norbeck Byway

East of Custer you'll enter *Custer State Park,* which at 71,000 acres and packed with fabulous hiking and wildlife, rivals some national parks. Be prepared to spend at least a day or two here, honking through one-way tunnels, circling pigtail bridges, and admiring the amazing rock formations along the Peter Norbeck Scenic Byway. Call (605) 255-4515 for more information.

Hop on the 18-mile *Wildlife Loop Road* early in the morning or close to evening for the best chance to view the park's famed bison herd (one of the largest in the country with about 1,300 animals), along with elk, mule deer, white-tailed deer, pronghorn antelope, burros (that are comically nosy

planearly tocamp

The park is so popular during the summer that its more than 300 campsites and camper cabins book up quickly. Plan ahead. Call (800) 710-2267 or go to campsd .com.

You can find 682 additional camp-sites and a cabin (wheelchair accessible), in the Black Hills National Forest's 30 campgrounds. Most have vault toilets. Go to usda .gov/activity/blackhills/recreation/ camping-cabins.

in begging for handouts), and coyotes roaming the prairies. Bighorn sheep and mountain goats can be spotted at the higher elevations, especially near Sylvan Lake or Blue Bell Lodge. Plan at least 45 minutes to an hour and a half to do the drive. Viewing is particularly good in the late spring when animals seek tender roadside grasses as snow melts or in the fall during breeding season.

Entering from the west on US 16A, detour south on SD 87 for two of the park's best scenic views. You can drive up to *Mount Coolidge* (elevation 6,000 feet) to see the fire tower or stop at the peaceful *Heddy Draw Overlook* for a picnic. On a sharp, blue-sky day, you can see clear to the Badlands from both. At Mount Coolidge you can also see Mount Rushmore and Crazy Horse. Bring your binoculars or change for the coin-operated ones. On the return to Highway 16A and heading toward Legion Lake, keep an eye out for the Badger Clark Historic Trail on the right. The Badger Hole was home of the state's first poet laureate, *Charles Badger Clark Jr.* (1883–1957), whose most popular poem is "A Cowboy's Prayer," which, incidentally, is frequently misprinted and rarely attributed to its author. After a tour of the four-room cabin where Clark spent most of his literary career, hike the trail and read his poetry at quiet stops amid the pines. The Badger Hole is open from 10 a.m. to 5 p.m. Memorial Day through Labor Day.

The *Black Hills Playhouse,* nestled in Custer State Park, offers top-drawer entertainment but is laid-back enough that you can show up in camping attire. This nonprofit professional summer stock theater has been entertaining

Custer Resorts

All of Custer State Park's resorts feel steeped in history, especially *Sylvan Lake Lodge* and the *State Game Lodge,* which served as a summer White House for President Calvin Coolidge. *Bluebell Lodge* and Legion Lake are more family- and budget-oriented. Check rates and make reservations for all of them at (888) 875-0001 or custerresorts.com.

AUTHOR'S FAVORITE HIKES

Black Elk Peak	**Roughlock Falls near Spearfish Canyon**
Cathedral Spires	
Little Devils Tower	**Sunday Gulch**

Black Hills visitors since 1946. A visit here can be a fun expedition for the theatergoer, especially kids who will love seeing a chipmunk scurry by or hearing soothing sounds from a nearby stream. The troupe presents four or five productions each summer, from plays such as *The Odd Couple* and musicals such as *Something Rotten*, to thrillers such as *The Curious Incident of the Dog in the Night-Time*. Shows begin at 7:30 p.m. Tues through Sat, with matinees on Wed and Sun at 2 p.m. Tickets are $35 for adults; those under 18 are free when two

The Black Hills Rock

Author Lisa Meyers McClintick writes about her family's experience with rock climbing: "My first rock-climbing experience was near the shores of Sylvan Lake in the capable hands of Daryl Stisser, who runs Hill City–based **Sylvan Rocks Climbing School and Guide Service** with his wife, Cheryl.

The outfitters get their share of adrenaline junkies and people who want multiday trips and the opportunity to climb Devils Tower, but many customers are first-timers. They range in age from preschoolers to gung-ho grannies.

'Most of climbing is from the neck up. It's achievable by many, many people,' Daryl Stisser says. 'And it's very empowering.'

The Hills also are ideal for beginners because the rocks are easy to reach with tapering summits that let you power a climb with leg muscles and balance rather than upper-body strength. The climbing school also provides the climbing gear anyone needs.

We learned quickly to scrutinize granite grays for tiny toe-holds and bits of quartz and feldspar to gratefully grab onto as we ascended. It was an amazing experience: scary, exhilarating, and surprisingly satisfying to be standing high above ground surrounded by the gentle whoosh of pines."

You can learn more about Sylvan Rocks Climbing School and Guide Service at (605) 484-7585 or sylvanrocks.com. If you need gear or maps, check out Granite Sports on Hill City's Main Street or call (605) 574-2121.

go with one paid adult. Call (605) 255-4141 or visit blackhillsplayhouse.com for more information.

Buffalo Rock Lodge & Cabins bed-and-breakfast sits between the playhouse and Keystone, 2 miles outside the state park and tucked onto Playhouse Road. Innkeeper Marilyn Daniels can trace her family's roots in the Black Hills back to her grandfather who helped build Custer State Park's State Game Lodge. Guests can enjoy a distant but clear view of Mount Rushmore while eating a hearty western breakfast on the deck among the pines. The fireplace, inset with a variety of local stones they've collected, provides the centerpiece of this spacious yet homey lodge. The three rooms range from $165 per night, with two large enough for families. Three cabins sleep 3 to 5 guests and are $95 per night. Call (888) 564-5634 or see buffalorock.net for more information.

A simple drive through Custer State Park can raise your adrenaline with electrifying spins and knock-your-socks-off views from the 66-mile-long ***Peter Norbeck National Scenic Byway,*** easily one of the top scenic drives in the nation. It comprises two brilliantly planned routes: the 14-mile ***Needles Highway*** and ***Iron Mountain Road.*** Drivers are meant to drink in the scenery and take their time, so make use of the pullouts, keep a camera handy, and watch for wildlife (in winter the Needles Highway is closed to allow snowmobiling and cross-country skiing).

If you want to slow down the scenery even more, head to ***Sylvan Lake Lodge,*** one of four historic lodges in the park and a hub for many of the park's best hikes. Guests can choose from cozy lodge rooms for $165 to $250 per night, or 11 cabins (the park has 50 cabins spread across four locations) from basic sleeping cabins ($200 per night for 2 people), to a housekeeping cabin that sleeps 6 for $365 per night, to one that sleeps 20 and has five full baths

The Other Black Hills

Ninety percent of the Black Hills are in South Dakota, but the mountains also grace Wyoming for 10 to 40 miles. Even though they're across the South Dakota state line, the towns of Devils Tower, Hulett, Upton, Newcastle, and Sundance are very much part of the Black Hills community.

The Wyoming segment of the Black Hills includes a distinct branch known as the Bear Lodge. This is the site of the country's first national monument, Devils Tower. The tower is actually a solitary stump-shaped igneous rock formation that looms 1,267 feet above the Belle Fourche River in northeastern Wyoming like a skyscraper against the rural landscape. The tower is popular with rock climbers and movie makers. Devils Tower was a location for the movie *Close Encounters of the Third Kind*.

for $1,400 a night. This magnificent mountain resort overlooks Sylvan Lake and the granite outcroppings of Black Elk Peak. It's considered Custer State Park's crown jewel and a favorite romantic destination, attracting weddings throughout the summer and anniversary visits ever after. You'll need to book early. Call (888) 875-0001 for reservations.

Sylvan Lake was created in 1881, when Theodore Reder built a dam across Sunday Gulch. By 1895 a Victorian-style hotel opened along its shores and remained popular until it burned to the ground in 1935. The current hotel opened in 1937, and a wing was added in 1991. The hotel features cozy lodge rooms, a lobby, a lounge, and a restaurant, the Lakota Dining Room, which specializes in native game entrees and seafood and gorgeous views of Black Elk. If you look closely, you'll just make out the historic stone fire tower on the top.

Feeling adventurous? Hike to **Black Elk Peak,** the state's highest point at 7,244 feet and the highest elevation east of the Rockies. Be prepared, though. This 6-mile trek is a challenge and a workout. The time Dorie and I hiked it, we met some horseback riders coming down the trail (horses can go up only so far and the riders have to go the rest of the way on foot). Some who take the trail find themselves gasping when they meet a set of stairs that lead to the crown of the mountain but, as is often said, the end is worth it—a spectacular 60-mile view of undulating forest and rocky peaks. Stand atop the historic stone fire tower to breathe in the clean, rarefied air and feel it ripple across you. Without question, Black Elk Peak has inspired people of all faiths. When he was only 9 years old, the Oglala holy man Black Elk had his first vision here. "Then I was standing on the highest mountain of them all, and round about beneath me was the whole hoop of the world," he said.

Southern Hills and Hot Springs

If you head south on US 385, you will enter the wonderful wild kingdom of **Hot Springs.** This small town (population 3,460) known for its woolly mammoths, fascinating architecture, a cool cave, and healing springs often ranks as a family favorite. Chalk it up to mammoth bones and the fascination of exploring underground.

You'll reach **Wind Cave National Park** 11 miles before hitting Hot Springs city limits. Keep an eye out for the sprawl of prairie dog towns along the way. While some consider them pests, kids will find them entertaining with the way they pop up and down, call out to others, whistle, bark, and play together—remember, they are wild animals.

Wind Cave's claims to fame include being the nation's seventh-oldest national park, having one of the country's few intact prairies, and, with 152 miles of explored passageway, is one of the longest caves in the world with a labyrinth of levels. It also has great examples of boxwork, gridlike formations as delicate as potato chips on the ceiling. Popcorn and frostwork formations also can be seen. Visitors can choose from five tours. Each highlights different sections of the cave and ranges from an easy, quick look to historic candlelight tours to a four-hour wild caving adventure. Tours run $10 to $12 for adults, and half-price for kids ages 8 to 16 and senior citizens. The Wild Cave tours are $30 and it's suggested that visitors wear old rugged clothing and gloves since a lot of crawling is involved; no one under 16 is allowed. If you are doing a cave tour, go early in the day or reserve your tickets ahead of time to avoid waits.

The tours require admission, but there is no fee to enter the park, check out visitor center exhibits, watch the 18-minute movie on Wind Cave, or explore the several hiking trails threading through the 28,000-acre wildlife preserve above ground. Look for bison, antelope, elk, and deer roaming the grassland and forests as you drive through the park. Park rangers also lead themed hikes that focus on birding and the prairie, a drive to the Sanson Buffalo Jump, or campfire programs at the park's Elk Mountain campground. The 61 campsites, two of which are handicap accessible, are on a first-come, first-served basis and cost $18 during the high season. Call (605) 745-4600 or visit nps.gov/wica to learn more.

Before European settlers came to Hot Springs, the Lakota named the area *wiwila-kahta,* or "valley of healing waters." By the late 1800s, Hot Springs and its mineral springs attracted trainloads of wealthy visitors who sought the therapeutic benefits of mineral springs. These days your best bet to experience the springs is a dip in the naturally warm water that flows up through the pebble bottom of **Evan's Plunge** (1145 North River St.; 605-745-5165; evansplunge .com). The 87-degree mineral spring water flows at a rate of 5,000 gallons a minute, enough to change the water in the pool every 90 minutes. Anyone seeking extra thrills can slip down the water slides or test their strength with the Tarzan rings. Two kids' pools, two hot tubs, food and drink, a sauna, and a steam room are also here, among other features. Admission to this giant indoor pool that's open year-round runs $10 to $14.

If you stroll on the Fall River Freedom Trail, you can also stick a bare foot into a waterfall and feel the water's warm temperature. It's also a good way to admire downtown's unique Romanesque revival architecture that uses the red, pink, and tan sandstone found on the outer rim of the Black Hills.

You can stay in the heart of downtown and have a pampered getaway at **Red Rock River Resort** (603 N. River St.). Built in 1891 and faced with locally-quarried red sandstone, the building was initially a commercial building. Now it's a four-story hotel and spa. Rooms are decorated in earth tones, and beds are heaped with down comforters. Minnekahta Spa, open to hotel guests and day visitors, offers a full menu of massages and amenities such as Korean-style heat rooms. Guest rooms are $95 to $165, depending on the season. Call (605) 745-4400 or visit redrockriverresort.com for more information.

History buffs will enjoy the ***Fall River County Historical Museum*** (300 N. River St.) in an 1893 building that was once a school. Admission is free. The museum is open 9 a.m. to 5 p.m. Mon through Sat, May 15 to Oct 15. For more information, call (605) 745-5147 or visit pioneer-museum.com.

Hot Springs' biggest attraction is mammoth in every sense of the word and packs a wow factor like few places can. More than 26,000 years ago, more than 100 mammoths were trapped and died in a sinkhole on the town's southeastern edge. Mark the ***Mammoth Site*** as a must-see on your Dakota travel agenda. It rests atop an excavation, which began when a 1974 housing project uncovered the white bones and tusks. Visitors can get a 30-minute guided tour that leads them around this mass graveyard where paleontologists still work excavating bones or preparing bones and casts in a downstairs laboratory. There also is a great museum with bones of other prehistoric creatures such as camels, short-faced bears, antelope, gray wolves, minks, white-tailed prairie dogs, and frogs.

The Mammoth Site is the only *in situ* (bones left as found) display of fossil mammoths in the US. It's especially exciting for kids ages 4 to 12, who can sign up for the ***Junior Paleontology*** program, which is held every day June 1 to Aug 15 for $11.06 per person. The 60- to 90-minute program lets kids experience a simulated dig, excavating casts of different mammoth bones and then trying to identify them. You'll never see a group of kids concentrating this hard and being this quiet anywhere. Digs are popular and limited to 16 participants, so reservations are highly recommended. Additional options include an Advanced Paleontology Program for kids 5 and older who learn excavating along with how to map and jacket a bone, for $11.06 per person. Program fees do not include general admission, which is $10.14 for adults 13 or older; $8.29 for seniors 60 or older; $7.37 for kids ages 4 to 12, and active and retired military. All fees here do not include tax.

Younger children can do a free dig in the visitor center, using brushes to sweep away sand from casts of mammoth teeth, which look a lot like the bottom of sneakers. The site is open daily except for major holidays. Visit the website (mammothsite.org) to view hours as they vary with the seasons, or call (605) 745-6017 for more information.

If you prefer a more recent slice of South Dakota history, fast forward from the Ice Age to when mustangs ran wild and Native American tribes thrived on the prairie. ***Black Hills Wild Horse Sanctuary*** offers private tours through its 11,000-acre private wilderness area where more than 500 horses roam free. Among its tours is the 3-hour Cross Country Tour which costs $250 each for a minimum 2 people. The 3-hour photography tour costs $600 per person, and its Mustang Meadows Tour and Stay Package is a two-night stay with private tour and lunch for $2,000 which is for one or two people. The sanctuary is about 15 miles from Hot Springs, following SD 71 south and turning right at Highland Road. For more information call (605) 745-5955 or visit wildmustangs.com.

Along the way, keep an eye out for the **Cascade Falls Picnic Ground** once you hit the S-curve on 71 (about 8 miles south of Hot Springs). It's a good old-fashioned swimming hole along the tumbling waters of Cascade Creek with a deep pool for adults and strong swimmers and two shallower pools for kids. Cascade Springs pumps out more water than any other natural spring in the Black Hills. It's also home to some rare botanical species. Check fs.fed.us for more information.

If you're craving more water than a mountain stream, head to **Angostura State Recreation Area** about 10 miles southeast of Hot Springs via Highway 385. The bluffs offer some of the prettiest campsites in the state with breathtaking views of the reservoir and Cheyenne River Valley. You'll see anglers looking for walleye, bass, and crappie, colorful sailing boats and paddlers on the water, and a sandy beach along the reservoir's 36 miles of shoreline. There are 4 campgrounds with 169 campsites, and 12 camping cabins that can accommodate 4 to 5 people each. For park reservations, call (800) 710-2267 or go to campsd.com.

Additional campsites are in nearby **Sheps Canyon Recreational Area,** the newest campground on Angostura Reservoir. It has 22 campsites, plus 11 more for those with horses. It also has a lodge and cabin. For information about Sheps Canyon, call (605) 745-6996 or visit campsd.com.

Privately owned **Angostura Resort** has 6 rental lodges, an outdoor pool, and a marina. Call (800) 364-8831 for more information about the resort.

If the Wild Horse Sanctuary or the area's scenic hills leave you yearning for a horseback ride, check out **Sage Meadow Ranch,** which offers private trail rides by reservation near Hot Springs. The ranch is spread across prairie and rolling hills. There's a 90-minute option for novices and beginners for $75 per person or a half-day ride for intermediate to experienced riders at $125 per person. A day-long ranch camp is $150 per person. Call (605) 745-4866 or go to sagemeadowranchllc.com for more information.

The Northern Hills

The abundant snowfall in the northern Black Hills makes it a winter sports mecca. Snowmobiling, cross-country skiing, and downhill skiing are popular choices, but you can find gambling, entertainment, Old West museums, and enough restaurants to provide something to do year-round—no matter what Mother Nature dishes out.

Even if you're not into motorcycles, the mass of people and machinery that roll through the Hills during the legendary **Sturgis Motorcycle Rally** offers a spectacle like no other. It's a full-blown, hard-core party during the first full week of August, averaging close to 500,000 attendees coming annually to this town of 6,943 people. The highest attendance was in 2015 when 739,000 showed up for the rally's 75th anniversary. The agenda can include anything from AA meetings, burger battles, and Miss Buffalo Chip Beauty Pageants, to wine tastings, Harley shows, and live bands. The rally attracts weekend warriors and biker gangs such as the Bandidos and fuels a few romances as well. In peak years, local officials have issued close to 200 marriage licenses during the rally. Naturally, the legendary event attracts its share of celebrities, too. Emilio Estevez, Mickey Rourke, and Neil Diamond are just a handful of the rich and famous cruising into **Sturgis** for this festival of chrome, leather, and heavy-metal thunder.

J. C. "Pappy" Hoel probably never pictured this when he started the Sturgis Rally in 1938 with only nine races and a less-than-capacity grandstand crowd. Sturgis, fortunately, has learned to handle the crowds. There are thousands of campsites available for the event, but anyone planning to travel through the Black Hills that week in August will need to make lodging reservations well in advance, pay up front, and be prepared to hear engines rumbling and echoing through tunnels and along scenic byways. For information about the rally, call (605) 720-0800 or visit sturgismotorcyclerally.com.

You can sample the spirit of the rally without the crush of humanity at **Sturgis Motorcycle Museum & Hall of Fame** (999 Main St.; 605-347-2001; sturgismuseum.com). It blends rally memorabilia, antique motorcycles, unique bikes, and rotating exhibits. The museum is open 9 a.m. to 5 p.m. daily, May through Sept; 10 a.m. to 4 p.m. daily, Oct 1 through Apr 30. It pays to bring a friend or two: Admission is $10 for one person, $15 for two, or $30 for five people.

The normally quiet community of Sturgis also is home to **Fort Meade Museum & Old Post Cemetery,** located 1 mile east of Sturgis on SD 34. Fort Meade was built in the shadows of the majestic Bear Butte, a landmark that made it possible for early-day travelers to find the fort. Cavalry and infantry stationed here beginning in 1878 were assigned to keep the peace in those turbulent years, and so the fort gained the nickname "The Peacekeeper Fort." The fort is open daily 9 a.m. to 5 p.m. May through Sept. Admission is $5 for anyone 12 and older. The 5-mile-long Fort Meade Back Country Byway is a gravel road that winds between Fort Meade near SD 34 and the 120-acre Black

Hills National Cemetery near exit 34 on I-90. Call (605) 347-9822 for more information.

Colonel Samuel D. Sturgis, a Union general during the Civil War, was commander of the 7th Cavalry and the first permanent post commander at Fort Meade. He was a member of the company that founded the nearby town that bears his name. His son 2nd Lt. James. C. Sturgis died at the Battle of the Little Bighorn in June 1876; his body was never recovered.

The Bureau of Land Management manages approximately 6,700 acres of the former Fort Meade Military Reservation, now the **Fort Meade Recreation Area.** Approximately one-third of this area is on the National Register of Historic Places, due to the numerous historical sites at Fort Meade, mostly remnants of early cavalry life, and the post cemetery. The area accommodates grazing, forestry, wildlife, and a variety of recreational uses that include camping, picnicking, horseback riding, and hiking. The 123-mile multi-use Centennial Trail also winds through this area.

Mato paha (bear mountain) is the name the Lakota gave what is now **Bear Butte State Park**, an outstanding geological formation located 6 miles northeast of Sturgis. Artifacts from 10,000 years ago have been found here, and the volcanic laccolith is still used today by Native Americans for religious ceremonies and vision quests. Visitors are asked not to disturb the bits of cloth and offerings of tobacco that have been left on trees in prayer. An easy hike will take you around Bear Butte Lake while the Summit Trail offers more of a challenge. The reward for climbing the summit and gaining about 1,000 feet in elevation is an expansive—and inspiring—view of four states and a deep appreciation for why this place is considered sacred. The park and trails are open year-round, and the Education Center at the base of the summit trail is open 8 a.m. to 6 p.m. May through Sept. It has a first-come, first-served campground with 15 non-electric campsites and 4 more for those with horses. Because of its natural and historical significance, Bear Butte was designated a National Natural Landmark in 1965. For more information, call (605) 347-5240.

didyouknow?

It was on Fort Meade's parade grounds that the "Star-Spangled Banner" was first played in an official capacity in 1892. What later became the national anthem was used during the evening military retreat ceremony.

Eighteen miles northwest of Sturgis, **Spearfish** stands out among the Black Hills communities for its love of the outdoors with scenic drives and stellar hikes, a quieter, more studious pace than nearby Deadwood or Sturgis, and the dose of culture with the High Plains Heritage Center Museum and Black Hills State University.

High Plains Heritage Center Museum (825 Heritage Dr.) honors old west pioneers with art and artifacts from North and South Dakota, Montana, Wyoming, and Nebraska. Outdoor displays include antique implements, a log cabin, a sod dugout, a one-room schoolhouse, live buffalo, longhorns, miniature horses, and an original Spearfish-to-Deadwood stagecoach. You can hear cowboy poetry, music, and presentations in the 200-seat theater with a view of four states from the upper balcony. The museum is open year-round 9 a.m. to 5 p.m. daily in the summer, with shorter hours in the winter. Admission is $10 for ages 16 and older; $3 for youth ages 6 to 15. The center is located off I-90 at exit 14. Call (605) 642-9378 or visit westernheritagecenter.com for more information.

Back in downtown Spearfish (population 11,609), you can visit the ***Matthews Opera House and Art Center*** (614 Main St.). Spearfish residents returned it to its original 1906 charm and use it for summer community theater performances and concerts at the 250-seat theater. Productions always have strong support from the college theater department. For a schedule of events and art gallery exhibits, call (605) 642-7973 or visit matthewsopera.com.

Walk across the footbridge at Spearfish City Park to discover the ***D.C. Booth Historic National Fish Hatchery and Archives*** (605-642-7730; fws.gov/dcbooth). One of the oldest operating hatcheries in the nation, it introduced trout to the Black Hills and at one point had coordinated all federal fisheries in the US. The underwater viewing area lets you watch rainbow and brown trout, or you can catch a hatchery tour that runs daily from 9 a.m. to 5 p.m. mid-May through mid-Sept. The Von Bayer Museum of Fish Culture, which has more than 185,000 artifacts of fish culture, honors the history of those who work in American fisheries. The museum and grounds, including the historic Booth House which superintendent D.C. Booth built in 1905 for himself and his family, are open year-round. It's a must-see place for families, especially with the free admission.

A 1.7-mile detour southwest of Spearfish gives you a look at the unique work of artist Dick Termes at ***Termesphere Gallery*** (1920 Christensen Dr.; 605-642-4805; termespheres.com). He paints artwork on spheres using a mathematical process.

It's also a good excuse to hop onto US 14A and cruise along the ***Spearfish Canyon National Scenic Byway***. The 19-mile drive is on one of the prettiest and least crowded byways in the Hills. Peak time to go is fall when the vibrant gold of birch and aspen look most striking against the dark green of pine and spruce and the earth tones of the steep canyon walls. Colors usually peak by mid-October.

Thirteen miles south of Spearfish at 10619 Roughlock Falls Rd., ***Spearfish Canyon Lodge*** provides top-of-the-line accommodations in the heart of the canyon. Rates start at $89 in winter and $154 in summer. Suites start at $197. The lodge's *Latchstring Inn Restaurant & Lounge* serves meals on the veranda with the fresh scent of pine trees in the air. Call (605) 584-3435 for more information.

While in the area, you must see the canyon's three wonderful waterfalls. All are easy to drive to with Bridal Veil Falls, which has a 60-foot drop, being the easiest to see—just step out of your vehicle in the parking area and that may be good enough. Another parking area south of there starts your journey on a footpath that descends into a canyon where you end up looking at the face of the 110-foot-high Spearfish Falls directly opposite you. Then there's Roughlock Falls where, once you park your vehicle, you can walk on paths, rocks, and boardwalks to see a good portion of this stream that has falls, cascades, and swirling pools. Taking a camera with you is almost a requirement here.

At a 5,760-foot elevation, *Crow Peak* has been a northern hills landmark for centuries. If you want to tackle the 7-mile trip there and back, grab a map from the Spearfish Ranger District (605-642-4622). The trail is 7 miles southwest of Spearfish on FR 214, also known as Higgins Gulch Road.

About 14 miles southeast of Spearfish on US 85, *Deadwood* buzzes with the colors and energy of a mini Las Vegas teamed with Old West grit and spirit. Walk anywhere in town, and you'll see the flash and hear the blings and dings of slot machines and gaming areas in the town's 26 casinos and gaming halls—many of which operate in Deadwood's historic downtown.

Its gambling habit goes back more than 100 years and helped the town flourish during the Gold Rush. There have been plenty of boom and bust times since then and a clear streak of bawdiness from early days of gunslingers, opium dens, and bordellos. This was one of the last places in the country to outlaw prostitution, in 1980, after more than a century of business.

By 1989, Deadwood (with a current population of 1,304) brought back gambling when the state voted to allow $5 bets. They've since increased those bets to $100, and the number (and size) of casinos grew steadily, rejuvenating the Victorian downtown that's nestled into a valley.

The tucked-away gem, the *Deadwood Social Club* (657 Main St.; 800-952-9398; saloon10.com), is earning rave reviews from its perch on the second floor above the famed *Old Style Saloon No. 10*. Its menu blends northern Italian specialties with South Dakota cuisine for choices such as buffalo ravioli, elk tenderloin, lightly smoked pheasant in a Tuaca cream sauce, and Buffalo New York strip loin. In the summer, you can dine on the outdoor patio. Call to learn more about this wonderful place.

On the main floor, Saloon No. 10 doubles as a lively bar and a museum with old photos, mining and ranching artifacts, and the infamous "death chair," where Wild Bill Hickok was shot and killed in a card game. He was holding a hand of aces and eights, known from then on as "The Deadman's Hand." The bar carries a wide assortment of beer, wine, and creations conjured up by the staff such as the Tipsy Buffalo and A Skrewy Russian.

The majestic ***Silverado Franklin Historic Hotel & Gaming Complex*** (709 Main St.; 605-578-3670 or 800-584-7005; silveradofranklin.com), also has a lot of history to bet on. The 1903, 81-room Franklin Hotel has been the choice of celebrities including luminaries such as Presidents William Taft and Theodore Roosevelt plus John Wayne, Buffalo Bill, Babe Ruth, Pearl Buck, Robert Kennedy Jr., and Mary Hart (a South Dakota girl, too).

You can learn all about Deadwood's legendary past with gambling and brothels and larger-than-life characters such as Wild Bill and Calamity Jane at the fascinating ***Adams Museum*** (54 Sherman St.). There's something here to interest everyone, with three levels of artifacts, including a rare plesiosaur dinosaur, folk art, vintage photographs, and the museum's famous Potato Creek Johnny's gold nugget. At 7.75 troy ounces, the nugget ranks as one of the largest ever found in the Black Hills. It was recovered from a sluice on Potato Creek in western Lawrence County in May 1929. The massive chunk of gold was tucked away from public view until 1995, when it was on public display for two days to celebrate the museum's 65th anniversary. It now is safely back in the bank, and a replica of the nugget is on display. The Adams Museum is open year-round from 9 a.m. to 5 p.m. daily May 1 to Sept 30; 10 a.m. to 4 p.m. Tues through Sat the rest of the year. Admission is by donation.

The Adams Museum is part of Deadwood History, Inc., a non-profit organization that has four properties and is adding a fifth in 2020. For more information, call (605) 722-4800 or visit deadwoodhistory.com.

Another part of the organization is the ***Historic Adams House*** (22 Van Buren St.). Built by Deadwood pioneers Harris and Anna Franklin in 1892, the house was purchased in 1920 by W.E. Adams, businessman, former mayor, and founder of the museum. After his death in 1934, his widow closed up the house, and it sat unused for nearly 60 years. In 1992, the Deadwood Historic Preservation Commission bought the house and $1.5 million was spent returning it to its former splendor. Many original furnishings are among the restored parts of the Victorian Queen Anne–style home. It sits in the so-called presidential neighborhood of Deadwood. Admission to the tour here is $10 for adults, $5 for ages 6 to 12, and free to members. Adams House hours are 9 a.m. to 5 p.m. May 1 to Sept 30; 10 a.m. to 4 p.m. Tues through Sat for the rest of the year. Call (605) 578-1714 or visit deadwoodhistory.com for details on the house.

The organization also owns the ***Homestake Adams Research and Cultural Center*** (150 Sherman St.; 605-722-4800) to preserve significant collections, papers, photographs, records, dissertation, and publications related to the history of the Black Hills.

In 2020, the organization opened another museum, ***The Brothel***, to recognize and preserve an important Deadwood establishment that was in business from 1876 to 1980. Also called the Beige Door Brothel, visitors are led on tours of the Shasta Rooms which feature period furnishings, men and women's clothing, and other memorabilia. Call (605) 722-4800 for more information.

The Days of '76 Museum (18 76th Dr.; 605-578-2872), the fifth property of Deadwood History, Inc., celebrates the area's history, tribes, legendary characters, rodeos and star riders, and its annual community celebration that brings horse-drawn wagons back down Main Street. This museum has more than 50 horse-drawn carriages, stagecoaches, and wagons, plus memorabilia and archives related to the Days of '76, a popular community event held annually since 1924. You can visit reproductions of businesses that were here long ago, as well as a livery and fire house. Museum admission is $8 for adults, and $3 for children.

When you're in the residential area near the Adams House, Deadwood feels like a sliver of San Francisco with steep streets and historic homes. If you follow Lincoln Street uphill, you'll arrive at ***Mount Moriah Cemetery,*** the final resting spot for some of the Old West's biggest legends, including Wild Bill Hickok, Calamity Jane, Sheriff Seth Bullock, and Potato Creek Johnny. Also

Deadwood: The HBO Version

If you want to see a TV version of Deadwood that is far grittier than most fictional accounts of the town, you can watch the HBO series *Deadwood* that aired from 2004–2006. The set looks like Deadwood, but it is actually a $5 million replica on the Gene Autry ranch in California.

The series captures life in Deadwood in 1876, just two weeks after Custer's Last Stand. The settlers, ranging from an ex-lawman, to a scheming saloon owner, to the legendary Wild Bill Hickok and Calamity Jane, share a restless spirit as they struggle to survive in this frontier town. The Emmy Award–winning show is not for the faint-hearted with an ample amount of profanity, nudity, and violence—but that was part of life in Deadwood. Oddly enough, in the real Deadwood, one of the young city's first laws was to prohibit profanity in public, contrary to what the show portrayed.

The short-lived series was so popular with fans that HBO released a made-for-TV film in May 2019, titled *Deadwood: The Movie*, featuring most of the original cast.

buried at Mount Moriah, with her parrot and her husband, is Madam Dora DuFran, Calamity Jane's gal pal. Dora ran brothels in the Black Hills in the 1920s and 1930s but was known for her humanitarian work as well. Melanie Griffith portrayed Dora in the 1995 made-for-TV movie *Buffalo Girls*. Cemetery admission is $2.

One mile north of Deadwood on US 85 is **Tatanka: Story of the Bison,** at the **Northern Plains Peoples Educational Center**. Its centerpiece is the stunning, larger-than-life bronze sculpture by local artist Peggy Detmers, featuring 14 bison being pursued by three Native American horseback riders. The center depicts the relationship between the bison and the Native Americans through exhibits and displays. Kevin Costner, who starred in and directed *Dances with Wolves*, founded the attraction, which includes costumes from the movie. Admission is $12 for adults 13 and older; $5 for kids ages 6 to 12; children under 6 free. For more information, contact (605) 584-5678 or visit storyofthebison.com.

Just a few miles from Deadwood is **Lead,** Deadwood's sister city. After seeing the glitzy Deadwood, Lead might look much more bare bones, but you can find eateries, galleries, antique stores, and the Homestake Opera House. Mining was once the mighty force in this town (which is pronounced Leed) until operations ceased in 2001. You can imagine the glory days, though, with a trip to the **Sanford Lab Homestake Visitor** (formerly the Homestake Gold Mine Visitor Center) to see the largest, deepest, and oldest underground gold mine in the Western Hemisphere. Founded in 1876 by three California investors, including George Hearst, the Homestake mine extends 8,000 feet below the surface of the Black Hills. In addition to the underground mine, Homestake operated the Open Cut surface mine, which was the original site of the Homestake claim. The summertime one-hour guided bus tour goes through the town of Lead before heading underground, taking a peek at surface operations and viewing the 1876 open-cut mine. Guides explain new and old mining technology, and you can learn more about the hoisting, crushing, and milling of gold-bearing ore. Tours are $9 for adults; $8 for seniors, military, and ages 6 to 17; and free for children 5 and under. Also, a family of four can enter for $30. For more information, call (605) 584-3110 or visit sanfordlabhomestake.com.

For more on the history of mining, the **Black Hills Mining Museum** (323 W. Main St.; 605-584-1605; blackhillsminingmuseum.com) takes a detailed look at mining activity in the Hills during the past 120 years, including a simulated underground level of the Homestake Gold Mine. Count on realism—the simulation was created by more than 140 miners and former mine employees. Open seven days a week May through Sept, museum admission is $12 for adults, $10 for seniors, and $6 for ages 13 to 17; free for children 12 and younger with adult.

Terry Peak Ski Resort on Lead's southwestern edge takes advantage of the 7,000-foot-plus elevation for thrills and maximum snowfall. You'll find 1,100-foot vertical drops, moguls, and snowboarding terrain with jumps, bumps, rails, half-pipes, and quarter-pipes. There also are plenty of runs gentle enough for beginning and intermediate skiers. For more information on ski packages, sleigh rides, and tubing, call (605) 584-2165 or visit terrypeak.com.

Twenty-one miles south of Lead and Deadwood on US 85 you'll find *Trailshead Lodge,* a popular pit stop for snowmobilers. They whoosh through powdery snow, wind through deep canyons, and weave through pines on roughly 350 miles of trails throughout the 1.3 million-acre Black Hills National Forest. Trailshead Lodge offers a convenient stopping point for gas, food, lodging, and a chance to thaw out as needed. Call (605) 584-3464 or visit trailsheadlodge.com for more information. You can rent snowmobiles here and at other area resorts and outfitters.

If you prefer quieter winter sports, cross-country skiers and snowshoe enthusiasts will find close to 60 miles of trails to explore, along with national forest lakes for ice-fishing and several open-water streams where fly-fishing is practiced year-round by anyone willing to tolerate the cold for a few good trout.

Northwestern Corner

The northwestern corner of South Dakota is not as familiar as the Black Hills (even to South Dakotans), but this is a perfect place to get away from it all. Tiny towns occasionally crop up on the plains landscape here, with winsome names such as Eagle Butte, Bison, Prairie City, Meadow, Buffalo, and Faith, which gained notoriety when a Tyrannosaurus rex named Sue was found there. Names reflect the ranching spirit and determination of early settlers. This is a place where people tip their hats to fellow drivers, give a friendly finger wave from the steering wheel, or offer a full-blown wave out the window as you pass on the rural roads. These are gestures of warmth you'll never see in a big city. Folks assume they know you, or your kids, parents, employer—you get the idea. The degrees of separation are mighty thin in these big open spaces. It's a fine welcome, no matter how it's delivered.

If you take US 85 north 9 miles from Spearfish, you'll find the western panorama of *Belle Fourche.* It means "pretty fork," honoring the confluence of the Belle Fourche and Redwater Rivers. Dakotans, by the way, say "Bell Foosh." The town of 5,553 people has two claims to fame.

First, there's a stone compass on a plaza that marks the town's distinction as the geographical center of the US. For those who want to be precise, according to a US Coast and Geodetic Survey, the actual center is at 44° 58' 2" N 103° 46' 17" W. To get there, drive 13.5 miles north of the US. 212/85 intersection on Hwy. 85 and then turn to the left (north) on Old Hwy 85 for 7.75 miles. That will get you close enough to say you're there. Respect private property.

Belle Fourche's second distinction is its ranching and cowboy culture. During its profitable era of big cattle drives from the late 1800s through the last roundup in 1902, the region attracted such notables as Butch Cassidy and the Sundance Kid. At the turn of the 20th century, Belle Fourche became known as the largest cattle-shipping point in the world. Cattle are still an important part of Belle Fourche's economy, but so are sheep, or more correctly their wool. Of the 25 million pounds of wool produced in the US annually, about 5 million pounds come into Belle Fourche where they are marketed to textile firms.

You can join in on the community's rough-and-tumble spirit July 3 to 5 for the annual **Black Hills Roundup Rodeo,** with fireworks, a carnival, and a historic parade. First held in 1918, this rodeo still attracts top Professional Rodeo Cowboy Association (PRCA) bull riders, bareback bronc riders, steer wrestlers, and other cowboys. Indeed, many Pro Rodeo athletes call Belle Fourche their home, including four-time World Bareback Riding Champion Marvin Garrett. For more information, visit blackhillsroundup.com or call (605) 723-2010.

A handsome addition to the town's tourism offerings is the 4,000-square-foot *Tri-State Museum* (415 5th Ave.; 605-723-1200; thetristatemuseum.com), which focuses on the early pioneer, rodeo, and Old West history of western South Dakota, eastern Wyoming, and southeast Montana. The museum houses more than 5,000 artifacts, rodeo memorabilia, historical records, antiques, collectibles, fossils, and an 1876 cabin.

Just 9 miles east of Belle Fourche, *Orman Dam* makes a fabulous playground for the water-skiing, boating, camping, fishing, or swimming enthusiast. The world's largest earthen dam when it was built, Orman Dam was constructed with the use of horses around the beginning of the 20th century to provide irrigation for a huge tract of sugar-beet farms downstream. Although corn, small grains, and alfalfa now dominate the agricultural scene, Orman Dam remains the area's primary dry-season water source. And there is plenty of water to go around: Behind the dam, the Belle Fourche Reservoir has 8,000 acres of water and 52 miles of shoreline.

Continue on US 85 north, and you'll drive through cattle country, where one-pony towns like Redig and Ludlow can be missed with the blink of an eye. The sanctity of space keeps travelers mindful. Just before the town of Buffalo, take SD 20 east to find one of the best-kept secrets in South Dakota. Long before he became president, Theodore Roosevelt hunted bear in the region now known as **Custer National Forest.** (He later established forest reserves in the Cave Hills and Slim Buttes areas.) Custer National Forest is probably the most forgotten forest in the state. Even natives have a puzzled look on their faces when it's mentioned, which is understandable; there's Custer State Park to the southeast, so another Custer moniker seems at first repetitious, but that does not detract from the beauty of this rustic area.

The 73,000 timbered acres in the northwestern part of the state are anomalous to the barren, outlying landscape. Ride and hike, but don't expect a guide or user-friendly visitor center to take you by the hand. You're in the deep forest now, and there are no designated hiking trails.

The **Cave Hills** section of the forest was once a popular hiding place for outlaws. Ludlow Cave, the largest of the caves, sheltered many bandits during the stormy days of the Dakota Territory. Native Americans once carved drawings into the sandstone, but sadly those have been covered over by subsequent visitors.

East of the Cave Hills lies the **Slim Buttes** section of forest, where lofty cliffs of limestone are split by dramatic canyons. The Slim Buttes battlefield is nearby, where Dakota veterans of the Little Bighorn battle were practically run over by the US Army. The Oglala, Cheyenne, Brulé, and Minneconjous were taken by surprise on September 9, 1876, and after suffering many casualties, they escaped during the night and took shelter high in the hills behind the limestone outcroppings.

Stay east on SD 20 and you'll eventually run into SD 73. Take SD 73 north, and you'll inch your way toward literature and legend. The first suggested stop on this stretch of highway is **Shadehill Recreation Area** (605-374-5114), one of South Dakota's largest reservoirs with 5,000 surface acres. In addition to the customary sporting opportunities one expects, the reservoir also boasts an intriguing historical marker on the southern shore. The marker describes the legend of Hugh Glass, who survived incredible odds and inspired the book *Lord Grizzly* by Frederick Manfred. In the late summer of 1823, at the fork of the Grand River, Glass was hunting with the William Henry Ashley fur party when he was attacked by a grizzly bear. Horribly maimed, they believed his injuries were fatal, so two members of the Ashley party were instructed to stay with him until he passed. However, after only a few days, the men took Glass's weapons and fire-making kit and left him for dead. Amazingly, a few days later, Glass crawled away from where he lay and began slowly heading to the southeast. He survived on insects, berries, and some buffalo meat acquired after driving away two wolves from a downed calf. It took Glass six weeks to crawl about 200 miles to Fort Kiowa on the Missouri River (near present-day

Chamberlain) in early October. He later tracked down the two men who had abandoned him. He forgave the younger one because of his youth. When he found the older one, who had enlisted in the army and was at Ft. Atkinson, Nebraska (north of present-day Omaha), Glass reportedly forgave him, too. Also in the area, the marking left by Custer's 7th Cavalry can be seen on a butte at Shadehill Reservoir.

Lemmon, (1,191 pop.) just 12 miles north on the South Dakota–North Dakota border, is the home of Kathleen Norris, another fine contemporary writer from the state. She captured the essence of small-town life in *Dakota: A Spiritual Geography*. Her collection of poetry, *Little Girls in Church*, also speaks from the heart. Other excellent writers of western South Dakota include Linda Hasselstrom, Virginia Driving Hawk Sneve, and Dan O'Brien. Also writing his way into the annals of history—and by different means—was Ed Lemmon, for whom the town was named. He was one of the first South Dakotans inducted into the prestigious National Cowboy Hall of Fame.

The Lemmon **Petrified Wood Park and Museum** (500 Main Ave.), five blocks north of US 12, has been around since the early 1930s when Lemmon men under the command of Ole S. Quammen put together this bizarre, yet intriguing blend of petrified wood and fossil sculptures across a city block. It was a labor of love for some and a necessity for others who were unemployed and depended on the project for sustenance during its construction. You can explore the 300-ton castle, a wishing well, a waterfall, and petrified wood cones up to 20 feet. You can envision

suethet-rex

The famed Tyrannosaurus rex named Sue was found in Faith, South Dakota, straight south of Lemmon. She's the state's most famous discovery and has a permanent home at Chicago's Field Museum.

trolls, or at least gnomes, feeling quite at home in this otherworldly place.

One of South Dakota's finest contemporary artists, John Lopez, has his home and studio on Main Avenue in Lemmon. Making metal sculptures out of scrap and almost anything else that's metal that he can lay his hands on, Lopez has created statues that stand from New York to California. One statue, featuring legendary rancher Ed Lemmon astride a horse, stands downtown here. Another life-size one, of Hugh Glass being attacked by the grizzly, is in the **Grand River Museum** (114 10th St. W; 605-374-3911; thegrandrivermuseum .com). A third Lopez sculpture, of a cowboy riding a triceratops, greets visitors as they drive up to the museum. The museum covers the history of the region, through displays of the fossilized remains of creatures that lived here millions of years ago to the Native Americans, homesteaders, and ranchers who came later. The museum also discusses the relationship between the scientific and Biblical timelines of events through the ages. Open May through Sept. Free admission, donations accepted.

Where to Stay in Western South Dakota

BELLE FOURCHE

AmericInn by Wyndham
2312 Dakota Ave.
(605) 892-0900
wyndhamhotels.com
Inexpensive

CUSTER

Bavarian Inn
855 N. 5th St.
(605) 673-2802
bavarianinnsd.com
Moderate

Rocket Motel
211 Mt. Rushmore Rd.
(605) 673-4401
rocketmotel.com
Inexpensive

Shady Rest Motel
238 Gordon St.
(605) 673-4478
shady-rest-motel.com
Inexpensive

DEADWOOD

Deadwood Gulch Resort
304 Cliff St.
(605) 578-1294
deadwoodgulchresort.com
Moderate

Deadwood Mountain Grand
1906 Deadwood Mountain Dr.
(605) 559-0386
deadwoodmountaingrand.com
Moderate

First Gold Hotel
270 Main St.
(605) 578-9777
firstgold.com
Moderate

Historic Bullock Hotel
633 Main St.
(800) 336-1876
historicbullock.com
Moderate

The Lodge at Deadwood
100 Pine Crest Ln.
(877) 393-5634
deadwoodlodge.com
Moderate

Mineral Palace Hotel & Gaming
601 Main St.
(800) 847-2522
mineralpalace.com
Moderate

HILL CITY

Best Western Golden Spike Inn
601 E. Main St.
(605) 574-2577
bestwestern.com
Moderate

Knotty Pine Cabin
23836 Emerald Pines Dr.
(605) 574-4462
emeraldpinesrefuge.com
Expensive

Mountains to Prairies B&B
200 E. Main St.
(605) 574-2424
mountainstoprairiesbb.com
Moderate

HOT SPRINGS

Flatiron Historic Sandstone Inn
745 N. River St.
(605) 890-1321
Moderate

KEYSTONE

Elk Ridge Bed & Breakfast
12741 Matthew Ct.
(605) 574-2320
erbnb.com
Moderate

K Bar S Lodge
434 Old Hill City Rd.
(605) 666-4545
kbarslodge.com
Moderate

LEAD

Barefoot Resort
21111 Barefoot Loop
(605) 584-1577
barefootresort.com
Moderate

Spearfish Canyon Lodge
10619 Roughlock Falls Rd.
(605) 584-3435
spfcanyon.com
Moderate

RAPID CITY

Black Forest Inn, B&B Lodge
23191 Hwy. 385
(605) 574-2000
blackforestinn.net
Moderate

Grand Gateway
1721 N. LaCrosse St.
(866) 742-1300
grandgatewayhotel.com
Inexpensive to moderate

Holiday Inn Rushmore Plaza
505 N. 5th St.
(605) 348-4000
rushmoreplaza.com
Moderate

The Rushmore Hotel & Suites
445 Mt. Rushmore Rd.
(605) 348-8300
therushmorehotel.com
Moderate

Silver Mountain Resort & Cabins
13350 Silver Mountain Rd.
(605) 342-2246
silvermountaincabinscom
Moderate

Summer Creek Inn and Spa
23204 Summer Creek Dr.
(605) 574-4408
summercreekinn.com
Moderate

Willow Springs Cabin B&B
11515 Sheridan Lake Rd.
(605) 342-3665
willowspringscabins.com
Moderate

SPEARFISH

Hampton Inn
240 N. 27th St.
(605) 642-3003
hamptoninn3.hilton.com
Moderate

Orchard Creek Cottages
514 Mason St.
(605) 642-4234
Moderate

STURGIS

Baymont Inn & Suites by Wyndham Sturgis
2721 Lazelle St.
(605) 347-4140
wyndhamhotels.com
Moderate

The Hotel Sturgis
1144 Main St.
(605) 561-0116
thehotelsturgis.com
Moderate

Where to Eat in Western South Dakota

CUSTER

Baker's Bakery & Cafe
541 Mt. Rushmore Rd.
(605) 673-2235
bakersbakerycafe.com
Inexpensive

Black Hills Burger and Bun Co.
441 Mt. Rushmore Rd.
(605) 673-3411
blackhillsburgerand
bun.com
Inexpensive

Bobkat's Purple Pie Place
19 Mt. Rushmore Rd.
(605) 673-4070
purplepieplace.com
Inexpensive

Buglin' Bull Restaurant & Sports Bar
511 Mt. Rushmore Rd.
(605) 673-4477
buglinbull.com
Moderate

The Custer Wolf
506 Mt. Rushmore Rd.
(605) 673-0653
custerwolf.com
Moderate

Sage Creek Grille
611 Mt. Rushmore Rd.
(605) 673-2424
sagecreekgrille.com
Moderate

Sylvan Lake Lodge
24572 Hwy. 87
(605) 574-2561
custerresorts.com
Moderate to expensive

DEADWOOD

**Chubby Chipmunk
Chocolates**
420 Cliff St.
(605) 722-2447
chubbychipmunk.com
Moderate

Mustang Sally's
634 Main St.
(605) 578-2025
Inexpensive

Pump House
73 Sherman St.
(605) 571-1071
Inexpensive

Silverado Grand Buffet
709 Main St.
(605) 578-3670
silveradofranklin.com
Moderate

Tin Lizzie
555 Main St.
(605) 578-1715
tinlizzes.com
Moderate

HILL CITY

**Bumpin Buffalo Bar &
Grill**
245 Main St.
(605) 574-4100
bumpinbuffalo.com
Moderate

**Chute Rooster Steak
House and Lounge**
850 Chute Rooster Dr.
(605) 574-2122
Moderate

Perky Pine Café
24063 Hwy. 385
(605) 574-2416
Inexpensive

SELECTED CHAMBERS OF COMMERCE

Belle Fourche Chamber of Commerce
509 Grant St.
Belle Fourche 57717
(605) 892-2676
bellefourchechamber.org

Custer Area Chamber of Commerce
615 Washington St.
Custer 57730
(605) 673-2244
custersd.com

Deadwood Chamber of Commerce
501 Main St.
Deadwood 57732
(605) 578-1876
deadwood.com

Hill City Chamber of Commerce
23935 Hwy. 385
Hill City 57745
(605) 574-2368
hillcitysd.com

Hot Springs Area Chamber of Commerce
801 S. 6th St.
Hot Springs 57747
(605) 745-4140
hotsprings-sd.com

Lead Chamber of Commerce
106 W. Main St.
Lead 57754
(605) 584-1100
leadmethere.org

Rapid City Convention & Visitors Bureau
512 Main St., Ste. 240
Rapid City 57701
(605) 718-8484
visitrapidcity.com

Visit Spearfish
603 N. Main St.
Spearfish 57783
(605) 717-9294
visitspearfish.com

Turtle Town
Confectionary
205 Main St.
(605) 574-4124
turtletown.com
Inexpensive

KEYSTONE

Powder House
Restaurant
24125 Hwy. 16A
(605) 666-4646
powderhouselodge.com
Moderate

Ruby House Restaurant
124 Winter St.
(605) 666-4404
rubyhouserestaurant.com
Moderate

RAPID CITY

Black Hills Bagels
913 Mt. Rushmore Rd.
(605) 399-1277
blackhillsbagels.com
Inexpensive

Botticelli's Ristorante
Italiano
523 Main St.
(605) 348-0089
botticelliristorante.net
Moderate

Colonial House
Restaurant & Bar
2501 Mt. Rushmore Rd.
(605) 342-4640
colonialhousernb.com
Inexpensive

Everest Cuisine
2328 W. Main St.
(605) 343-4444
theeverestcuisine.com
Moderate

Philly Ted's
Cheesesteaks and Subs
502 Main St.
(605) 348-6113
Inexpensive

ROCKERVILLE

The Gaslight
13490 Main St.
(605) 343-9276
thegaslightrestaurant.com
Moderate

SPEARFISH

Dough Trader Pizza
Company
543 W. Jackson Blvd.
(605) 642-2175
Moderate

Green Bean Coffeehouse
304 N. Main St.
(605) 717-3636
spearfishgreenbean.com
Inexpensive

STURGIS

Jambonz Grill & Pub
2214 Junction Ave.
(605) 561-1100
Inexpensive

Loud American
Roadhouse
1305 Main St.
(605) 720-1500
loudamericanroadhouse
.com
Inexpensive

WALL

Red Rock Restaurant
506 Glenn St.
(605) 279-2388
Moderate

Western North Dakota

Called the "Dean of the Western Writers," Wallace Stegner once said that the West is America, only more so. In North Dakota you're privileged to experience an inconceivably huge chunk of the real West. There is no drugstore-cowboy posturing here. Ranchers work tirelessly, as do the oil industry workers who have come from around the country to work hard and support families back home, although many of those families have moved here.

The traveler will find long, lonely stretches of land—just like those that the settlers and Native Americans of the past encountered—west of the Missouri River. Towns steadily grow to accommodate oil industry workers; you might see the flame of a natural gas flare on the horizon, and lightning strikes in the jagged peaks of the Badlands can ignite ancient coal veins that smolder for years.

It serves the soul well to roam over the plains of North Dakota. To feel small. To feel vulnerable. To find strength. To breathe deeply and embrace the wide-open landscape as it ripples to the horizon. The self-reliance espoused by Ralph Waldo Emerson years ago is infectious in North Dakota. As Teddy Roosevelt once said, "My experience when I lived and

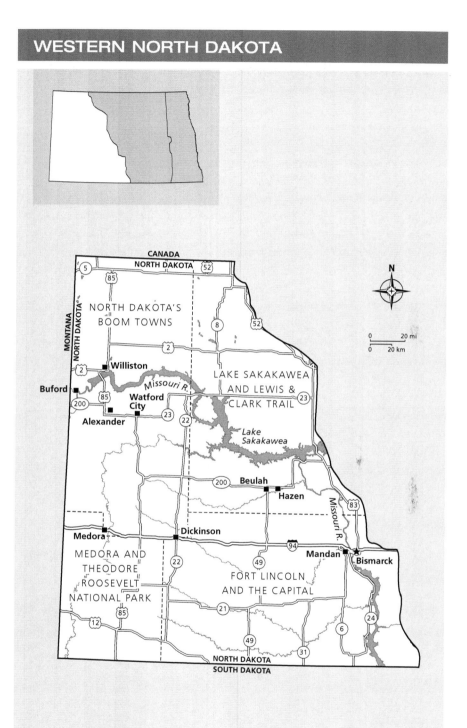

CANADA
NORTH DAKOTA

MONTANA

NORTH DAKOTA

NORTH DAKOTA'S BOOM TOWNS

Williston

Buford

Watford City

Alexander

Missouri R.

LAKE SAKAKAWEA AND LEWIS & CLARK TRAIL

Lake Sakakawea

Beulah

Hazen

Missouri R.

Medora

MEDORA AND THEODORE ROOSEVELT NATIONAL PARK

Dickinson

FORT LINCOLN AND THE CAPITAL

Mandan

Bismarck

NORTH DAKOTA
SOUTH DAKOTA

N

0   20 mi
0   20 km

worked in North Dakota with my fellow ranchmen, on what was then the frontier, was the most important educational asset of my life."

Medora

South Dakota may have Mount Rushmore and Badlands that look like a galactic moonscape, but when North Dakota pulls out its big guns for tourism promotion, you can be sure that **Medora** will hover at the top of the list. For families, Medora offers a sweet nostalgia trip, a throwback to friendly small towns and tourism from an earlier generation and providing a charming hub for exploring North Dakota's kinder, gentler Badlands. Still rugged and awe-inspiring, the Badlands are also rounder, greener, and filled with more wildlife than what you see in South Dakota's Badlands.

The frontier town of Medora was founded in 1883 and named for the wife of the ambitious Marquis de Mores, a French nobleman whose thirst for adventure was matched only by his intense desire to be the richest financier in the world. When he and his beautiful wife arrived in the tiny, tough railroad town of Little Missouri, he envisioned a unique meat-processing scheme that would process and ship meat—rather than cattle—in refrigerated train cars to the East Coast. Local residents called de Mores "the crazy Frenchman," yet it was Little Missouri that became a deserted pile of splinters when de Mores built his town of Medora and had a population of 251 only a year later. In addition to the meat-packing plant, it boasted a newspaper, a brickyard, several stores and saloons, a hotel, and St. Mary's Catholic Church.

The marquis often entertained neighbor Theodore Roosevelt at his 26-room chateau that overlooked Medora. De Mores and the man who would be president did not always see eye to eye on everything, but they did agree on socializing over iced champagne. De Mores's dreams proved to be farfetched,

BEST ATTRACTIONS IN WESTERN NORTH DAKOTA

Dakota Dinosaur Museum	Maltese Cross Cabin
Fort Union Trading Post National Historic Site	Medora Musical
	Theodore Roosevelt National Park
Lake Sakakawea	Tobacco Gardens

however, and he shut down the meat-packing operation in 1886. He and his wife returned to France the following year. Medora became another pale western ghost town when the wicked winter of 1887–1888 wiped out most of the ranchers' herds. The De Mores's home, with its sweeping views of the valley, along with historical exhibits and the towering brick chimney from the slaughtering plant, remind today's visitors of Medora's big dreams and ill-fated beginning.

The elegantly appointed, two-story de Mores chateau is now the **Chateau de Mores State Historic Site.** Lavish furnishings, Oriental carpets, and fine details in this frame house greeted the family when it arrived in 1884. For three years the family occupied the home seasonally, returning to New York during the winter months. The marquis and his wife loved hunting, music, and art. The chateau was given to the state in 1936. The interpretive center and chateau are open for tours daily from Memorial Day through Labor Day. The interpretive center is open Tues through Sat year-round. Tours are $10 for adults; $3 for children 6 to 15. Call (701) 623-4355 for seasonal hours or visit history.nd.gov/historicsites/chateau.

Medora's revival began in 1958, when the **Burning Hills Amphitheatre** was built and the drama *Old Four Eyes* was presented to mark Roosevelt's 100th birthday. Four years later, history buff and businessman Harold Schafer reignited de Mores's dream and brought the town back to life, this time as a premier vacation destination. In 1986 the Schafer family donated its holding in Medora to the Theodore Roosevelt Medora Foundation, a public, nonprofit organization that operates the public attractions and provides a one-stop spot for visitors. For more information, call (701) 623-4444 or visit medora.com.

In the summer of 1995, the **Harold Schafer Heritage Center** (335 4th St.) opened to tell the story of Schafer's engaging life at his Gold Seal Company (which sold Mr. Bubble bath, Glass Wax, and Snowy Bleach worldwide) and as the promoter of Medora, the state's leading tourist attraction. The center's **Sheila Schafer Gallery** shows art exhibits each year.

The biggest ticket around is still the **Medora Musical,** which began in 1974 and still serves up a rollicking song-and-dance variety show peppered with patriotism, a few special effects, cowboys on real horses, aw-shucks humor, history, and North Dakota pride. It might look a little schmaltzy at first glance, but the spirit of it pulls you in, especially in its jaw-dropping setting carefully nestled into the Badlands. The dramatic escalator ride into the 2,900-seat amphitheater alone can trip its share of "wows" from first-time visitors.

If you're a seasoned musical-goer, consider adding on a behind-the-scenes tour that starts at 6:30 p.m. before the show. Tour tickets are $7 for adults; $3 for students. Tours begin at the **Medora Musical Welcome Center** and last about 40 minutes. Tickets to the musical are $38 to $42 for adults; $17 to $21 for students 7 to 17. Preschoolers are always free, and kids under 7 are free Wed and Sun. Tues and Thurs, seniors get 15 percent off ticket prices. Showtime is 7:30 p.m. nightly in the **Burning Hills Amphitheatre,** with performances running Memorial Day through Labor Day weekend.

It's easy to make a full evening of a musical outing. You can start by watching chefs plunge steaks speared by pitchforks into vats of boiling oil—a pitchfork fondue—before dining on the nearby Tjaden Terrace with some of the most scenic views anywhere.

Be sure to try the **Farmhouse Café** (314 Pacific Ave.; 701-623-3105), which serves mainly American food. Try the croissant French toast or the Bad-lands nachos for breakfast and a burger or Indian tacos for later. This restaurant like many others in Medora has only seasonal hours and is closed during the winter months.

Once a seasonal hotel, **Rough Riders** (301 3rd Ave.; 701-623-4444) underwent a major expansion in the early 2010s, adding 68 new rooms and a conference center which allows it to stay open year-round. The original eight historic rooms were also updated during the renovation. Despite the new construction, the hotel kept its Victorian western look (oak armoires, shower tiles with Teddy Roosevelt's ranch brand), while adding the modern comforts of pillow-top beds and flat-screen TVs. If you want the best room, ask for No. 501, a king corner suite with seven windows facing the Badlands. Or try No. 503 with a balcony, where you can pretend you're Theodore Roosevelt giving his presidential pitch in 1900.

The biggest winter event is the **Old-Fashioned Cowboy Christmas** the first weekend in December, with most of the events taking place in the

What's in a Name?

On March 2, 1861, President James Buchanan signed the bill creating the Dakota Territory. It originally included the area covered today by both Dakotas, as well as Montana and Wyoming. The word *Dakota* means "friend" in the Dakota language.

Beginning about 1887, efforts were made to bring Dakota into the Union as both a single state and as two states. The latter was successful, and on November 2, 1889, North Dakota and South Dakota were admitted.

Since President Benjamin Harrison went to great lengths to obscure the order in which the statehood proclamations were signed, the exact order in which the states entered is unknown. However, because of the alphabetical position, North Dakota is often considered the 39th state.

community center. The highlight is sleigh or hayrides, but the event also includes an antiques and crafts show, as well as a Christmas quilt show, a family Christmas dance, ice skating, a cowboy poker game, cowboy poetry, and a Best of the West doll show. The kids are entertained with a children's story hour and a chalk-art drawing session. To round off the activities, the chamber hosts a traditional Christmas supper, Western Parade of Lights, outhouse races, and a cowboy Christmas jamboree. In conjunction with all the holiday wonderment, the chamber honors a veteran each year.

Just about everything in Medora sits within easy walking distance, including a handful of shops ranging from candy stores and a bookshop to western wear. **Rough Riders Gift Shop** features jewelry, including Landstrom's original Black Hills gold and sterling silver.

Look for Teddy Roosevelt's historic **Maltese Cross Cabin** (315 2nd Ave.) by the national park's visitor center. When Roosevelt first came to the Badlands, he was an asthmatic young man who scoured the wild ravines—in bad weather for two weeks—until he finally found and shot a bison. The adventure thrilled Roosevelt so much that before he left he bought a cattle ranch named Chimney Butte about 7 miles south of Medora, near the Little Missouri River, and renamed it the Maltese Cross Ranch.

At Roosevelt's request, ranch managers built a 1½-story cabin complete with shingle roof and cellar. In its day the cabin was considered a mansion, for it had wooden floors and three separate rooms. The steeply pitched roof, an anomaly on the Dakota plains, provided an upstairs sleeping loft for ranch hands. You can see the desk at which Teddy wrote his book *Hunting Trips of the Ranchman,* which he completed between 1884 and 1885. The rocking chair in the living room was his favorite piece of furniture. During the Roosevelt presidency the Maltese Cross Cabin was exhibited in Portland, Oregon, and St. Louis, Missouri. It was then moved to the capitol grounds in Bismarck and finally relocated to its present site and renovated in 1959.

didyouknow?

The highest point in the state of North Dakota is straight south of the national park near the tiny town of Amidon. **White Butte,** south of town and east of US 85, rises to 3,506 feet. You can pitch a tent about 16 miles south of it at Butte View State Campground.

When Roosevelt returned to North Dakota for the second year after the buffalo hunt, it was for far grimmer reasons. His wife and mother had died within hours of each other, and Roosevelt was inconsolably grief-stricken. In a move to further isolate himself from civilization and his own pain, he bought another cattle operation, the **Elkhorn Ranch,** 35 miles north of Medora. The

Riding Tall in the Saddle

When in Theodore Roosevelt National Park, do as Teddy did—go on horseback. The South Unit of the park features more than 80 miles of marked horse trails, and endless unmarked trails carved by the park's buffalo herd. Riders are permitted in all areas of the park except for the camping and picnicking areas and nature trails. A group horse campground is available in the South Unit by reservation, and backcountry horse camping is allowed. Be on the lookout for bison, wild horses, longhorned cattle, elk, and deer. To get closer to the land here, cinch up a ride with the *Medora Riding Stables,* which offers one- and two-hour long guided rides through the surrounding lands including some to the top of a butte. Open Memorial Day to Labor Day, 7 a.m. to 3 p.m. For more information, call (701) 623-4444.

ranch buildings no longer exist but interpretive signs tell where the house and outbuildings were. You can visit the ranch, but be aware that it can be reached only on rough dirt roads. Call the visitor center at (701) 623-4466 for conditions before attempting the trip.

Teddy's cattle ranches during the late 1800s let him practice and nurture his philosophy of practical conservation. He also was aware of the problems of the West and possessed the rugged spirit of its settlers, an enviable asset when he became president in 1901. His time in North Dakota greatly shaped his groundbreaking conservation efforts that helped national parks and the nation's wildlife thrive in the 20th century.

Theodore Roosevelt National Park

"It was still the Wild West in those days . . . and ours was the glory of work and the joy of living," Theodore Roosevelt said of North Dakota. The former president knew the Badlands intimately, and his passion for these endless buttes and clay-streaked bluffs inextricably pulses throughout the region. You'll start to understand it with that first sweeping glance across *Theodore Roosevelt National Park's Painted Canyon* overlook and rest area just off I-94. To truly appreciate the landscape, you need to enter the park, hike its buttes, watch bison take a dirt bath in a wallow, and photograph majestic wild horses as they trot alongside a curve in the Little Missouri River. Within the park is one of the world's largest petrified forests, and it's best to inquire with a ranger to learn how to get there.

The park is divided into three distinctly different units: the South Unit (accessible from Medora via I-94), the Elkhorn Ranch site, and the North Unit,

BEST ANNUAL EVENTS IN WESTERN NORTH DAKOTA

MAY

Cowboy Poetry Gathering
Medora
(701) 623-4910

JUNE

The Fort Union Trading Post Rendezvous
Williston/Buford
nps.gov/fous

JULY

The Roughrider Days Rodeo
Dickinson
roughriderdaysfair.com

DECEMBER

Old-Fashioned Cowboy Christmas
Medora
(701) 623-4910

which can be reached via US 85 near **Watford City.** Although the park is open year-round, some portions of the road system may be closed during winter. The park includes 110 square miles of Badlands and is considered one of the nation's least crowded gems. Since the withdrawal of an ancient salt sea 130 million years ago, rain, wind, and the Little Missouri River have shaped a curious, mystical landscape in the Badlands. Exposed seams of lignite coal create a band of black below one ridge. On another butte, clay is baked into red scoria, the result of smoldering lignite, ignited by lightning strikes or prairie fires. The burning of lignite beds through the ages has helped lend color as well as shape to the Badlands, as the baked rocks become more resistant to erosion than the neighboring layers. Painted canyons, ash coulees, and broad cottonwood river bends are breathtaking. Be sure to watch for the cannonball concretions at a pullout on the North Unit's loop drive.

North Dakotans like to call the park Rough Rider Country, and no doubt it was the rough-and-tumble lifestyle of the West and the starkness of the North Dakota Badlands that primed the young Roosevelt for a much larger role later in his life, that of a Rough Rider leading his men to battle in Cuba. The **Medora South Unit Visitor Center** (315 2nd Ave.) will formally introduce you to Teddy, and if you haven't already fallen madly in love with the former president, you certainly will here. While the presidential history is fascinating, the highlight for most visitors is the national park's awe-inspiring 36-mile scenic loop drive through the wide expanse of the park's South Unit. For more information, call (701) 623-4466 or visit nps.gov/thro.

Along this paved road you will see panoramic views of the Badlands with plenty of opportunities to get out and hike through this 46,158-acre section. A word to the wise: Drive carefully and make sure you're not in a hurry. On my first visit to the park, a herd of bison took its sweet time crossing the road. A few shaggy males rumbled so close to our vehicle and seemed so huge, it was like we were in a sardine tin. Don't even think about getting out to shoot a photo unless it's from the car or a good distance away with a telephoto lens. They look tame (and even slow) until you see a National Park Service clip of ignorant tourists getting swiftly head-butted like a game-winning field goal.

You'll likely see elk and deer in the park, as well, especially during early morning or late afternoon drives when wildlife is most active. Park rangers can clue you in on where the wild horses were recently spotted and show you where to watch for prairie dog towns. The prairie dogs are especially entertaining as they interact and pop up and down in their intricate towns. They may seem cute and timid, but do keep your distance to avoid painful bites

Hit the Maah Daah Hey Trail

Writer Lisa Meyers McClintick describes how she felt traveling on this trail one time: "My first taste of mountain biking was on a section of the 144-mile **Maah Daah Hey Trail** near Medora. It took almost 30 minutes to ease the death grip I had on the brakes. When I finally relaxed and let myself speed down the hills and let momentum carry me up new ones, it was an exhilarating breakthrough. I've been hooked ever since."

People come from across the nation to tackle this trail, following the iconic posts marked with the simple outline of a turtle. In the Mandan language, *maah daah hey* means "a place that will be around for a long time." We can only hope so. While the scenery isn't as colorfully intense as the red rock mountain biking mecca in Moab, Utah, North Dakota makes up for it with solitude and only slightly more muted colors in this gorgeous and challenging terrain.

One section, "The Deuce," climbs buttes and zig-zags through switchbacks in the 30-mile extension south from Sully's Creek State Park to the US Forest Service's Burning Coal Vein Campground. The trail also is popular with horseback riders.

The trail extends north to the USDA Forest Service Dakota Prairie Grasslands CCC Campground in McKenzie County 15 miles south of Watford City on Highway 85 and one mile west on Forest Road 842. For maps or more information, contact the US Forest Service McKenzie Ranger District at (701) 842-8500 or fs.fed.us, or the Maah Daah Hey Trail Association at mdhta.com.

Dakota Cyclery (701-623-4808; dakotacyclery.com) offers great introductory experiences for beginners and families, along with bike rentals, shuttles, and anything an expert will need, from repair parts to having your gear waiting at your campsite when you're ready for an epic ride. They're open 9 a.m. to around 5:30 p.m. daily from mid-May through Oct.

Vibrant Souvenirs

Pottery lovers head 25 miles west of the national park on I-94 to visit **Tama Smith**'s studio (127 E. Main St.; prairiefirepottery.com) in the tiny border town of Beach. A self-proclaimed "fire potter," Smith's most distinctive palette of colors is prairie fire. The mix of brilliant red, rich ochre, and earthy browns grace her pots, vases, mugs, and other practical works of art.

Her studio is open 8 a.m. to 6 p.m. daily through the summer, and 9 a.m. to 5 p.m. Mon through Sat, Oct through Dec. Call (888) 229-9496 for winter hours.

---

or disease. Also be on the watch for prairie rattlesnakes, which might strike if surprised on the trails.

The North Dakota Game and Fish Department urges people not to touch wildlife, especially baby animals that appear to be abandoned. It is illegal to take wild animals home, and captive animals returned to the wild will lack the necessary survival skills. Motorists also should watch for deer along roadways throughout the entire region—not just the park. June and November are the peak months for deer-vehicle accidents when deer are more on the move.

If you take US 85 north from Belfield, you're well on your way to the North Unit of Theodore Roosevelt National Park. The highway first will take you through **Grassy Butte,** where you can find the **Old Sod Post Office.** Construction materials were scarce in 1912, so the Grassy Butte Post Office was built of logs and sod. The building was used until 1964. Now listed on the National Register of Historic Places as a historic site, the building serves as a museum that is filled with sundry antiques and relics from the 1800s and early 1900s. The museum is open 9 a.m. to 4 p.m. July 1 through Labor Day, and weekends from Memorial Day through June. Admission is free. Call (701) 863-6604 for more information.

In the less-visited North Unit of Theodore Roosevelt National Park, the buttes are taller and certain areas are heavily forested. Squaw Creek (1.1 miles) and Caprock Coulee (1.5 miles) nature trails are self-guided and interpret the Badlands, coulees, and breaks. Upper Caprock Coulee, Achenbach, and Buckhorn Trails will take you into the backcountry. A 14-mile scenic drive has turnouts with spectacular views and interpretive sites.

North Dakota's Boom Towns

Oil has boomed in northwestern North Dakota. The epicenter? **Williston,** which fittingly dubbed itself "Boomtown" in 2014. Small wonder, its population soared from 16,083 in 2010 to 26,968 in 2015 after which it dropped to 25,621 two years later. However, it's on the rise again, peaking at 27,096 in 2019. Officials estimate that the oil reserves in the Bakken formation, which stretches under much of northwest North Dakota, is now 30 to 40 million barrels. Also, the US Geological Survey estimates 1.85 trillion cubic feet of associated/dissolved natural gas, and 148 million barrels of natural gas are in the Bakken formation.

Dickinson has experienced a similar but slower growth, rising from a population of 17,998 in 2010 to 22,739 in 2019, making it a micropolitan (a community between 10,000 and 50,000). After some tough years of trying to meet the high demand for housing as workers flooded to oil fields from across the nation, housing has stabilized. For travelers, that means it's possible to get a hotel room again. The roads and fields may look a little more crowded with oil trucks and equipment, but you'll also find more places to eat and more things to do as the entire region grows. Remember, the natural beauty of national wildlife refuges, state parks, Lake Sakakawea, private ranches, and quirky attractions endure and beckon people to explore oil country.

Watford City, pop. 6,523, which bills itself as a slice of the New Old West, provides a gateway to the northern section of Theodore Roosevelt National Park and to the Bakken oil field as it sprawls west and north. You can get a feel for the grit and masculinity of the area with a hand-cut steak, western-themed food, and a slice of community history through old photos on display at **Outlaws' Bar and Grill** and Six Shooters' Showhall. The historic theme includes a coatroom jail cell. Call (701) 842-6859 or visit outlawsbarngrill.com for details.

You can see North Dakota's largest fossil at **Long X Visitor Center and Pioneer Museum** (100 2nd St. SW; 701-444-5804). The petrified bald cypress tree stump is estimated at 17,000 pounds and measures about 6 feet in diameter and 8 feet tall. The 60-million-year-old fossil was discovered in the Badlands south of Watford City during an archaeological dig in 2001. You'll also find tourist information and the **Pioneer Museum of McKenzie County,** which has added an oil exhibit. The new exhibit, which pays homage to North Dakota's jump to No. 2 in US oil production, includes a replica oil rig, industry information, and replicas of drilling bits. Hours are 10 a.m. to 5 p.m. Mon through Sat. Free admission. Call (701) 444-2990 for more information.

Swing into the **McKenzie County Heritage Park** for a look at how hunters, trappers, and pioneers survived life on the northern plains. Or follow US 85 back south to some of the state's best modern hunting and fishing grounds. Mourning dove, sharp-tailed grouse, Hungarian partridge, and ring-necked pheasant are just some of the upland bird hunting opportunities. Wing-shooters take to the fields and prairie water holes on the first of September, as mourning dove hunting traditionally kicks off North Dakota's shotgun season. Drive almost anywhere among the rolling green grasslands, and you'll be sure to see and hear the honk of pheasants.

Belfield, some 18 miles east of Medora and the Badlands south unit, is a magnet for weary travelers and hunters with *Trapper's Kettle* restaurant and gift shop. It incorporates the hunting/trapping theme throughout its decor and menu. Authentic traps serve as door pulls in the restaurant, and the cedar dining tables have inlaid traps. Examples of taxidermy of almost every animal imaginable seem to stare vacantly in the dining areas. The hearty and well-prepared food is stick-to-your-ribs good here. Pan-fry dishes and mini-kettle soups also hit the spot. Prices are moderate. Call (701) 575-8585 or visit trapperskettle.com.

hunting101

For more information on resident and nonresident hunting requirements and licenses, call the *North Dakota Game and Fish Department* at (701) 328-6300 or check out the website gf.nd.gov.

Bright orange is the fall fashion color of choice in these parts as hunters remind their buddies to reset watches to mountain standard time and team up to land the biggest bucks. White-tailed deer are found almost everywhere, but the mule deer tend to cluster in the jagged country of the Badlands and other broken terrain. Lightning-swift pronghorn inhabit the western borders of the region, and the regal white elk and bighorn sheep confine themselves primarily to the Badlands and the Killdeer Mountains.

Catch a Rodeo

Nearly 60 rodeos throughout the state attract hundreds of cowboys each year. The word *rodeo* is actually derived from a Spanish word meaning "roundup." The history of the rodeo traces back to the 1800s when most ranches had untamed horses (or broncos). Cattle outfits often challenged one another to bronc-riding contests in which cowboys could prove their mettle. Eventually someone reckoned there would be good money to be made if there was an admission charge to see the contest between the bronc and the cowboy.

Rodeos remain a popular, breathtaking event in North Dakota and South Dakota. Basically, there are four types of rodeo: high school, college, amateur, and professional. For a listing of rodeos in North Dakota, check the North Dakota Rodeo Association's website at ndrodeo.com.

Dickinson (19 miles west of Belfield off I-94) has surged from 16,325 people in 2009 to 22,186 by 2017. It still hangs onto its cowboy and cowgirl personality, and considers itself the rodeo capital of North Dakota with one of the state's biggest events—*Roughrider Days Rodeo*—and additional festivities during the Fourth of July weekend.

Dickinson's biggest claim to fame for most visitors is its **Badlands Dinosaur Museum**, a fantastic earth science museum that features dinosaur bones found in North Dakota, including a complete triceratops, which lived in the Badlands when they were a swampy and warm area, and a duck-billed edmontosaurus. Ten other full-scale dinosaurs, a complete fossil rhino, and rocks and minerals are impressive displays as well. Located right on I-94 at 200 E. Museum Dr., it's part of the Joachim Regional Museum complex. It is open 9 a.m. to 5 p.m. daily Mon through Sat, and Sun noon to 5 p.m. Memorial Day

Enchanted Highway

About 20 miles east of Dickinson at exit 72, a 110-foot-tall sculpture of Canada geese looms over the interstate, dwarfing the cars that pull over to admire it and drawing attention to one of America's most interesting, quirky, and endearing stretches of roadside art: the 32-mile *Enchanted Highway*. This ribbon of rural road stretches from the freeway to tiny *Regent* with North Dakota–inspired sculptures pulling you forward as they rise from the wide-open rolling landscape about every 10 to 15 miles.

Former teacher and school principal Gary Greff was worried his hometown of Regent (pop. 156) would disappear like so many other farm-dependent towns. One day he saw drivers pulling over to snap pictures of a giant figure of a man created out of hay bales. He then dreamed up the idea of metal sculptures. With no welding or formal art training, he finished the first sculpture of a tin family made from used farm equipment in 1991 and erected it a few miles outside of Regent. Since then, he has built and installed seven more sculptures, each more complex and artsy than the last. Look for Teddy Roosevelt, 60-foot-tall pheasants, deer, Canada geese, and the delightful "Fisherman's Dream," featuring a lively group of fish made from recycled scrap metal, oil well pipes, drums, and tanks. Go ahead and ham it up beneath the 40-foot-tall grasshoppers, which represent one of the Midwest's most devastating plagues. You can lighten the mood with a B-movie moment, looking miniature and posing with mock looks of terror beneath the Godzilla-size grasshoppers.

Despite the allure of the Enchanted Highway, Regent remains a tiny town but chockfull of charm and appeal with a Metal Magic gift shop and Greff's newest creation, the *Enchanted Castle* (607 Main St.; 701-563-4858), a themed hotel featuring a steakhouse and tavern, built in the town's former brick school.

The Great Survivor

As many as 60 million bison once roamed over one-third of the entire land mass of North America. It was not unusual for a herd to contain 4 million animals and cover an area 50 miles long and 20 miles wide.

On the Dakota prairies, bison provided food, clothing, shelter, arrow points, ropes, and ornaments for the Native Americans who lived on the plains. As late as 1866 a huge herd of bison estimated at 100,000 was sighted 18 miles north of Fargo. Often mistakenly called buffalo, bison are not related to the true buffalo of Africa and Asia. Their ancestors, wild cattle that found their way across the now-vanished land bridge from Siberia to Alaska, came to North America during the Pleistocene era.

Prized for their meat and hides and as trophies, bison were hunted almost to extinction; by 1891 the US bison population had been reduced to a mere 541 animals. The species was saved from annihilation by concerned conservationists, ranchers, and lovers of the outdoors who protected the remaining bison, gradually replenishing their number and building today's herds.

through Labor Day. Admission is $6 for adults; $4 for children 3 to 12. For more information, call (701) 225-3466 or visit dickinsonmuseumcenter.com.

A self-guided tour of the ***Joachim Regional Museum and Prairie Outpost Park*** gives you an idea of how rugged pioneers settled southwestern North Dakota. The museum offers tours of a Norwegian *stabbur* (storage house), a Germans-from-Russia homestead house, a one-room schoolhouse, a railroad depot, a church, and other buildings that reflect the area's ethnic and immigrant past. For more information call (701) 456-6225 or visit dickinson museumcenter.com.

If you travel 3 miles west on I-94, then 1 mile south, you'll be at ***Patterson Reservoir*** (701-225-2074), ideal for swimming, fishing, boating, camping, and picnicking during the summer. The reservoir is part of the Missouri River Valley reclamation project. The park is open daily June through Aug.

Back on the interstate, two exits east of the Enchanted Highway is ***Richardton,*** population 538. The twin spires of its historic ***St. Mary's Catholic Church*** (418 3rd Ave. W) are quiet testaments to the faith that has steadfastly guided Dakotans through lean and prosperous times. Benedictine monks built this stunning structure a century ago on what's known as Russian Ridge, which stretches for dozens of miles and divides the Heart River basin in the south from the Knife River basin in the north. The original church and its immovable central altar are the focal point amid the vaulted ceilings, original medallion paintings, ornate altars, and more than 50 stained-glass windows. St. Mary's is a wonderful example of Bavarian-Romanesque–style architecture.

Today, the church is lovingly tended to by monks living in the Assumption Abbey, which is connected to the church. They warmly welcome visitors. Be sure to see their gift shop, printing facility, wine cellar, church, and library. Nuns of the Benedictine order at nearby Sacred Heart Monastery also welcome visitors. Call (701) 974-3315 for an appointment or visit assumption abbey.com.

Lewis and Clark Trail

Whether you head north of Theodore Roosevelt National Park or follow the Missouri River from the east, you'll find many of North Dakota's most historic and storied places by following the *Lewis and Clark Trail* (lewisandclarktrail .com).

The explorers and their crew bravely headed across uncharted territory to seek a route from St. Louis to the Pacific Ocean, meticulously recording their discoveries and adventures along the way. The Lewis and Clark Trail comprises two developed highways along the Missouri River. The highway numbers—1804 and 1806—appropriately match the years that the explorers entered and returned to North Dakota. ND 1804 follows the eastern side of the Missouri River, while ND 1806 follows the western side. Historical sites and recreation can be discovered along both banks of the river.

On the far western border of the state, astounding history unfolds at the *Fort Union Trading Post National Historic Site* (701-572-9083; nps.gov/ fous), which stands near the confluence of the Yellowstone and Missouri Rivers

Glorious Golf Courses

North Dakota has three of the nation's top golf courses, which frame up some of the state's most stunning scenery. It costs $165 to play all of them with the Triple Golf Challenge.

The Links of North Dakota (701-568-2600; thelinksofnorthdakota.com) boasts a pure links style, taking advantage of gently rolling bluff-tops overlooking Lake Saka-kawea west of Williston on ND 1804.

Hawktree Golf Club (3400 Burnt Creek Loop; 701-355-0995; hawktree.com) near Bismarck also takes a links-style approach with greens tucked into the Burnt Creek Valley and framed in native grasses.

Bully Pulpit Golf Course (800-633-6721; medora.com), 3 miles south of Medora, looks the most dramatic with vibrant greens tucked into orange, red, and ochre colors of the Badlands.

in the town of **Buford.** Open daily year-round, the site is accessible from ND 1804, a 24-mile drive southwest from Williston. From 1829 to 1867, the Fort Union Trading Post was the "vastest and finest" of a string of trading posts along the northern rivers. In a typical year more than 25,000 buffalo robes would change hands here, along with iron tools, guns, blankets, and other manufactured goods. Twenty-foot-high whitewashed palisades, anchored by two-story stone bastions, surrounded Fort Union. Capitalist John Jacob Astor reasoned that the imposing structure would impress the local Native Americans. Here, Scots, Germans, French, and Spanish bargained with the Assiniboine, Crow, Cree, Blackfoot, and Sitting Bull's Hunkpapa band of Lakota.

Much of what we have learned about the cultures of the Native Americans who lived on the northern plains comes from Fort Union's adventurous staff and often rich-and-famous guests. John James Audubon, Germany's Prince Maximilian, and renowned artists George Catlin and Karl Bodmer left lasting legacies in their paintings, sketches, and words about this incredible mosaic. You can enjoy the rich tapestry of culture and feel like a part of the past by timing a visit with the annual Rendezvous festival in June. The site is free and includes tours of Bourgeois House and visitor center and the Trade House with living history actors throughout the summer.

Trade flourished here until smallpox ravaged most of the trading tribes. The friendly trade ultimately ended when Fort Union was occupied by the 30th Wisconsin Infantry in 1864. The fort is open from 8 a.m. to 6:30 p.m. from Labor Day through Memorial Day, and from 9 a.m. to 5:30 p.m. in the off-season. The red-roofed Trade House, filled with replicated goods and a costumed interpreter acting as an 1850s trader, is open from 10 a.m. to 5 p.m. Memorial Day through Labor Day.

Fort Union dismantled the private enterprise to help construct the military's **Fort Buford,** now a state historic site about a mile upstream. The fort is probably best known as the place where Hunkpapa leader Sitting Bull surrendered in 1881. Chief Joseph also surrendered here after defeat in the Nez Perce War. Buildings here date from the 1870s. The site is open mid-May through mid-Sept. Admission is $5 for adults and $2.50 for children and includes admission to the **Missouri–Yellowstone Confluence Interpretive Center** (701-572-9034; history.nd.gov) half a mile away. The center is open year-round and includes exhibits on geology, prehistoric times, geography, and the impact of people, the river, and roads through the area. The best attraction, though, is the chance to see the same magnificent views that Lewis and Clark saw as they reached the confluence.

Twenty-two miles northeast of Fort Buford on ND 1804 is **Williston,** a proud energy town at the epicenter of the oil boom. Locals will assure you

Famous North Dakotans

Theodore Roosevelt isn't the only famous person to have kicked up his boots in North Dakota. Some famous North Dakotans include:

Warren Christopher, who served as deputy secretary of state in the Carter administration and was awarded the Medal of Freedom on January 16, 1981. In 1993, Christopher was sworn in as the 63rd US secretary of state.

Angie Dickinson, who has appeared in more than 50 major movies and television productions, but is best known for her roles in the movie *Dressed to Kill* and the TV series *Police Woman*.

Phil Jackson, who will go down in National Basketball Association history not only for his dynamic leadership, but also as the only person to both play for and coach teams (New York Knicks, Chicago Bulls, and Los Angeles Lakers) to titles for the NBA and the Continental Basketball Association.

Louis L'Amour, the award-winning western author and screenwriter, who published more than 400 short stories and more than 100 novels. He wrote 65 TV scripts and sold more than 30 stories to the motion-picture industry, including *Hondo*, starring John Wayne.

Roger Maris, baseball's former single-season home-run king, who hit 61 home runs during the 1961 season while he was a member of the New York Yankees.

Lawrence Welk, who became one of the greatest entertainers in the world through his weekly TV show featuring his distinctive "champagne music."

Cara Mund, born in Bismarck, North Dakota, in 1994, is the first contestant from North Dakota to be crowned Miss America in 2018. She has organized the annual North Dakota Make-a-Wish Fashion Show for the past 12 years.

this isn't the city's first economic boom, and you can glimpse the town's past throughout the summer at the **Frontier Museum** (6330 1st Ave. W; 701-580-2415; thefrontiermuseum.org), northwest of Spring Lake Park. The complex comprises a 1910 rural church, complete with furnishings, 2 modern buildings filled with artifacts, a 1903 two-story house filled with antique furniture, an 1887 grocery store, a restored Great Northern Railway Depot from the town of Alamo, and a complete country school.

Another Great Northern Railway Depot, this one at 1 S. Main St., is where Amtrak's Empire Builder stops twice a day. Built in 1910, the depot's interior and exterior were restored in 2010 to its original look. Since the oil boom, Williston has become the state's second busiest Amtrak station with 28,062 passengers using the passenger service in 2018. Only Minot, with 30,405 passengers, has more travelers.

The **Williston Tourist Information Center** is at 212 Airport Rd. Contact the Williston Convention and Visitors Bureau for more information, (800) 615-9041 or visitwilliston.com.

Williston sits off the west end of **Lake Sakakawea**, an artificial widening of the Missouri River named for the young Shoshone woman who guided the intrepid explorers Lewis and Clark from North Dakota to the Yellowstone River in 1805. Garrison Dam, built between 1947 and 1953, created the lake that's 200 miles long and covers 909 square miles. North Dakota's largest lake draws thousands of visitors each year for superb sailing, camping, hunting, and fishing.

Head 19 miles southeast of Williston on Highway 1804 to reach **Lewis and Clark State Park** on Lake Sakakawea. The explorers were here on April 17, 1805, and you can likewise enjoy the area by land or water. There's a marina and excellent fishing, including walleye, sauger, and northern pike, along with rare pallid sturgeon and ancient-looking paddlefish. The 490-acre park also has a campground, sleeping cabins, and a swimming beach. Winter visitors can snowshoe or cross-country ski, enjoying clear views of the Badlands' rugged buttes in the distance. Go to parkrec.nd.gov/parks/lcsp, or call (701) 859-3071 for more details.

If all the Lewis and Clark sites leave you yearning for adventure, the folks at **Lund's Landing Marina & Lodge** (701-568-3474; lundslanding.com) 23 miles east of Williston on SD 1804 will take guests canoeing or kayaking on the same routes Lewis and Clark followed along Lake Sakakawea. Packages include lodging in their cedar cabins, plus breakfast, lunch, and evening meals that are likely topped off with their beloved juneberry pie a la mode. Open 9 a.m. to 5 p.m. Tues to Sat, Apr through Nov; 9 a.m. to 5 p.m. Tues to Fri the rest of the year. Closed Mon and Sun.

On the south shore of the lake, **Tobacco Garden Bay** was once a stop for steamboats. It's now home to **Tobacco Gardens Resort and Marina** (701-842-4199; tobaccogardens.com), with a restaurant, more than 100 campsites, 2 cabins, a bait shop, and playgrounds. Nearby, the 2.5-mile **Birnt Hills Trail** offers lovely scenic views of Lake Sakakawea. The name Tobacco Garden Bay is derived from the Lakota and Assiniboin name for the reed that grew in the area.

Fort Berthold Reservation is home of the Three Affiliated tribes (Hidatsa, Arikara, and Mandan) on Lake Sakakawea. The boundaries for the reservation have changed many times since its inception in 1880, and today the reservation encompasses 980,000 acres of tribally and individually owned lands. Historically, the Mandan and Hidatsa were a peaceful and agricultural group, stable and not as nomadic as the other Native Americans living on the plains. The Arikara, previously part of the Pawnee, separated from their relatives on the Loup River in Nebraska, worked their way north, and eventually joined the Hidatsa and Mandan. At present about 5,387 of the tribes' members live on the reservation.

The **Three Affiliated Tribes Museum** is located on the Fort Berthold Reservation about 4 miles west of New Town on ND 23. One exhibit at the museum honors Fort Berthold World War I veterans. At that time Native Americans were not allowed to vote, yet they valiantly volunteered to serve their country. Memorabilia, photographs, and a 48-star US flag are highlights in the display. The museum's Eaton collection has records of Native American and treaty lands of tribes in North Dakota plus maps used to verify tribal land claims against the US between 1946 and 1957. The Cross collection examines tribal government in relation to the time when the Garrison Dam was being built from 1947 to 1953. The Wilson collection relates to the region after the completion of the dam. The museum is open mid-Apr through Oct. Call (701) 627-4477 or visit mhanation.com for more information.

You can get a feel for the vastness and beauty of the tribes' historic communities with a visit to the **Knife River Indian Villages National Historic Site** that commemorates Native Americans. The remains of the villages arc along the banks of the Knife and Missouri Rivers, approximately 60 miles north of Bismarck. This is one of the oldest inhabited sites in North America, dating back 9,000 years. The Hidatsa and Mandan, two of the oldest tribes on the continent, lived here in earth lodges, planting and harvesting gardens of corn, squash, beans, and sunflowers, which they exchanged in an ever-growing trading network between tribes. The locally produced Knife River flint has been traced to villages in the far southeastern part of the US. In the winter of 1804 to 1805, they were gracious hosts to Lewis and Clark and the Corps of Discovery, appointed by President Thomas Jefferson to explore and document America's new Louisiana Purchase territory. The Corps, which departed from near St. Louis, comprised 45 men operating a 55-foot keelboat and five other boats. After arriving in North Dakota for the winter, the explorers met the teenage girl Sakakawea (the Dakotas' alternate spelling of Sacagawea). She helped guide them through her native Shoshone lands as they searched for a water route to the Pacific Ocean. In April 1805 the group left Fort Mandan to continue the westward expedition. Lewis and Clark returned to North Dakota in August 1806 on their way back to St. Louis.

Knife River Indian Villages are part of North Dakota's American Legacy Tour. This world-class archaeological park boasts an earthen lodge at the modern visitor center. Trails lead to three village sites, where remnants of earth lodges and scattered bones and tools are easily seen. Ten miles of hiking and Nordic ski trails offer opportunities to view wildlife. The center is open 7:30 a.m. to 6 p.m. Memorial Day through Labor Day; excluding federal holidays, the center is open 8 a.m. to 4:30 p.m. the remainder of the year. For more information, go to nps.gov/knri or call (701) 745-3300.

Ready for another detour? Take ND 49 North to **Beulah,** which prides itself on being the Energy Capital of North Dakota—and for good reason. The Freedom Mine, the largest lignite mine in the nation, delivers more than 15 million tons of coal a year, also fuels the nearby Antelope Valley Station, the Leland Olds Station, and the **Great Plains Synfuels Plant.** The synfuels plant consumes about 18,000 tons of lignite each day, turning the coal into 160 million cubic feet of synthetic natural gas. The natural gas is piped to Iowa and distributed to the eastern US. To tour Freedom Mine, phone (701) 873-2281. To tour the synfuels plant or the Antelope Valley Station, call (701) 223-0441 or email tours@BEPC.com.

Fort Mandan in **Washburn** (38 miles north of Bismarck) ranks among the best Lewis and Clark sites, re-creating the Corps of Discovery's winter camp with interpreters explaining their daily life and how they prepared to keep heading west in the spring. Admission is $8 for adults; $5 for students K through college, and is also good for admission into the nearby North Dakota **Lewis and Clark Interpretive Center.** Among its treasures are a canoe hand-carved from a cottonwood trunk, exhibits on steamboats and frontier trade, and the Berquist Gallery with rare watercolors from Swiss artist Karl Bodmer and written observations from German Prince Maximilian, who both traveled through the area in 1833 and lived among the Native Americans. Hours are 9 a.m. to 5 p.m. daily, Apr through Sept; 9 a.m. to 5 p.m. Mon to Sat, Oct though Mar. For more information, call (701) 462-8535 or visit parkrec.nd.gov/lewis-clark-interpretive-center.

Another jumping-off point for the adventurous is the **Cross Ranch Nature Preserve,** managed by the Nature Conservancy. The ranch is located 30 miles north of Mandan via ND 1806 (a gravel road). This 5,600-acre nature preserve has mixed grass prairies, Missouri River floodplain forest, upland woody draws, and a bison herd. You can hike along self-guided nature trails. The preserve is open year-round to the public. Activities include bird watching, canoeing, wildlife viewing, and cross-country skiing. Call (701) 794-8741 for more information.

The adjacent **Cross Ranch State Park** has a visitor center, 4 log cabins, 70 campsites (both electrical and modern and backcountry), 3 yurts, plus picnicking and fishing along one of the last free-flowing, undeveloped stretches of the Missouri River. Visit parkrec.nd.gov/cross-ranch-state-park or call (701) 794-3731 for more information.

Fort Lincoln and the Capitol

Most people think of South Dakota and Montana when they hear the name George Armstrong Custer, and for good reason. He led the army expedition into the Black Hills of South Dakota, where he had been sent to quell rumors of gold on parts of Lakota land. Instead he found that the prospectors' tales of extractable quantities of gold throughout the area were bona fide. Later, he and many of his troops were killed at the famous Battle of the Little Big Horn in Montana. Prior to these illustrious times in history, however, Custer was a young Civil War hero stationed at Fort Lincoln in what was then the Dakota Territory.

You can visit Custer's home at the **Fort Abraham Lincoln State Park**. The only thing dry about these tours might be a sample of hard tack or spicy jerky. The park in **Mandan** has some of the best living-history actors around, adding a sense of fun with stories on food, manners, day-to-day operations, and old-fashioned gossip from 1875 before the battle. You also can see the central barracks, the commissary store, the blockhouses standing guard over the old fort, and the cemetery where the marked graves of soldiers tell stories never found in history books. The park has monthly themed guided hikes year-round. Every weekend in Oct is a Haunted Fort replete with decorations and scary characters. Visit hauntedfort.com for more information.

The story of ill-fated Custer isn't the only legend at Fort Abraham Lincoln State Park. Mandan settled **On-a-Slant Village** from 1575 to 1781 with a population once as high as 15,000. They farmed miles of Missouri River bottomland from 10 or 12 fortified cities here on the Slant River. The villages were empty and wiped out by disease by the time Lewis and Clark visited. At the pinnacle of their wealth and power, the Mandan built remarkably cozy, round earth lodges, like those seen at Knife River. On-a-Slant Village shows traces of 75 lodges, including the large ceremonial lodge that is 84 feet in diameter. Visitors also can capture the spirit of the time through trail rides. For more information, call (701) 667-6340 or visit parkrec.nd.gov/Parks/FLSP.htm.

In downtown Mandan, the **Five Nations Arts Museum** (400 Main St.; 701-663-4663; fivenationsarts.org) brings the talent of local tribes into the present tense. Inside, the soothing sounds of Native American music can be heard, and an amazing selection of native arts and crafts admired. Located in the former Lewis and Clark Hotel which was built in 1917 with pressed brick and white enamel trimmings, the gallery carries the work of more than 200 artists from the Mandan, Hidatsa, Arikara, Turtle Mountain Band of Chippewa, Lakota, and Dakota tribes. The gallery is open 10 a.m. to 5 p.m. Mon through Sat.

Just across the Missouri River from Mandan, you'll find **Bismarck,** the state capital and, with 72,865 people, the second-largest city in North Dakota. Located at a natural ford of the Missouri River, Bismarck served as an early-day steamboat port. It was named for German chancellor Otto von Bismarck in hopes of encouraging German investment in the railroad.

For a sense of its history, head downtown to check out its growing number of restaurants and boutiques such as **Boutique 23** at 201 W. Main Ave. You'll find plenty of casual, fun eateries, but a fine selection of elegant dining, too.

Among Bismarck's most venerable eateries is **Peacock Alley** (422 E. Main Ave.; 701-255-7917; peacock-alley.com). The former Patterson Hotel was once the off-hours headquarters for state and national politicos and hosted Theodore Roosevelt, Calvin Coolidge, John F. Kennedy, and Lyndon Johnson when they swept through on presidential campaign stops. It's still a posh gathering place, yet with a down-to-earth attitude. Entrees include shrimp pappardelle, a cowboy rib eye using Dakota beef, sides such as buffalo fries, and prime-beef sandwiches with homemade potato chips. Leave room for desserts such as fresh gelatos and baked blueberries with a sugary crust crowned with homemade gelato.

For more cuisine worthy of an elegant date night, there's the **Pirogue Grille** (121 N. 4th St.; 701-223-3770; piroguegrille.com). The chef constantly alters the menu to reflect seasonal, fresh ingredients. Choices might include a walleye sampler, house-made venison sausage, a wild rice salad, and bison medallions. For dessert, you can find everything from an artisanal Midwest cheese plate to chokecherry and chocolate praline ice cream. It's a worthy splurge.

If warm weather has you craving a meal on an open patio, try the **Edwinton Brewery** (411 E. Main Ave.; 701-222-8075; edwinton.com), in a mission-style depot built in 1900. Besides offering its own brews (some are seasonal), it serves sandwiches, gyros, truffle fries, burgers, flatbreads, salads, and desserts.

For refreshments under the open sky, visit the Lüft Rooftop Beer Garden at **Humpback Sally's** (510 E. Main Ave.; 701-425-0844; humpbacksallys.com) where its credo is good drinks including innovative cocktails, great food such as bacon cheeseburger eggrolls, and a huge sky overhead.

No trip to Bismarck would be complete without at least a walk or drive past the **State Capitol** (600 E. Boulevard Ave.; 701-328-2480). Actually, I wonder why we put in its address as it should be easy to find, being the tallest inhabitable building in the state. Some call it the Skyscraper of the Plains. Still, if you take 6th Street north 10 blocks, you'll run into Boulevard Avenue and be at the foot of the grand 19-story capitol, which is topped with an observation tower. Built in the 1930s, the capitol boasts an art deco interior as fashion-forward now as it was then, with exotic wood paneling, stone, and metal. It's open year-round, and free tours are available every two hours from 9 a.m. to 3 p.m. Mon through Sat, and 1 p.m. and 3 p.m. on Sun. The public is to use the capitol's south entrance which, on weekends, opens at 10 minutes prior to tour times.

In 2014, the **North Dakota Heritage Center** (612 E. Boulevard Ave.; 701-328-2666; statemuseum.nd.gov) expanded considerably with the addition of 97,000 square feet that has since allowed the center to continue its already impressive exhibits on prehistoric times and the ice age, Native Americans of the plains, the Old West, pioneers, and bonanza wheat farms, while expanding to include more of the past century with World War II, emerging energy industries, and more. Keep an eye out for unique artifacts including a buffalo hide tipi, a mastodon skeleton, and the museum's famous mummified dinosaur that has been seen around the world. Many activities are hands-on (smell a buffalo wallow) and appeal to kids. An area called the Treehouse is designed for preschool through 3rd-grade visitors. The museum's open 8 a.m. to 5 p.m. Mon through Fri; 10 a.m. to 5 p.m. Sat and Sun. Admission is free.

Just a few blocks south is the **Former Governor's Mansion State Historic Site** (320 E. Ave. B). This restored Victorian mansion was occupied by the state's first families from 1893 to 1960. Interpretive exhibits and governors' portraits now occupy this elegant three-story structure. Tour the mansion for free. It's open 10 a.m. to 5 p.m. Mon through Fri, and noon to 4 p.m. Sat and Sun, mid-May through mid-Sept. For information about hours between Oct and May or other concerns, call (701) 328-9528 or visit history.nd.gov/historicsites/fgm.

oldredoldten

If you're itching to ditch the interstate and take the road less traveled on the way west from Mandan to Dickinson, grab the *Old Red Old Ten Scenic Byway*. It slows the pace and the scenery with pretty buttes, wildlife, prairie, and small towns. Go to oldredoldten.com for more information.

To see the great state of North Dakota in a similar fashion to Lewis and Clark over 200 years ago, hop aboard the **Lewis and Clark Riverboat,** a 150-passenger boat. The riverboat offers daily excursion cruises, dinner cruises with pizza or barbecue, sunset cruises, and special events for the entire family from Apr through Sept. Snacks and beverages are available on all cruises. The riverboat is located at 1700 N. River Road, which is at exit 157 off I-94. Cruise prices start at $10 for kids (ages 4 to 12) and $15 for adults. Call (701) 255-4233 or visit lewisandclarkriverboat.com for more information.

BEST BISMARCK-MANDAN FAMILY ATTRACTIONS

Dakota Zoo
602 Riverside Park Rd.
Bismarck
(701) 223-7543
dakotazoo.org

Fort Abraham Lincoln State Park
4480 Fort Lincoln Rd.
Mandan
(701) 667-6340
park/rec.nd.gov/Parks/FLSP.htm

Fort Lincoln Trolley (seasonal)
1989 3rd St. SE
Mandan
(701) 663-0918

North Dakota Heritage Center and the Capitol Grounds
612 E. Boulevard Ave.
Bismarck
(701) 328-2666
history.nd.gov

Papa's Pumpkin Patch
5001 Fernwood Dr.
Bismarck
(701) 222-1521
papaspumpkinpatch.com

Raging Rivers Waterpark
2600 48th Ave. SE
Mandan
(701) 663-3393
ragingriverswaterpark.com

Speaking of boats and Lewis and Clark, immediately south of the riverboat's parking lot, you can walk on a full-size replica of their keelboat at Keelboat Park which lies alongside the Missouri River. Colorful, 30-foot tall interpretations of Lewis, Clark, and Sakakawea stand at the park's entrance.

North Dakota is again timelessly joined to South Dakota through the *Standing Rock Reservation,* which extends into both states. The people of the Standing Rock Sioux tribe are part of the Yanktonai and Teton Sioux Nation, which formerly controlled a vast domain that extended from the James River in North Dakota and South Dakota west to the Big Horn Mountains of Wyoming. In 1868 the Treaty of Fort Laramie reduced this area to the Great Sioux Reservation, setting the boundaries of a 25-million-acre tract that covered all of South Dakota west of the Missouri. When gold was discovered in the Black Hills, Congress ratified an invalid agreement and took the Black Hills shortly thereafter. The Great Sioux Reservation was broken into six small reservations in 1889, one of which is Standing Rock (formerly called the Grand River Agency), situated on the North Dakota–South Dakota border between the Badlands and the Missouri River. On the western edge of Fort Yates, located on the Missouri River on the North Dakota portion of the Standing Rock Indian Reservation, is the original gravesite of renowned Hunkpapa Lakota spiritual leader Sitting Bull.

You can arrange a tour of the reservation and sites along the Standing Rock Scenic Byway at the Sitting Bull Visitor Center on the Sitting Bull College Campus in Fort Yates. The center is open from 8 a.m. to 4:30 p.m. Mon through Fri. Call (701) 854-8125 for more information about the visitor center, which is also a good place to check for campsites or rooms at Prairie Knights Casino and Resort or to check on powwows, rodeos, and other special events in the area. For information about Prairie Knights Casino and Resort, call (800) 425-8277 or visit prairieknights.com.

Where to Stay in Western North Dakota

BISMARCK

AmericInn by Wyndham
3235 State St.
(701) 353-0436
Moderate

Expressway Suites
180 E. Bismarck Expy.
(701) 222-3311
Inexpensive

Radisson Hotel
605 E. Broadway Ave.
(701) 255-6000
Moderate

Wingate by Wyndham Bismarck
1421 Skyline Blvd.
(701) 751-2373
Moderate

BOWMAN

North Winds Lodge
503 Hwy. 85
(701) 523-5641
Inexpensive

MANDAN

Baymont by Wyndham Mandan Bismarck Area
2611 Old Red Trl.
(701) 663-7401
baymontmandan.com
Moderate

MEDORA

AmericInn by Wyndham
75 E. River Rd. S
(844) 581-4982
Moderate

Badlands Motel
501 Pacific Ave.
(701) 623-4444
Moderate

WILLISTON

Four Points by Sheraton Williston
7115 2nd Ave. W
(701) 609-5490
Moderate to expensive

Missouri Flats Inn
213 35th St. W
(701) 572-4242
missouriflatsinn.com
Moderate

Where to Eat in Western North Dakota

BISMARCK

Blarney Stone Pub
408 E. Main Ave.
(701) 751-7512
blarneyirishpub.com
Moderate

Bread Poets
106 E. Thayer Ave.
(701) 222-4445
breadpoets.com
Inexpensive

Fireflour Neapolitan Pizza & Coffee Bar
111 N. 5th St.
(701) 323-9000
fireflourpizza.com
Moderate

Laughing Sun Brewhouse and Pub
1023 E. Front Ave.
(701) 751-3881
laughingsunbrewing.com
Moderate

SELECTED CHAMBERS OF COMMERCE

Bismarck–Mandan Convention and Visitors Bureau
1600 Burnt Boat Dr.
Bismarck 58503
(701) 222-4308
discoverbismarckmandan.com

Bottineau Convention and Visitors Bureau
519 Main St.
Bottineau 58318
(701) 228-3849
bottineau.com

Dickinson Convention and Visitors Bureau
72 E. Museum Dr.
Dickinson 58601
(701) 483-4988
visitdickinson.com

McKenzie County Tourism
100 2nd Ave. SW
Watford City 58854
(701) 444-2804
visitwatfordcity.com

Williston Convention and Visitors Bureau
212 Airport Rd.
Williston 58801
(701) 774-9041
visitwilliston.com

The Walrus Restaurant
1136 N. 3rd St.
(701) 250-0020
thewalrusrestaurant.com
Moderate

DICKINSON

Brickhouse Grille
2 W. Villard St.
(701) 483-9900
brickhousegrilleonline.com
Moderate

JD's BBQ
789 State Ave.
(701) 483-2277
Moderate

MEDORA

Cowboy Cafe
215 4th St.
(701) 623-4343
Moderate

Little Missouri Dining Room
440 3rd St.
(701) 623-4404
Moderate

Theodore's Dining Room
301 3rd Ave.
(701) 623-4444
Moderate to expensive

WILLISTON

Basil Restaurant Sushi Bar and Asian Bistro
16 E. Broadway
(701) 572-6688
basilwilliston.com
Moderate

Gramma Sharon's Family Restaurant
1501 16th St. W
(701) 572-1412
grammasharons.com
Inexpensive to moderate

Williston Brewing Company
in The El Rancho Hotel
1623 2nd Ave. W
(701) 609-5439
elranchowilliston.com
Moderate

The Williston Steakhouse
408 1st Ave. E
(701) 572-0544
thewilliston.com
Expensive

Central North Dakota

With woods to explore, lush lakes, prairie potholes, and an international garden of incredible magnitude, central North Dakota lures its share of visitors. They come for the world-class birding and outdoor activities, the chance to immerse themselves into the German-Russian or Nordic character of early pioneers, to walk the childhood paths of celebrities, and to experience Native American culture and rare opportunities such as seeing the albino bison the Dakota consider sacred. No matter which direction you point your vehicle, look for the vast patchwork of wheat and brilliant sunflowers that thrive in North Dakota's glacial soils and listen for the songbirds and waterfowl that gather along rivers, potholes, and lakes.

If you enjoy unique graveyards, check out **St. Mary's Church and Cemetery** in Strasburg. On the National Register of Historic Places, the cemetery is distinguished by ornate iron crosses marking graves—another nod to the area's German-Russian heritage and its craftsmanship.

East of Wishek on ND 13 is the tiny town of **Kulm,** hometown of actress Angie Dickinson and near one of the more haunting sites in the state. **Whitestone Hill Battlefield Site** was the site of North Dakota's most deadly clash of Native

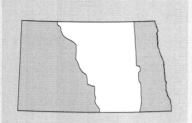

International
Peace Garden

CANADA

NORTH DAKOTA

TURTLE MTS.

(83)

(5)

(5)

(281)

(1)

Bottineau

Dunseith

DEVILS LAKE AND
THE RENDEZVOUS
REGION

TURTLE MOUNTAINS

Minot

(2)

Rugby

(2)

(20)

Devils Lake

(14)

(3)

(52)

(200)

(200)

(52)

Carrington

JAMES VALLEY

HAWK'S NEST

(14)

(3)

Jamestown

(94)

(1)

(3)

GERMANS-FROM-
RUSSIA POCKET

James R.

(13)

Linton

(13)

Kulm

(281)

Wishek

Strasburg

(11)

N

0   50 mi

0   50 km

South-central North Dakota: Germans-from-Russia

Start in the southern corner of central North Dakota, an easy jaunt from Fort Yates to the home communities of North Dakota's German-Russians: Strasburg, Wishek, Linton, and other area towns.

Their European homelands are no longer in Germany. They left Alsace (then a German province, now part of France) around 1804 and resettled in Ukraine to farm and escape the Napoleonic Wars. In 1808–1809 another wave of immigration created Roman Catholic communities along the Kutschurgan River in Russia, with names brought from Germany: Strassburg, Baden, and Selz. Those names arrived in North Dakota with yet another wave of immigration, fueled by overpopulation and Russian desires to turn the Germans into Russians. The name **Strasburg** underwent its second spelling change (Strasbourg, Strassburg, Strasburg), and Selz was bestowed upon two towns, the first of which, near Hague, disappeared. The second, in Pierce County, is still a thriving community. Black Sea Germans, or *Russlanddeutsch,* as they are called, are so far removed from Germany that the customs and language they preserve are ancient history in present-day Germany. Whereas French and Scottish immigrants quickly assimilated into North Dakota society, the Black Sea Germans maintained their cultural identity longer and were generally aloof to community involvement.

Nowadays the residents are eager to share their food and festivities. Oktoberfest, a traditional event in Germany, is replicated in many communities in south-central North Dakota, as well as in the western part of the state. The town of **Wishek,** for instance, has paid homage to fermented cabbage every October since 1925 with its **Sauerkraut Days.** Schoolchildren get out of school early for the free wiener-and-kraut lunch. If kraut's not

Americans and US Cavalry. It's truly off the beaten path, a 23-mile detour that heads 15 miles south of Kulm on ND 56, then east on an unimproved road.

The battle lasted about two hours as General Alfred Sully's troops attacked a tipi camp of Yanktonai, some Dakota, Hunkpapa Lakota, and Blackfeet (Sihasapa Lakota) from September 3 to September 5, 1863. The camp was said to have consisted of 400 lodges, or 2,000 to 5,000 people, of which about 1,000 were warriors. The attack was part of a military mission to punish participants of the Dakota Uprising of 1862 that had raged through Minnesota's Minnesota River valley and across the prairie toward the Dakotas. By sunset an estimated 150 to 300 warriors, women, and children had lost their lives, and 156 were taken prisoner. The army lost considerably less—22 men died, 50 to 60 were wounded. Sully ordered his troops to burn what the villagers had left behind, and the soldiers destroyed 300 tipis and up to 500,000 pounds of dried buffalo meat—the winter supplies that had been gathered by those who had been in the village. There are memorials to both sides of the battle on-site, along with your style, try *knoephla* soup (spelled many ways, but the soup is always buttery with potatoes and dumplings) and *fleischkuekle*, a beef-filled pasty, or pierogi. The festival is replete with food and drink, and you can hear the oompah-pahs of polka throughout the community.

The family histories of the people who live here are strikingly similar to that of "wunner-ful, wunnerful" Lawrence Welk, the famous Champagne Music Maker. Welk's father had grown increasingly unhappy with life in Russia, and in 1892 he and his wife came to America. Their voyage was financed by an uncle who ran a store in Strasburg. Lawrence Welk was born in 1903, and he spoke only German until he was 21 years old. This was not uncommon for children of German-Russian descent, as parents were reluctant to send their children to school, only allowing them to attend when their work was finished on the farm. Welk was the sixth of nine children, and on his 21st birthday he left for Bismarck. He played his accordion at weddings and dances until his great break came in 1955 with a chance to appear on national TV.

Welk's birthplace, officially known as the **Welk Homestead State Historic Site** (845 88th St. SE) is nestled among wheat fields north of Strasburg. Although the home is made of dried mud brick, called batsa, a technique that had been used in Russia, its 3-foot-thick walls have white siding on the exterior and wallpaper inside. Note the exterior stairs, the only way to go between the first floor and the second-floor bedroom used by Welk and his three brothers. The site includes a summer kitchen, barn, buggy house, granary, and blacksmith shop. Welk died in sunny southern California in 1992, the year the homestead restoration was completed to its 1920s condition.

It is open Thurs through Sun from 10 a.m. to 5 p.m. Memorial Day through Labor Day and by appointment. Admission is $5 for adults; $3 for children ages 6 to 15. For more information call (701) 336-7777.

a self-guided tour and a small museum, picnic area, and playground. The North Dakota Historical Society operates the free museum mid-May to mid-Sept, Thurs through Mon. The local Whitestone Historical Society hosts an annual summer event at the site to commemorate the battle. For more information, call (701) 328-3508 or visit history.nd.gov/historicsites/whitestone.

Jamestown and James River Valley

Jamestown, nestled in the valley where the James and Pipestem Rivers meet, is appropriately known as Buffalo City, and you can't miss seeing its *"World's Largest Buffalo"* sculpture that stands 26 feet tall and weighs 60 tons. It was built in 1959 and was gradually surrounded by historic buildings that the community thought should be saved. That collection grew into the *Frontier Village* (404 Louis L'Amour Ln.) and attracts over 100,000 people each year. A post office, trading post, 1881 church, fire department, jail, and barbershop are

Go Birding Along the Central Flyway

North Dakota is a world-class paradise for birds, with more than 70 National Wildlife Refuges—more than any other state. More than 320 species and an estimated 53 million songbirds, shorebirds, birds of prey, wading birds, upland birds, and nesting waterfowl make their home here in the summer, and even more make it a rest stop on their way north or south, using the Missouri River and the Central Flyways.

What also makes this area unique is its convergence of eastern and western species and the thriving prairie potholes that polka-dot the landscape east of the Missouri River. Check out one of the many birding hot spots throughout the valley.

Arrowhead National Wildlife Refuge, Carrington (25 miles northwest of Jamestown on US 281), has a 5.5-mile auto tour with viewing areas for waterfowl, shorebirds, dancing sharp-tailed grouse, grassland, and songbirds. The 16,000-acre refuge is also known for sightings such as downy woodpeckers, greater yellowlegs, and belted kingfishers. Look for migrating snow geese in the fall. A self-guided automobile tour affords breathtaking views of duck broods in summer and migrating snow geese in fall. Call (701) 285-3341 or visit fws.gov/refuge/arrowwood for more information.

Chase Lake National Wildlife Refuge, Woodworth, is one of the country's oldest refuges, established by President Theodore Roosevelt in 1908 to protect American white pelicans, which were threatened at the time. Today, it's home to America's largest nesting colony of white pelicans. Call (701) 752-4218 or visit fws.gov/refuge/Chase_Lake for more information.

Lake Alice National Wildlife Refuge, Cando, is known for thousands of geese and ducks that use its open waters during spring and fall migration as they pass through the Devils Lake region. Call (701) 662-8611 or visit fws.gov/refuge/Lake_Alice for more information.

Long Lake National Wildlife Refuge, Driscoll, is one of the nation's best birding spots, noteworthy for its 2-mile-wide, 16-mile-long lake that draws more than 20,000 shorebirds for a rest stop while migrating or for breeding. Similarly, up to 30,000 Canada geese, 10,000 to 15,000 sandhill cranes, and up to 50,000 ducks visit here, too. You may be able to spot sandhill and rarer whooping cranes in Mar or Apr or reserve a spot in a blind

just some of the structures that re-create small-town life in the 1800s and are open to the public during the summer months. If you have children, be sure to take the stagecoach ride so they appreciate the modern wonders of paved roads and shock absorbers. There are pony rides and western shootouts, too. Hours are 8 a.m. to 8 p.m. daily, Memorial Day weekend to Labor Day, and 10 a.m. to 6 p.m. after Labor Day through Sept. Admission is by donation.

One of the favorite stops at the Frontier Village is the writing shack of famed western novelist and Jamestown native **Louis L'Amour,** the highest-selling western author of all time. Louis Dearborn L'Amour (1908–1988) wrote to watch the sharp-tailed grouse do its mating dance on the prairie or watch grebes doing their mating dance on water. Sept and Oct also are peak bird-watching months. You can watch birds from the public roads or "the butte" a mile east of Highway 83 on the lake's north side. Call (701) 387-4397 or visit fws.gov/refuge/long_lake for more information.

Lostwood National Wildlife Refuge, Kenmare, lies along what's called the Missouri Coteau with rolling and steep hills covered in rich prairie that includes more than 700 plant species and harbors grassland birds such as the threatened piping plover, grasshopper sparrow, Sprague's Pipit, and Baird's sparrow. It's considered globally important by the American Bird Conservancy. Close observers might also be able to spot close to 200 ancient tipi rings across the landscape. For more information, call (701) 848-2722 or visit fws.gov/refuge/lostwood/.

Even if you aren't heading to a wildlife refuge, keep the binoculars handy. Take the roads less traveled and follow the scenic bluffs of the Missouri River. You're sure to spot a wealth of winged creatures.

Birds unique to the pristine prairies include the western grebe (also known for its comical upright two-grebe dance across the water—known as water weaving), ferruginous hawk, western meadowlark, dickcissel, Hungarian partridge, sharp-tailed grouse, upland sandpiper, marbled godwit, clay-colored sparrow, and the chestnut-collared longspur.

Several endangered or threatened birds have been documented in North Dakota by the US Fish and Wildlife Service, including the interior least tern, bald eagle, whooping crane, peregrine falcon, and piping plover. For details on the refuges, including maps and trails, go to fws.gov/mountain-prairie.

You can get complete details on the best birding hot spots in the region of Steele, Carrington, and Jamestown by calling (888) 921-2473 or checking out birdingdrives.com. The site includes 6 birding routes pulled together by bird experts.

If you like to have company and enjoy the expert eye of a guide, you can find several birding festivals and workshops in late May and early June.

For information on the **International Adventure Trail,** a network of 15 notable birding sites in North Dakota and southern Manitoba, go to internationaladventuretrail.org.

117 books and is best known for his frontier books, such as *Mustang Man, The Sackett Brand, Ride the Dark Trail,* and *The Daybreakers.* More than 30 of his books became movies, including *Hondo,* with John Wayne; *Shalako,* starring Sean Connery; and *The Burning Hills,* which featured Tab Hunter and Natalie Wood.

If you want to learn more about the man who lassoed the American West spirit with words, walk the ***Louis L'Amour Trail*** in Jamestown where he is warmly remembered. The first stop is the Dakota Territory Courthouse, where L'Amour's father worked as the county and the state veterinarian. He

BEST ATTRACTIONS IN CENTRAL NORTH DAKOTA

Devils Lake

International Peace Garden on the US border

National Buffalo Museum

North Dakota Birding Trail

Turtle Mountains

also doubled as a deputy sheriff for several years. The courthouse is located at 5th Street and 3rd Avenue Southeast in Jamestown. The Stutsman County Memorial Museum (located in the Lutz Mansion) and the Jamestown City Hall are next along the trail, then the *L'Amour Family Home Site.* This is where L'Amour's boyhood home originally stood at 113 3rd Ave. SE. The home was later moved to another part of Jamestown and structurally changed. The First United Methodist Church, the Alfred Dickey Library (one of the young boy's favorite places), Franklin Grade School, and Walz Pharmacy, once owned by L'Amour's friend Reese Hawkins and stocked with all of the writer's books, also are highlighted along the trail.

didyouknow?

Louis L'Amour wasn't Jamestown's only world-famous firstborn. Norma Deloris Egstrom, better known as the singer *Peggy Lee,* was also born in Jamestown, on May 26, 1920.

L'Amour's writing reflects his Dakota roots. "The sort of men and women it took to open the West were the kind of whom stories were told. Strongly individual, willing to risk all they possessed as well as their lives, they were also prepared to fight for what they believed was theirs," he wrote in *The Sackett Companion.*

L'Amour is the only writer to receive the Presidential Medal of Freedom and the Congressional Gold Medal. Besides writing, he worked as an elephant handler, a professional boxer, a seaman, and a journalist.

An attractive brochure charting the Louis L'Amour Trail is available at the *Jamestown Visitor Center* (404 Louis L'Amour Ln.; 800-222-4766 or 701-251-9145). They also have information on the area's 30 miles of hiking and biking.

While at Frontier Village, you should be able to see the herd of about 30 bison that absolutely deserves a closer look. They belong to the *National Buffalo Museum* (500 17th St. E; 701-252-8648; buffalomuseum.com), just next door to the Frontier Village. For 20 years, the museum had a rare white buffalo,

Legend of the White Buffalo

The white buffalo is sacred to the Lakota people. Legend says the White Buffalo Calf Woman brought them their most sacred pipe. This beautiful woman in a white buckskin dress spent four days and four nights showing the Lakota how to smoke the pipe, on which a bison calf was carved on one side. As the White Buffalo Calf Woman left, she walked in the direction of the setting sun, stopped, and rolled over four times. The first time, she got up and became a black buffalo; the second time, a brown buffalo; the third time, a red buffalo; and the fourth time she rolled over, she became a white buffalo. This buffalo walked on farther, stopped, and after bowing to each of the four directions of the universe, disappeared over the hill.

which is revered by Native Americans, some of whom made pilgrimages here to see her and left hundreds of prayer ribbons on the fence of her enclosure. White Cloud gave birth to several calves including a white one named Dakota Miracle. White Cloud died in 2016 but returned to the museum the next year as a full taxidermy mount. Dakota Miracle died in a fall in 2019. Beside the bison grazing in the pasture, the museum exhibits a 10,000-year-old bison skull and a complete skeleton of an ancestor to the modern bison. It also has artifacts relating to the bison throughout the years and a Hall of Fame to honor people who have helped preserve and restore this icon of the US. The museum is open 8 a.m. to 8 p.m. daily, Memorial Day through Labor Day, and 10 a.m. to 5 p.m. Mon to Sat during the rest of the year. Admission is $8 for adults; $6 for seniors; $6 for ages 5 to 14; and under 5 for free. There is no admission to visit the Prairie Winds Gift Shop.

At the north end of town on US 281, the ***Fort Seward Historic Site and Interpretive Center*** which overlooks Pipestem Lake, sheds light on the early military history of the region when three army companies were stationed

BEST ANNUAL EVENTS IN CENTRAL NORTH DAKOTA

JULY

North Dakota State Fair
Minot
(701) 857-7620
center.ndstatefair.com/

SEPTEMBER

Norsk Høstfest
Minot
(701) 852-2368
hostfest.com/

here. The free center is open daily 10 a.m. to 6 p.m. Memorial Day through Labor Day, although the grounds and picnic area are open year-round. Homesteading by covered wagon is commemorated each year in the ***Fort Seward Wagon Train***. Participants don mandatory pioneer costumes during a one-week wagon train reenactment each June. The wagon train was first organized in 1969 as a one-time experience, but promoters found it so worthwhile they made it a yearly event. The wagon train starts rolling at the crack of dawn, and it averages 3 to 4 miles per hour. At the end of the day, singing and storytelling around the campfire foster camaraderie, pioneer style—a memorable family affair. For more information, call (701) 251-1875 or visit covered-wagon-train .com. In the off-season, call (701) 251-9145.

The ***Stutsman County Memorial Museum*** (321 3rd Ave. SE; 701-252-6741) is housed in the George Lutz mansion, a monument to the early-day history of the area. Four floors in the stately brick museum, which was built in 1907, are devoted to the culture and life of the early pioneers. The first floor, with a complete dining room, kitchen, and butler's pantry, highlights items that a pioneer homemaker might have used. Military life and the railroad's strength in the state are featured on the second floor, and pioneer medicine, wildlife, and church relics round out this eclectic collection on the third floor. A room in the basement has been turned into a claim shanty. Many visitors love the home's art nouveau–style stained glass and Tiffany lamps the best. If you want to learn more about history, be there at 2 p.m. Sun, June through Aug for Front Porch Chats. The free museum is open Mon through Fri from 10 a.m. to 5 p.m., and Sat and Sun from 1 to 5 p.m., Memorial Day through Sept 30.

Just north on US 281, the 840-acre ***Pipestem Dam and Lake*** offers year-round recreational opportunities, and the lovely lake fascinates birders, boaters, anglers, and others. Conservation of wildlife and the natural environment is a major objective of the US Army Corps of Engineers, and 4,200 acres of creek valley and rolling upland at Pipestem are home to a wide variety of wildlife and waterfowl. The natural setting has been enhanced by selective planting of more than 250,000 trees around the lake.

For swimming, camping, fishing, and boating, head to the ***Lakeside Marina and Recreational Area*** (3225 E. Lakeside Rd.; 701-252-1183) by the Jamestown Dam. Tent and trailer camping sites are available. There is a fee for some activities. Open early May through mid-Oct.

North on US 281 and 52 is ***Carrington,*** which, like most of the communities in North Dakota, can trace its development to the arrival of the railroad. By 1882, the Northern Pacific line ran through the yet unnamed prairie settlement. Agriculture formed the base for Carrington's early and present-day economies. It's home to the state-of-the-art ***Dakota Growers Pasta Co.,*** which makes

Nicknames for North Dakota

Peace Garden State: the official license-plate nickname inspired by the International Peace Garden since 1957.

Flickertail State: referring to the Richardson ground squirrel that flicks or jerks its tail while running or just before entering its burrow.

Roughrider State: referring to the first US Volunteer Cavalry that Theodore Roosevelt organized to fight in the Spanish American War. In fact, the Roughriders included several North Dakota cowboys.

more than 150 kinds of pasta from durum wheat harvested by more than 1,100 third- and fourth-generation growers in the region. It has become the largest pasta manufacturer in North America.

It's also home to the charming **Dakota Sun Gardens and Winery,** a destination for relaxing among flowers, buying summer fruits, and sipping wines made by owners Bruce and Merleen Gussiaas since 2010. They sell or make wine from familiar fruits, such as rhubarb, raspberries, plums, and cherries, but you'll also find elderberry, aronia berry, chokecherry, and haskap. You can also grab a glass of lemonade and sit on the patio by the 1950s octagonal grain bins. Call (701) 674-3623 or visit dakotasungardenswinery.com for information on visiting.

Pipestem Creek Bed and Birding offers a fresh combination of a birding getaway and a taste of a working small grains farm. Owner Ann Reimers Hoffert grew up on the 5,000-acre farm and started a specialty grain business with edible decor for birds when she moved back. Rustic rooms can be found in two historic granaries or guests can rent one of two houses that sleep 6 to 11 people. Call (701) 652-2623 or go to pipestemcreek.com.

History and art buffs, be sure to check out the **Putnam House** (533 Main St.), an American Foursquare home built in 1907 by Thomas Nichols Putnam, the area's pioneer lumberman, and his wife, Clara Belle Putnam. The 4,300-square-foot home is testament to the precise craftsmanship and architecture of the turn of the 20th century. The grand staircase is a breathtaking focal point, and the dining room features a built-in oak buffet with leaded glass doors. It's more than majestic, though. It's also a rural cultural and community center, providing an inspiring setting for summer concerts on the wraparound porch, art exhibits, and hands-on classes in stained glass, jewelry, ethnic cooking, and more. For details and upcoming events, call (701) 652-1213 or go to putnamhouse.org.

All Creatures Great and Small

As you are traveling along the highways and byways of North Dakota, be on the lookout for small brown and white roadside signs featuring binoculars, which indicate one of the state's 80-plus roadside viewing areas.

Watch the birds and beasts from a distance with good-quality binoculars, a spotting scope, or a telephoto lens. If the animals you are watching are watching you—with their heads up and ears facing your direction—or are nervous, you are probably too close or moving too quickly. Remember, sometimes the best observation and photo blind is in your car.

Obviously, be kind to these bashful critters. Patience will reward you. Keep quiet and wait for animals to return to or enter an area. The early and late hours of daylight are generally the best times to watch and photograph most wildlife.

Detour straight east of Carrington to Cooperstown for a sobering look at the Cold War era with the ***Ronald Reagan Minuteman Missile State Historic Site*** (also known as Oscar Zero). The facility is 4 miles north of Cooperstown at 555 113 ½ Ave. NE along ND 45. Visitors can descend 50 feet into a concrete capsule to the launch control center for 10 Minuteman Missiles, each warhead packing more destructive power than what was dropped on Hiroshima and Nagasaki at the end of World War II. The site was one of 15 command centers and 150 missile sites spread out over 6,500 square miles and manned by the Grand Forks Air Force Base. It was set up to defend the country at the peak of the Cold War that began in the mid-1960s. The sites were decommissioned starting in 1991 after the Strategic Arms Reduction Treaty. It's open 10 a.m. to 6 p.m. daily Memorial Day through Labor Day, and shorter hours in Apr, May, Sept, and Oct. Nov through Mar it's open by appointment only. Admission is $10 for adults; $3 for children. Call (701) 797-3691 or go to history.nd.gov/historicsites/minutemanmissile for more information.

Devils Lake and the Rendezvous Region

Head an hour north of Carrington on US 281 to reach the emerald waters of ***Devils Lake*** at the crossroads of ND 19 and ND 20. Don't let the name fool you. This spring-fed lake was called *mni wak'án* by the Dakota, which meant "water" and "pure source." The name could also mean "spirit" or "sacred." Early settlers conflated "spirit" with the high salinity of the water which was bad for drinking and wound up naming the body of water Devils Lake and the name has stuck. The state's largest natural lake covers more than 70,000 prairie acres and nurtures forests of hardwood oak, ash, and elm that provide year-round recreation. Walleye and white bass are the top draws, and yellow perch are found in winter. Migrating geese, ducks, and sandhill cranes take over the skies each spring and fall. Devils Lake State Parks comprises three parks and recreation areas. Call (800) 766-4015 or visit parkrec.nd.gov/grahams-island-state-park for more information.

On the south shore of Devils Lake, ***Sullys Hill National Game Preserve*** shelters swans, bison, elk, deer, prairie dogs, and other wildlife with its native habitat. Worth noting: It started out as a national park in 1904 but was redesignated a big game preserve in 1921. Don't miss the quarter mile hike up a hill to beautiful lake overlook (closed in the winter along with the Devils Lake Vista Loop) and bring binoculars for the 4-mile auto tour open daily. In the winter, you can ski the trails. Stop in the visitor center, open noon to 4 p.m. daily (except Tues) for maps, exhibits, and a look at native species swimming in the 180-gallon aquarium. The preserve is 12 miles southwest of the town of Devils Lake on ND 57. Admission is free. Call (701) 766-4272 or visit fws.gov/refuge/sullys_hill_national_game_preserve for information.

Thirteen miles southwest of Devils Lake on ND 57, one of the best-preserved military outposts west of the Mississippi is found at the ***Fort Totten State Historic Site.*** The fort was built in 1867 to protect the overland route to Montana and was the last outpost before 300 miles of wilderness. It later became a Native American boarding school with up to 400 students, a health care facility for tuberculosis, and then a reservation school. The grounds are open year-round, 8 a.m. to 4:30 p.m. Mon through Fri. The museum and the 17 original buildings can be enjoyed 9 a.m. to 5 p.m. daily Memorial Day to Labor Day, or by appointment on weekdays in the off-season. Admission is $6 per adult and $3 for children 6 to 15; children 5 and under are free. In the summer months, check out performances, which are usually musicals, at the Fort Totten Little Theatre (701-662-8888). For more information on the state historic site, call (701) 766-4441 or visit history.nd .gov/historicsites/totten.

To get a firsthand frontier experience, stay at the ***Totten Trail Historic Inn*** (701-766-4874; tottentrailinn.com) which was built in 1868. The bed-and-breakfast inn is right on the historic site and is furnished in period style (1870–1910). Its ten rooms are available year-round, with prices ranging from $100 to $135. Some rooms have a private bath each, and others share a bath with one other room. A stay includes breakfast and a Victorian-style afternoon tea in a lovely dining room. Proceeds fund continuing renovations at the fort.

Minot

The town of *Minot,* like other growing North Dakota cities, has welcomed a wave of almost 10,000 newcomers in a handful of years thanks to the oil boom. But even with over 47,370 residents, the population seems small when fall arrives and the town's size almost doubles over the five days of its much-loved annual *Norsk Høstfest* (701-852-2368; hostfest.com). An estimated 55,000 visitors from around the region and the country gather to celebrate North America's largest Scandinavian festival, where you can catch a heady whiff of cardamom-spiced sweet breads, tap your feet to fiddles, and enjoy the kaleidoscope whirl of dancers in ethnic costumes. Held each fall since 1978, the Hostfest brings in big-name entertainers on 7 stages including the 4,500-seat Great Hall of the Vikings. About 150 artisans and craftsmen with everything from delicate silver jewelry to sturdy tine boxes are here too. Bite into favorite desserts such as *lefse, rommegrot,* rosettes, and *krumkake* or bravely sample the infamous lutefisk. For multicourse fine dining, reserve a seat at En to Tre, where chefs from the Scandinavian countries prepare a buffet with traditional dishes such as smoked salmon, shrimp, herring, lingonberry preserves, roasted meats, cold plates, flatbreads, and cheeses to be savored by Norwegians and non-Norwegians alike.

The Scandinavian Heritage Center (1020 S. Broadway; 701-852-9161; scandinavianheritage.org) is the world's only outdoor living museum dedicated to preserving the ethnic heritage of the five Scandinavian countries. Buildings on the premises include a visitor center; a *stabbur* (storage house) from Telemark, Norway; a Finnish sauna; Danish windmill; Dala horse; Stave church museum; an eternal flame brought to North Dakota from Norway; and a 230-year-old house from Sigdal, Norway. Hours vary by season.

didyouknow?

Norwegians accounted for a large number of the immigrants who came to North Dakota. Seventy-five percent of the soil in their homeland was not suitable for agriculture, so it was natural these Norwegians sought the fertile farmland of North Dakota. Only Ireland lost a greater percentage of its people to America.

The must-go summer event is the *North Dakota State Fair* in Minot. How big is it? Think of it by the numbers: nearly 300,000 visitors; 46,000 competitive exhibits; 600 vendors; at least two dozen buildings; 46,000 competitive exhibits, seven free stages; nine days of fun; and three nights each of rodeo contests and car and truck competitions. The grandstand that opened in 2010 holds 18,000 spectators for a rockin' time when big names arrive for concerts. Call (701) 857-7620 or visit the website at ndstatefair.com for details on upcoming events. Also on the fairgrounds is the Ward County Historical Society Pioneer Village and Museum.

Among the eateries generating the best buzz for great food in the region is **10 North Main** (10 Main St. N; 701-837-1010; 10northmain.com). This urbane, upscale restaurant has scrumptious offerings—including smoked duck, vegetables in curry cream sauce over rice, squash ravioli, margarita pasta, and crème brulée.

The 19-acre **Roosevelt Park Zoo** (1219 Burdick Expy. E; 701-857-4169; rpzoo.com), the oldest zoo in North Dakota, is the home of a black-footed penguin collection. No doubt these flightless seabirds enjoy the chilly temperatures during North Dakota winters. Among the zoo's 200-or-so animals are spider monkeys, kangaroo, amur tiger, bears, reindeer, snow leopard, giraffe, llama, and even a rare okapi. The feathered friends count a laughing kookaburra, trumpeter hornbill, a variety of finches, and an eastern screech owl and a bald eagle among their numbers. In 2019, the zoo opened a new habitat for its lions, giving them 16 times the room of their former enclosure. Concessions, a children's zoo, a gift shop, and an educational center also are part of the zoo. Open daily (weather permitting) 10 a.m. to 8 p.m. May through Aug; 10 a.m. to 5 p.m. in Sept; 10 a.m. to 3 p.m., Mon to Sat in the winter. Admission from May through Sept is $9 for adults; $8 for college students, military, and seniors; and $5.50 for ages 3 to 12. Admission is less from Oct through Apr.

The Roosevelt Park and Zoo is the fifth point along the 2.5-mile **Riverwalk,** a walking and biking trail that starts at the **Railroad Museum** (19 1st St. NE; 701-852-7091). The museum presents the history and progression of the railroad through photographs, model railroad layouts, and other memorabilia from 1886 to the present. It's free and open 10 a.m. to 2 p.m. Sat. A three-fifths-scale train, **Magic City Express,** is located at the north end of Roosevelt Park. Pulled by a miniature steam locomotive, it travels down a mile-long track in about 12 minutes.

The second point of interest is the **Lillian and Coleman Taube Museum of Art** (2 N. Main St.; 701-838-4445; taubemuseum.org). The Minot Arts Association renovated the former Union National Bank building as a center for the visual arts, educational programs, and cultural and social events. Hours are 10:30 a.m. to 5:30 p.m. Tues through Fri; 11 a.m. to 4 p.m. on Sat.

As you traverse the Riverwalk, you will also discover **Val's Cyclery** (222 E. Central Ave.) where Rocky and Rory Schell continue the cycling and fitness tradition started by their father, Valentine, in 1960. For more information, call (701) 839-4817 or visit valscyclery.com.

Eastwood Park is the next stop. This is a splendid place to check out the architectural styles of homes from Minot's early days: Princess Anne, English Tudor, and arts and crafts. In 1986 the neighborhood was designated a National Historic District.

Other sites along the Riverwalk are Lowe's Garden Center (701-839-2000) housed in a replica of an early North Dakota train depot; North Dakota State Fair and All Seasons Arena; and MotorMagic, the largest motor sports festival in the Upper Midwest which takes place every Labor Day weekend at the fairgrounds.

For more information about Riverwalk or what's along it, call the Minot Convention and Visitors Bureau at (701) 857-8206 or go to visitminot.org.

The *Ward County Historical Society Pioneer Village and Museum* (701-839-0785; wardcountyhistoricalsociety.com) was on the fairgrounds for a long time but moved to a new location north of the town of *Burlington* (pop. 1,206) in the summer of 2019. Now located at 8181 Hwy. 2/52, the Pioneer Village and Museum is a collection of 12 preserved and restored historic buildings, housing vintage automobiles and thousands of artifacts that illuminate the region's past. Put the emphasis on "restored." The museum is open Memorial Day to Labor Day.

didyouknow?

12,217 jobs are attributed to aviation activity in North Dakota with a payroll of $505 million.

The state has 8 commercial airports and 89 public airfields.

$1.56 billion of economic activity is created each year by North Dakota aviation.

In 1928, North Dakotan Carl Ben Eielson flew across the Arctic Ocean with Australian Hubert Wilkens, becoming the first men to do so.

Minot Air Force Base has about 7,600 residents 13 miles north of the city and was built in the 1950s. With aviation a large part of North Dakota's economy—especially here—it makes sense to check out the *Dakota Territory Air Museum*, which is adjacent to the northwest corner of the *Minot International Airport* (100 34th Ave. NE), which has the state's newest and largest commercial terminal. The museum features civilian and military aircraft from 1928 to the present. If you love things that fly, this is the place to be. You'll find civilian aircraft, from a replica of the Wright Flyer, the world's first heavier-than-air aircraft, to a 1928 Waco to a 1946 Piper J-3 Cub, as well as a Lockheed T-33 jet trainer, a Douglas C-47 World War II transport, and a P-51 Mustang, considered the premier piston-engine fighter of WWII. Also prominently displayed—and still operational—is the Minot Airport beacon, which guided pilots in the area from 1949 to 1993. Admission is $10 for adults;

$5 for ages 6 to 17; free for those younger than 5. The museum is open from 10 a.m. to 5 p.m. Mon through Sat, and from 1 to 5 p.m. Sun, mid-May through mid-Oct. Call (701) 852-8500 or visit dakotaterritoryairmuseum.com for more information.

Turtle Mountains and Border Region

One of the prettiest places to take a fall drive is along the 28-mile **Des Lacs River Valley,** which kisses the Canadian border and stretches southeast along US 52 to Kenmare, about 50 miles northwest of Minot.

Hop onto the 12-mile scenic drive along Des Lac Lake from near the Baden overpass to a picnic area 5 miles northwest of Kenmare. There are several scenic pullouts and 13 interpretive panels about the area, famous for vast fields of wheat and cheery sunflowers (North Dakota trails only South Dakota in the production of sunflowers). In the town of **Kenmare**, look for the 1902 **Old Danish Mill,** a restored flour mill with millstones that weigh 1,800 pounds. The mill's interior was damaged by arson in early 2019 but it has been lovingly brought back to its original self. This mill is one of only three Danish windmills in the US.

For a truly stunning sight, head to the **Des Lacs National Wildlife Refuge** one mile west of Kenmare. While it's great for picnics, hikes, and birding year-round, it's best known as a staging area for up to 300,000 snow geese as they gather and prepare for migration. Kenmare hosts **Goosefest** in October to celebrate the gathering. The refuge also is a sanctuary for moose, elk, bison, and pronghorn. A small visitor center and an observation platform equipped with binoculars are at the refuge. Call (701) 835-4046 or visit fws.gov/refuge/des_lacs for more information.

About 90 minutes east of Kenmare and only about 20 miles south of the Canadian border, the bustling community of **Bottineau** serves as the gateway to the Turtle Mountain area. Visitors come for every season at **Lake Metigoshe State Park,** a wooded natural area with numerous lakes, making the area one of North Dakota's most popular year-round vacation spots. That should be no surprise, snugged up to the Canadian border and having 12 miles of multi-use trails, nearly 4 miles of snowmobile trails, and 2 miles of trails for canoes. It also has two lodges, three cabins, a yurt, and two group dorms. If you're going in the summer, check for performances by the water-ski show team, the Club de Skinautique, which practices and performs on Lake Metigoshe. For more information about this wonderful 1,551-acre park, call (701) 263-4651 or visit parkrec.nd.gov/lake-metigoshe-state-park.

It doesn't hurt that it's also a short drive to the **International Peace Garden**, which drew 50,000 people when it was dedicated on July 14, 1932.

Juneberry Ice Cream

For one of North Dakota's best summer treats, head to the Dairy Dipper, an old-fashioned ice cream parlor at **Pride Dairy** (517 Thompson St.; 701-228-2216; pride-dairy.com) in Bottineau. They make juneberry ice cream—which is rare to find outside of North Dakota—along with flavors like cherry chocolate chip and a coffee ice cream made with locally roasted Mojo beans. It's no wonder that USA Today once named it as one of the top 50 ice cream parlors in the US. If you travel with a cooler, you can load up with butter and cheeses, along with juneberry and chokecherry syrups, and more.

This lavish garden on the border commemorates peace between Canada and the US. Dr. Henry J. Moore, a horticulturist from Islington, Ontario, Canada, conceived the idea for the garden when he was on his way home from the 1928 annual meeting of the National Association of Gardeners, a US organization. He thought it was a fitting tribute to the peaceful existence between the two countries.

The proposal was approved at the association's 1929 meeting, and the search began for an appropriate site. Moore liked what he saw when visiting the Turtle Mountains. After a plane ride over the area, he remarked: "What a sight greeted the eye. Those undulating hills rising out of the limitless prairies are filled with lakes and streams. On the south of the unrecognizable boundary, wheat fields everywhere; and on the north, the Manitoba Forest Preserve. What a place for a garden!"

The tablet on a cairn of native stone reads: TO GOD IN HIS GLORY . . . WE TWO NATIONS DEDICATE THIS GARDEN AND PLEDGE OURSELVES THAT AS LONG AS MAN SHALL LIVE WE WILL NOT TAKE ARMS AGAINST ONE ANOTHER. The two countries chose a place situated on ND 3, the longest north–south road in the world, and about centrally located on the continent of North America. The garden's main axis straddles the US-Canada border which lies on the 49th parallel that runs east and west here. The famous Floral Clock that greets visitors just inside the main entrance is 18 feet in diameter and sprouts between 2,000 and 5,000 flowers, depending on the clock's design which changes annually. In the last few years, the site has attracted an average of about 150,000 visitors annually.

The border walk through the Formal Gardens is a one-of-a-kind chance to see an enormous carpet of flowers in bloom across two nations. The 1.5-mile walk takes you past fountains, pools, cascades, the Perennial Garden, Arbor Garden, arboretum, bell tower, Sunken Garden, Conservatory, and Visitor Center. The Four Peace Towers that stood over the border for 35 years were removed in 2017 because weather had taken its toll on them. There are no plans to replace the towers.

If you visit between July 15 and Aug 15, you'll be dazzled by hundreds of orange and yellow Asiatic lilies. Most gardens hit their peak color in August. Self-guided driving tours will allow you to see Lake Udall on the US side and Lake Stormon on the Canadian side.

One of the most touching displays at the garden is the 9/11 Memorial Site, which pays tribute to the more than 2,800 lives lost in the September 11, 2001, terrorist attacks. On June 3, 2002, the International Peace Garden received ten 10-foot girders from the World Trade Center wreckage. The girders lie at rest at the 9/11 Memorial Site as an everlasting reminder of the human tragedy that occurred one quiet September morning in New York City, Pennsylvania, and Washington, DC.

The park isn't only for the green thumbs in the family; it's also the perfect spot for the culturally inclined. The *International Music Camp* is held annually each summer at the park, featuring Saturday concerts with guest conductors and an old-time fiddlers' contest. The camp has seven sessions in June and July.

asprawling tributetopeace

The International Peace Garden has:

2,339 acres of gardens

150,000 annuals

5,000 flowering shrubs

300 shade and flowering trees

6,000 cacti in a conservatory

The International Peace Garden is one of the prettiest spots in the nation for picnicking, camping, or just sitting back and absorbing the scents and beauty of nature. The grounds are open daily, with camping available May through mid-Oct. For detailed information, call (888) 432-6733 or visit the website at peacegarden.com.

To get to the garden from Bottineau, travel 13 miles east on ND 5 until you reach Dunseith; then take US 281 north for 13 miles.

If you drive US 281 south back to Dunseith, check out the quirky Wee'l Turtle statue, made from more than 2,000 tire rims. Then take US 281 east approximately 18 miles, which will take you right through Belcourt, near the lovely town of *Rolla* and the heart of the magnificent Turtle Mountains.

Peace among nations is nothing new in this territory. Ancient tribes became nations of Mandan, Hidatsa, Arikara, as well as Yanktonai, Sisseton, Wahpeton, Pembina Chippewa, Cree, and Metis. Each had its own culture, yet many worked together during years of peace and years of turmoil and change.

Crossing the Border

If you plan to travel between Canada and North Dakota at any of the 18 border crossings, heightened security measures mean you'll need a passport or a US passport card. The card, a slimmed down version of a passport, is good for travel in Canada, Mexico, and the Caribbean. Apply for one and find out more about customs procedures at travel .state.gov.

The best way to avoid delays and hassles when crossing the international border is to be prepared.

In either direction, customs officials will ask you where you live, your citizenship, the purpose of your trip, how long you intend to stay, and if you have any goods to declare. There may be questions about alcohol, tobacco, and firearms. If you made a duty-free purchase, state how much you bought. When returning home, you may be asked what you have purchased, so it's a good idea to save your sales slips and pack your items so they can be easily inspected at the border. Oral declarations are the general rule.

24-hour Ports of Entry:

- **Pembina, North Dakota,** and **Emerson, Manitoba**
  I-29
  (701) 825-5800

- **Dunseith, North Dakota** (International Peace Garden), and **Boissevain, Manitoba**
  US 281
  (701) 263-4460

Their traditions, philosophies, and spirituality have made an unparalleled contribution to the sumptuous cultural landscape of North Dakota.

The ***Turtle Mountain Band of Pembina Chippewa*** live in the wooded, rolling hills of north-central North Dakota. Their ancestors came from the Great Lakes region in the late 1700s, essentially pushed west by the fur-trade business. As trappers, voyagers, entrepreneurs, and caretakers of the land, the Pembina Chippewa formed enduring relations with other indigenous and European peoples, most significantly the Cree and the French. The Chippewa and Metis (who are descendants of indigenous Native American and those who came from Europe) people built and developed North Dakota's oldest still-existing community: ***Pembina,*** located east of the Turtle Mountains and tucked into the far northeast corner of the state. The Red River Valley and northern North Dakota were the choice hunting territories of the Pembina Chippewa after the 1800s. As part of the continuing westward migration and following a stir of treaty making, Chief Little Shell III brought his band across the Dakota prairie

- **Portal, North Dakota, and North Portal, Saskatchewan**
  US 52
  (701) 926-7500

- All other ports of entry are open daily with varied hours.

Ports of Entry with Shorter Hours:

All other ports of entry on the North Dakota-Canada border are open daily with varied hours.

- 8 a.m. to 4 p.m.
  Hansboro

- 8 a.m. to 9 p.m.
  Saint John and Westhope

- 8 a.m. to 10 p.m.
  Neche and Walhalla

- 9 a.m. to 5 p.m.
  Ambrose, Antler, and Hannah

- 9 a.m. to 7 p.m.
  Carbury

- 9 a.m. to 10 p.m.
  Fortuna, Maida, Noonan, Northgate, and Sherwood

- 11 a.m. to 7 p.m.
  Sarles

to the Turtle Mountains, an area much like the woodlands of Minnesota. On December 21, 1882, the *Turtle Mountain Indian Reservation* was established. It is now located on 84,500 acres in Rolette County, where the community of Belcourt is situated. If you wonder, Pembina is an Ojibway word for a bush with bright red berries and is a type of viburnum which grows in the area.

You can explore some of this history at the *Pembina State Museum* with more than 100 million years of regional history. There's also a 7-story viewing tower for an eagle's eye view of the landscape. Call (701) 825-6840 or go to history.nd.gov/historicsites/pembina for more information.

The reservation is surrounded by the beautiful *Turtle Mountains,* which offer endless recreational opportunities that include cultural centers, gaming facilities, powwows, fishing, swimming, skiing, golfing, and sundry community-sponsored events. Named the Turtle Mountains 200 years ago by explorers, these hills, flecked with lovely lakes, have long been home to native tribes. One of the safest bets for accommodations and entertainment is the

enchantedforests

The oak and aspen forests of the Turtle Mountain State Forest provide refuge to a variety of birds, including rugged grouse, magpies, and vireos. Also commonly seen are deer, moose, and small mammals such as squirrels, woodchucks, raccoons, and snowshoe hares.

Sky Dancer Hotel & Casino (866-244-9467; skydancercasino.com), located 5 miles west of Belcourt on US 281. The hotel, which is operated by the Turtle Mountain Band of Chippewa, features 194 guest rooms, the Miikana Buffet and Grill, and a 37,000-square-foot casino with poker and blackjack tables, bingo, and 700 slot machines.

Six miles east of Belcourt on US 281 is Rolla, which hosts the annual *International Ragtop Festival* on Main Ave each July. The three-day salute to America's automotive gem—the convertible—rolls out a parade, rock 'n' roll concerts, and other activities. For more information call (701) 477-3610.

Twenty-three miles south of Rolla on Highway 30 is the *Dale and Martha Hawk Foundation Museum*, with North Dakota's largest collection of antique farm machinery and the only known working Hackney Auto Plow, which looks as beautiful as the day it rolled out of the manufacturer's doors in 1912. The collection is housed in several historic buildings, including a church, a store, and a schoolhouse. Open 9 a.m. to 5 p.m. Mon to Sat, and 1 to 5 p.m. Sun, May through Sept. Camping also is available. Call (701) 583-2381 or visit hawk museum.org for more information.

Where to Stay in Central North Dakota

BOTTINEAU

Norway House
815 11th St. E
(701) 228-3737
Inexpensive

Quilt Inn and Suites
10722 Lake Loop Rd.
(701) 263-6500
quiltinn-lakemetigoshe.com
Moderate

DEVILS LAKE

Fireside Inn and Suites
215 Hwy. 2 E
(701) 662-6760
Inexpensive

JAMESTOWN

Lakeview Meadow
8280 31st St. SE
(701) 252-5100
lakeviewmeadow.com
Expensive

MINOT

Clarion Hotel Convention Center
2200 Burdick Expy E.
(701) 852-2504
Moderate

Dakotah Rose Bed & Breakfast
510 4th Ave. NW
(701) 838-3548
dakotahrose.com
Moderate

Hawthorn Suites by Wyndham
800 37th Ave. SW
(701) 858-7300
Moderate

Hyatt House Minot
2301 Landmark Dr. NW
(888) 882-1234
hyatt.com
Moderate

Noble Inn
1009 20th Ave. SE
(701) 837-1500
nobleinnhotels.com
Moderate

Where to Eat in Central North Dakota

DEVILS LAKE

Cedar Inn Family Restaurant
445 US 2 W
(701) 662-8893
cedarinndl.com
Inexpensive

White House Café
425 College Dr. S, #9
(701) 662-4852
whitehousecafedlnd.com
Inexpensive

MINOT

Badlands Grill Restaurant and Bar
1400 31st Ave. SW
(701) 852-7335
blgrill.com
Moderate

Broadway Bean and Bagel
1701 S Broadway
(701) 839-2732
broadwaybean.com
Inexpensive

Souris River Brewing
32 3rd St. NE
(701) 837-1884
sourisriverbrewing.com
Moderate

ST. MICHAEL

Dakotah Buffet
(Spirit Lake Casino)
7889 Hwy. 57
(701) 766-4747
spiritlakecasino.com
Moderate

SELECTED CHAMBERS OF COMMERCE

Bottineau Chamber of Commerce
519 Main St.
Bottineau 58318
(701) 228-3849
bottineau.com

Devils Lake Convention and Visitors Bureau
208 Hwy. 2 W
Devils Lake 58301
(701) 662-4957
devilslakend.com

Jamestown Tourism Center
404 Louis L'Amour Ln.
Jamestown 58401
(701) 251-9145
discoverjamestownnd.com

Minot Convention and Visitors Bureau
1020 S. Broadway
Minot 58701
(800) 264-2626
visitminot.org

Eastern North Dakota

As you travel toward the North Dakota–Minnesota border, the alluvial **Red River Valley** defines the history and economy of the far eastern third of North Dakota and has been dubbed the "Breadbasket of the World." It is one of the greatest agricultural regions in the world and is often compared with the Valley of the Nile.

The Red River Valley is the remnant of glacial **Lake Agassiz,** and its waters flow into the Hudson Bay and eventually into the Arctic Ocean. The valley varies from 10 to 40 miles in width from north to south along the border of North Dakota and Minnesota and is relatively flat, with an average elevation of 900 feet. Rich chernozem (black) soils are found in the Red River Valley; promoters in the 1800s hailed the valley as the Garden of Eden, conveniently omitting the fact that early spring flooding or a lack of water coupled with a short growing season could be less than idyllic.

North Dakota's livelihood, nonetheless, has always depended upon its soil, and that soil has made the state the land of plenty, whether in agriculture, crude oil, or lignite (a brown variety of very soft coal). North Dakotans simply call this long eastern corridor of woodlands in the north and agricultural bounty in the south "The Valley."

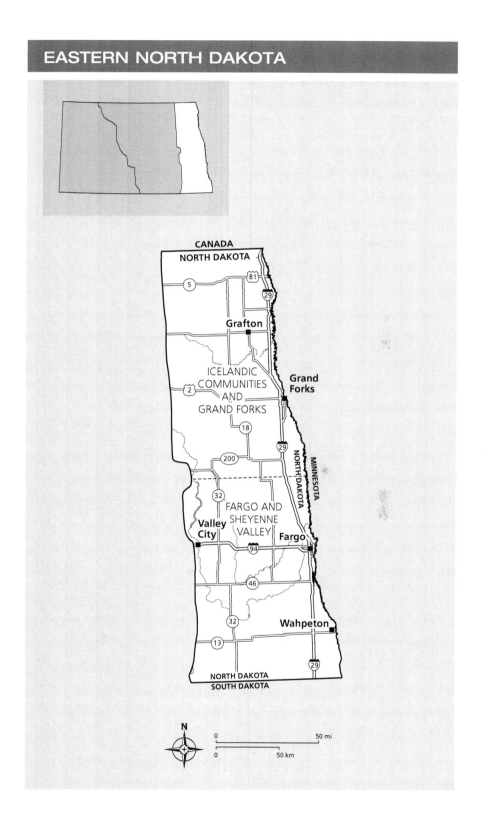

CANADA
NORTH DAKOTA

Grafton

ICELANDIC
COMMUNITIES
AND
GRAND FORKS

Grand
Forks

NORTH DAKOTA

MINNESOTA

FARGO AND
SHEYENNE
VALLEY

Valley
City

Fargo

Wahpeton

NORTH DAKOTA
SOUTH DAKOTA

N

0   50 mi

0   50 km

In the very northeast corner of the state, the four communities of Walhalla, Pembina, Langdon, and Cavalier successfully meld various traditions and nationalities. The largest Icelandic settlement in America is located within the region—providing a fascinating chapter in the rich history of the frontier West.

Icelandic Communities

The towns of Mountain, Gardar, Hallson, Svold, and Akra were settled in 1873–1879 by Icelanders coming from a sister colony in Gimli, Manitoba. After traversing the fertile Red River Valley, the immigrants reached the Pembina Escarpment, a hilly wooded region that overlooks the valley. They put down roots and thrived here. Quality education for their children was paramount to the settlers, and the vision was not only to assimilate into this new world but also to become its leaders. Icelandic pioneers and other ethnic groups are remembered in the Pioneer Heritage Museum which has the historic Akra Hall community center, the one-room Cranley School, Hallson Church with its high spire, and the Gunlogson Homestead (begun in 1882) at *Icelandic State Park* near Cavalier. Set on the shore of Lake Renwick, the 912-acre park offers year-round activities from hiking and swimming to cross-country skiing on groomed trails and snowshoeing. A 3-mile trail leads through the *Gunlogson Nature Preserve,* the state's first dedicated nature preserve, where more than a dozen rare types of plants, wildlife, and birds exist. They include bishop's cap and the pileated woodpecker, so keep a sharp eye out for them and others such as the western wood-peewee, which is the size of a small sparrow. The park also has a beach, campground, and 3 seasonal sleeping cabins. For more information call (701) 265-4561 or visit parkrec.nd.gov/icelandic-state-park.

If you feel you haven't seen enough historical buildings, then go across the highway from Icelandic State Park to the grounds of the *Pembina County Historical Museum*. Among its 11 structures are a 1930s barn, an 1882 homestead, blacksmith shop, a Great Northern depot that has been nicely restored, and St. Anthony's Church. Three buildings house the collection of some of the first machines used on the farms in North Dakota. The museum is open from 8 a.m. to 6 p.m. daily, Memorial Day through Labor Day; closing time is 5 p.m. during the winter. For more information, call (701) 265-4691 or visit cavaliernd.com/museum.

Despite the similar name, *Pembina State Museum* is its own entity and about 25 crow miles to the northeast. On the north side of the city of *Pembina,* (pop. 554), actually, the museum is possibly the last building in North Dakota before reaching the border crossing about two miles north of the city. The museum has displays showing the periods of time in this region from the Cretaceous period to the present day, 100 million years later, in the permanent gallery. Above all else here is the museum's 7-story observation tower which offers views of up to ten miles in any direction including up and down the valley of the Red River, one of the few north-flowing rivers in the US. Admission to the museum is free, but there is a charge for going up the tower: adults $2; ages 13 to 18 $0.50; 12 and younger free. Open 9 a.m. to 6 p.m. Mon through Sat and 1 to 6 p.m. Sun, mid-May through mid-Sept. It closes an hour earlier during the rest of the year. For more information, call (701) 825-6383 or visit history.nd.gov/historicsites/Pembina.

If you prefer grander accommodations, head a mile east of nearby Mountain on ND 3 to *221 Melsted Place Bed & Breakfast.* This elegant house on a historic farmstead was built in 1910 by Sigurdur Magnussen Melsted, an engineer, businessman, farmer, and active citizen. He built the impressive estate for his wife, Rosa, her parents, and their 10 children. In July 1995, it hosted Olafur Grimsson, the president of Iceland, who stayed in its Matriarchal Suite, an original bedroom for the maternal grandparents. It's appointed with an ornate golf-leaf headboard and a king-size bed. Three other bedrooms are available for guests. Savor sweets at the inn's Chocolate Festival in February; enjoy the sight of swans at the Spring Celebration in April; tour the haunted granary in October; or enjoy sleigh rides, Victorian teas, and candlelight dinners during the Christmas season. Room rates run from $80 to $120 a night. Amenities include a spa, evening bonfires, and a host of nature activities, including bird-watching, stargazing, and berry picking. For more information, call (701) 993-8257 or visit melstedplace.com.

Go with the Flow

The fact that the Red River flows north cost three escaped convicts their bid for freedom in 1978. After breaking out of the Douglas County Jail in Omaha, Nebraska, by shimmying down a 109-foot rope of braided sheets, the men—one of whom had taught himself to fly light aircrafts by reading instruction manuals while incarcerated—made their way to a small airport in southwest Omaha early one morning, stole a twin-engine light aircraft, and flew it north.

Not wanting to land in Canada, the pilot landed near Pembina, although a bystander said the landing was not the smoothest he had seen. He added that the men emerged from the plane, some laughing nervously.

They had planned to cross the border into Canada on foot, so they walked toward the Red River. Most rivers in North America flow to the south, so the escaped prisoners headed upstream in the direction they thought was north. But the Red River flows south to north, meaning that they were actually heading south, farther into the US when they were captured by border patrol agents that same day.

thestateflower

In **Mountain** you'll find the oldest Icelandic church in America. Built in 1884, the Vikur Lutheran Church has a stained-glass window depicting the Icelandic flag. Visitors from Iceland have remarked how it resembles churches in their island-nation. The town also hosts the largest Icelandic festival in the US every August. Over the years, the festival, called The Deuce of August, has not only attracted thousands of visitors and participants but five Icelandic prime ministers. For information, visit thedeuce.org.

If you drive three miles north of Mountain on ND 32 and look to the west, you cannot help but see the second-tallest building in North Dakota, after the capitol. Looming over the small Cavalier Air Force Station, the building houses a special system called phased array radar which can electronically steer its radar beams to scan different parts of the sky and space over northern North America without the antenna moving. Said to be able to spot an object the size of a basketball 3,000 miles away, it tracks up to 20,000 objects daily, ranging in size from particles of space debris to giant satellites. Don't hold your breath in hopes of being able to visit this facility, which has US and Canadian military members; it has opened its gate to the public only about a half dozen times since it was built in 1977. Still, it generates lots of comments among those seeing it for the first time while they drive the nearby highways.

One-and-one-half miles northeast of **Walhalla** on ND 32, the **Gingras Trading Post State Historic Site** preserves the home and trading post established by prominent Metis trader Antoine B. Gingras in the 1840s. Gingras was one of the signers of the charter of Winnipeg. His hand-hewn oak-log home and store are among the few tangible remains of the fur trade in the Valley of the Red River of the North. Admission to the grounds is free although the buildings were closed as of 2018. For more information, call (701) 825-6840 or visit history.nd.gov/historicsites/gingras.

BEST ATTRACTIONS IN EASTERN NORTH DAKOTA

Bagg Bonanza Farm

Fargo Theatre

Fort Abercrombie State Historic Site

Pembina State Museum

Today Walhalla is more of a vacation outpost. ***Frost Fire Ski Park Ski Resort*** (11950 County Hwy. 55) is a fully developed ski area, with 2 chairlifts, a lodge, and spectacular views. It also has three mountain bike trails with plans to open more along with a mountain bike terrain park. During the

didyouknow?

The Pembina River is North Dakota's only whitewater river, offering excellent paddling through the Pembina Gorge.

summer, its theater's musicals draw audiences from near and far. The covered amphitheater, on the slopes of the heavily wooded Pembina Gorge, sees sellout crowds who like to come early, shop in the crafts barn, and grab lunch before the curtain rises. For information call (701) 549-3600 or visit frostfirepark.org.

Grand Forks Area

Grab I-29 south from Pembina, and you'll follow the Red River Valley to the heart of ***Grand Forks***, the state's oldest community and third-largest city at about 57,056. The junction of the Red River of the North and the Red Lake River has been a meeting place for centuries—first for Native Americans who camped and traded there, then for French, British, and American fur traders who ambitiously peddled and paddled their wares across the continent. The regional population of about 103,000 encompasses North Dakota's Grand Forks and Minnesota's East Grand Forks, established on the opposite river bank in 1870 by steamboat captain Alexander Griggs.

The population first grew dramatically after the Great Northern Railroad came to town in 1880. From the 1880s to 1910, pine logs were floated down the Red Lake River or brought in by rail to sawmills in the city. Many homes in Grand Forks were built of regal white pine from the immense forests of northern Minnesota. Through the years, Grand Forks has remained the center of trade and processing for an agricultural area rich with wheat, potatoes, sugar beets, and livestock. The communities are also bolstered by a thriving state university, an air force base, and world-class sports facilities.

Locals are mighty proud of the ***Alerus Center*** (1200 42nd St. S), which hosts conventions, arena concerts, exhibitions, meetings, and sporting events—especially as home to University of North Dakota football. To arrange a walking tour of the center, call (701) 792-1200.

You don't have to be a sports fan to be bowled over by UND's $100 million ***Ralph Engelstad Arena*** (701-777-4167; theralph.com). The luxurious 400,000-square-foot, five-story arena, with seating for 11,700, is truly the envy of the NCAA. Chalk it up to an Italian marble lobby, cherrywood leather-padded seats, and 300 television sets that can even be found in the bathrooms so fans won't miss a bit of the action. Underneath the nation's largest center-hung video, the arena hosts family shows, ice events, concerts, and games featuring the Division I 8-time National Champion men's hockey team. Also, on-site are a pro shop and a Fighting Hawks Museum. The **Betty Engelstad Sioux Center**, a 50,000-square-foot expansion to the arena, houses 4 regulation-size practice volleyball and basketball courts, all of which can be converted into one main game court.

For devoted bakers, the state-owned **North Dakota Mill and Elevator** has been a Grand Forks fixture, supplying high-quality patent flours since 1922. It offers a mind-boggling array of choices such as extra fancy durum, high-gluten flours, pancake mixes, wheat germ, and spring wheat tailored for tortillas and pizza crusts. Most of it goes to food manufacturers, such as those who make pasta or crackers, but you can find some basic flours on grocery shelves. The mill can process more than 100,000 bushels of wheat a day or add value to 34 million bushels of hard spring and durum wheat each year. With an addition in 2014, the company became the largest wheat mill in the United States. For more information, visit ndmill.com.

Although Grand Forks lost several downtown buildings to the flood and fire of 1997, many remaining structures reflect the innate style and grace of the architects who shaped the city at the turn of the 20th century. You'll find architectural styles that include art deco, classical revival, colonial revival, Romanesque, Greek revival, and Dutch colonial.

A better lure than architecture—think creative food and drink—gets most people to the lively downtown that runs along 3rd Street and parallel to the river and flood memorials. In an 1893 building at the other end of the block, **The Toasted Frog** (124 N. 3rd St.) drew fans with its regional, trendy dinners and eventually expanded to Bismarck, as well. They specialize in wood-fired cooking, serving Moroccan-spiced lamb burgers, an open-face pheasant melt, and Gorgonzola and beef tips pizza. Appetizers include fried cheese-wrapped pickles, of course, frog legs, and buffalo wings. Call (701) 772-3764 or visit toastedfrog.com for more information.

Sky's Fine Dining (322 DeMers Ave.) is becoming a favorite for fine diners seeking 1907 Roast Caraway Duck, honey miso glazed sea bass, and Voodoo Pasta. Call (701) 746-8970 or visit skyscloud9.com.

didyouknow?

In 1893 miller Frank Amidon invented Cream of Wheat as a creamy white porridge that became a hot cereal staple in kitchens across the Midwest—especially on cold winter mornings.

Beyond downtown and at the west end of University Avenue, the ***University of North Dakota*** (UND) reigns as the state's largest school and its oldest after being started in 1883. It feeds the minds of close to 15,000 students. Many of them are drawn to its highly respected medical and law schools and its internationally known John D. Odegaard School of Aerospace Sciences.

The ***North Dakota Museum of Art,*** located on the UND campus in a renovated gymnasium, is renowned for its cutting-edge contemporary art and human-rights exhibitions. Its collection spans art in all media starting with the early 1970s, including the visual history of the region. The museum has concentrated on the works by Native American artists. Leave time to browse the eclectic gift shop with ethnic gifts, children's books, jewelry, and artwork. Also, the menu at the museum's café changes often. The museum is open 9 a.m. to 5 p.m. Mon through Fri, and 1 to 5 p.m. Sat and Sun. Admission is free. For more information, call (701) 777-4195 or visit ndmoa.com.

madein northdakota

If you're seeking the perfect souvenir or gift, check prideofdakota .com for a guide to North Dakota grown and created products.

Also on the UND campus, the ***Chester Fritz Auditorium*** is a 2,300-seat venue for a wide array of performances, from country acts and classical music to Russian ballet and Broadway shows. There's a permanent photo gallery of past performers at "The Fritz," world-renowned for acoustic brilliance. Call (701) 777-3076 or go to und.edu/chester-fritz-auditorium.

Families can continue the prehistoric theme at ***Canad Inns Destination Center*** (1000 S. 42nd St.) and connected to the Alerus Center. There are 14 kid-themed rooms with bunks and murals with dinos, mermaids, or the galaxy, plus a few themed Jacuzzi rooms with Egyptian, Japanese, Mayan, and Dakota

Crunch into Chippers

Enjoy Red River Valley potatoes in an addictive new way at Widman's. Grand Forks' **Widman's Candy Shop** (106 S. 3rd St.; 701-775-3480) and Carol Widman's **Candy Co.** (4325 13th Ave. S; 701-281-8664) in Fargo. They drench salty, crispy potato chips in smooth, sweet milk, or dark chocolate made from a family recipe and call the tasty treats "chippers." They put a North Dakota twist on other chocolates, too, pouring almond bark across nutty sunflower seeds and coating roasted flax seed in dark chocolate. Enjoy the sweet goodness.

decor. The hotel's 40,000-square-foot water park is North Dakota's largest. Non-guests also are welcome to use the water park. Call (701) 772-8404 or go to canadinns.com/stay/grand-forks for current prices and details.

For a history lesson, check out the Campbell House where Thomas Campbell lived and was dubbed the "Wheat King of America" in the early 1900s. He earned his nickname because of the enormous farm acreage he owned. His white, clapboard structure at 2405 Belmont Rd. shares space on the old family ranch with an original 1870s post office, a 1920s one-room schoolhouse, a carriage house, the original log Grand Forks post office, and the *Myra Museum.* The house and property were deeded to the historical society in 1971 and used to house a variety of local artifacts. Buildings are open daily mid-May through mid-Sept, from 1 to 5 p.m. Call (701) 775-2216 for more information.

Near downtown is the *Flood Memorial Marker* (3rd St. and 1st Ave.), a stone obelisk that shows the heights of different floods that have inundated the city. The 1997 flood, the greatest flood known to hit this area since 1826, combined with a fire to destroy 11 downtown buildings plus dozens of apartment units. Its waters reached more than two miles inland, forcing the evacuation of most of Grand Forks and all of East Grand Forks, Minnesota, and went on to the north, destroying much in Manitoba and Winnipeg, Canada. Built in a greenway, the marker is sometimes in the water as the Red River continues to periodically flood.

For an easy weekend getaway and perfect place to introduce children to fishing, check out *Turtle River State Park* 22 miles west of Grand Forks on US 2 in the breathtaking Turtle River Valley. You can borrow fishing gear at the park office and try catching rainbow trout in the river. Not your thing? Hike, mountain bike, or return in the winter for cross-country skiing and sledding. Camping spots and rustic cabins are available May through Sept. For more information, call (701) 594-4445 or visit parkrec.nd.gov/turtle-river-state-park.

Fargo

Hit I-29 and head south to *Fargo,* which has soared in population to 127,833 from 96,319 ten years ago—and is clearly keeping its claim as North Dakota's largest city and hippest metropolitan area. The metro area, which includes West Fargo and Moorhead, Minnesota, just across the Red River, has a population of 229,000. The town's roots are firmly in agriculture, playing a role as a vital trade and distribution center for sugar beets, wheat, and livestock produced in the rich soils of the surrounding valley. But it's diversified by many other industries, too, including health care and companies such as Microsoft.

Fargo wears its heritage like a badge of honor and brings the past to life with events like **Pioneer Days** during the third weekend in August. Head to **Bonanzaville,** a restored and extensive pioneer village of more than 45 buildings from the early 20th century. The 12-acre village includes a Plains Indian Museum, train depot, machinery shed, church, general stores galore, log cabins, and even a hangar for historic planes. Plan to spend at least a few hours here or you'll miss the fun details like the telephone company offering local calls in exchange for "two eggs or five cents."

Bonanzaville is named for the large and well-capitalized Bonanza farms (not to be confused with the ranch of 1960s TV fame) that were built by early railroad boosters as a way to attract settlers to this "slice of Eden in the West." Sure enough, settlers followed with their plows and dreams. Between 1879 and 1886, about 100,000 people, many of them Scandinavian and German, came to live in Dakota Territory. This period became known as the Dakota Boom, well, perhaps the First Dakota Boom. Several of the Bonanza farms endured to the early part of the 20th century—the last threads in the fabric of a powerful era in agriculture.

Bonanzaville's visitor center does a great job commemorating what was one of North Dakota's most colorful eras. The village (located 4.25 miles west of I-29 on Main Avenue or via I-94, exit 343) is open daily Memorial Day

didyouknow?

Fargo was established in 1871 where the Northern Pacific Railway crossed the Red River. Its first name was Centralia, but the town later was renamed to honor William George Fargo, who was founder of Wells Fargo and Co. and one of the railroad's directors. Low railroad freight rates and the land's incredible wheat-producing potential attracted settlers.

Fargo and Fame

Ah, geez. Thanks to Hollywood, saying you're from Fargo can elicit a snicker and flashbacks to the darkly comic and cultish *Fargo* movie (1996). It doesn't help that *Fargo* came back as a 2014 TV series. You can find T-shirts that say, "Yes, I'm from Fargo. No, it's not like the movie" or "You betcha." *Fargo* fans can pose with the infamous wood chipper from the movie at the Fargo-Moorhead visitor center. They even provide the furry hats with ear flaps. If you head downtown to the funky Fargo Theatre, you can pose with "Wood-Chip Marge," an 8-foot-tall chainsaw carving of the movie's heroine, Marge Gunderson, a role that scored Frances McDormand a best actress Oscar.

through Labor Day. Admission is $12 for adults; $10 for seniors and military; $6 for kids 6 to 16; free for military. Call (701) 282-2822 or go to bonanzaville .org for details and special events such as Christmas on the Prairie.

Children can have their own lesson on the merits of agriculture through the **Children's Museum at Yunker Farm** (1201 28th Ave. N; 701-232-6102). Here they can see a display of live bees, then crawl through a honeycomb section designed just for them. The exhibits were constructed to involve kids in more than 50 demonstrations and hands-on experiments. Housed in a renovated, 1876 red brick farmhouse (it was the first brick residence in Dakota Territory), the museum is naturally inviting. The 55-acre grounds include a playground, a pumpkin patch, nature trails, and a community garden. Admission is $5 for children and adults. Train rides are $5 and a whirl on the carousel is $0.50. Open 10 a.m. to 5 p.m. Mon through Sat, and 1 to 5 p.m. Sun. It's closed on Mon during the school year.

For hip, sophisticated fun, head to **downtown Fargo.** On balmy Thursday nights, it might be lined with the vibrant colors and throaty rumbles of classic cars. Pick any night, though, and you'll find Broadway hopping with restaurants, upscale stores, and the glowing neon of ultra-trendy The Hotel Donaldson on one end and the art deco **Fargo Theatre** marquee on the other.

The renovated Fargo Theatre at 314 Broadway hums with the artsy, quirky spirit that has helped independent films thrive in the last decade. They added a second 99-seat theater in 2009, giving patrons the choice of two movies each night when the theater isn't hosting dance groups, comedians, bands, and orchestras. The theater opened in 1926 as a vaudeville and silent-film hall. There are still a handful of rare talents, local men who can improvise the sound effects and background music for silent films with the theater's rare, still-functioning Wurlitzer pipe organ. Your best bet for hearing it is attending the annual **Fargo Film Festival** in early March. Expect to be confounded when trying to choose what movies, out of the 100 offered, during the five-day event. Call (701) 239-8385 or visit fargotheatre.org.

For the best view of downtown, head up to Sky Prairie Lounge and watch the sunset from **The Hotel Donaldson**'s rooftop gathering place at 101 N. Broadway. It's open to the public 5 to 10:30 p.m. on balmy evenings, Mon through Sat. Guests in the 17-room boutique hotel each enjoy the work of a different artist and can use the hot tub on the rooftop. The centerpiece of its premiere room—No. 17—is a Japanese soak tub with water cascading from the ceiling. The hotel boasts some of the area's most creative dining with an emphasis on local ingredients. Splurge on five spice salmon served on rice noodles and cabbage in tamari sauce and scallion oil, or lunch in the more affordable HoDo Lounge that offers a bison burger as well as a burger with a patty made of wild rice and barley. Call (701) 478-1000 or visit hoteldonaldson .com for more information.

For a newer option in rooftop dining and tasty food, head to **Rhombus Guys** (606 Main Ave.; 701-540-4534; rhombusguyspizza.com), a Grand Forks favorite that has expanded to Fargo. You'll find choices like the meat-laden T-Rex or vegetarian Backpacker and even a s'mores dessert pizza.

It would take weeks to check out all the superb dining in Fargo, but even if you've run out of time, at least grab a to-go item from **Nichole's Fine Pastry** (13 S. 8th St.; 701-232-6430; nicholesfinepastry.com). They create such artful fruit pastries, tarts, and layer cakes—you'll definitely want a photo. Cool down a hot day with a creamy gelato or tart sorbet in flavors such as spicy ginger, tangy rhubarb, or blood orange. The cafe serves sandwiches, soups, and salads, too.

If you like edgy, Native American, or contemplative art, head to the elegantly renovated, turn-of-the-20th-century warehouse that's home to the **Plains Art Museum** (704 1st Ave. N; 701-232-3821; plainsart.org). It hosts regional, national, and international exhibits, large permanent collections, special events, performances, and art classes. The largest art museum in North Dakota is open 11 a.m. to 5 p.m. Mon, Tues, Wed, and Fri; 11 a.m. to 9 p.m. Thurs; 10 a.m. to 5 p.m. Sat. Closed Sun. Admission is free.

baseballlegend

Fargo athlete **Roger Maris** vaulted to fame when he joined the New York Yankees and hit 61 home runs during the 1961 season, breaking the long-standing record of the great Babe Ruth. At the Roger Maris Museum exhibit at West Acres Shopping Center, you'll see actual film of Roger's last 12 homers of 1961, along with his uniforms, baseball equipment, and other memorabilia. Call (701) 282-2222 for more information.

You can see the white peaks of the **Hjemkomst Center**, Historical and Cultural Society of Clay County, Minnesota, from the North Dakota side of the Red River, but you have to cross the bridge to Moorhead, Minnesota, to see the **Hjemkomst Viking Ship,** a replica built by Robert Asp, a Moorhead school counselor whose dream was to sail it to Norway. Leukemia took him before he could, but his family completed the harrowing, adventurous, and historic Atlantic crossing, traveling from Duluth, Minnesota, to land in Bergen, Norway, in 1982. You can get up close to the 76-foot-long ship (its name means "homecoming" in Norwegian), watch a movie about it, and also go outside to tour the impressive Hopperstad Stave Church, modeled after a stavkirke in Vik, Norway. To get the best feel for these Nordic cultures—through sights, music, costumes, Viking-age crafts, and food—time a visit with the Scandinavian Festival the last weekend in

A Spirited Dakota Road Trip: Beer, Wine, and Vodka

Looking for your new favorite drink? Here's just a sampling of the many regional breweries, distillers, and vineyards:

Drekker Brewing Company (1666 1st Ave. N; drekkerbrewing.com): hand-crafted beers in Fargo

Fargo Brewing Company (610 University Dr. N; fargobrewing.com): artisan beers in Fargo

Maple River (630 Front St., Cassleton; mapleriverwinery.com): wild plum and native fruit wines, rhubarb, chokecherry, and other fruit-infused vodkas, cordials, and fruit brandies. Maple River Winery also operates Maple River Distillery 2 doors away (4 N. Langer Ave.; mapleriverdistillery.com)

Red Trail Vineyard (redtrailvineyards.com): wines made from northern varietals along the Old Red Trail along the Maple River valley in Buffalo

For more information and additional sites, check out the North Dakota Beer and Wine Trail Brochure at ndtourism.com or contact the North Dakota Grape Growers Association at ndgwa.org.

June, which hosts a Viking Village in the park to the center. For more information about the center and the festival, call (218) 299-5511 or go to hcscconline.org.

You can soak up much more art and culture, especially theater and musical performances, with three universities calling the Fargo-Moorhead area home: Concordia College and Minnesota State University at Moorhead and North Dakota State University at Fargo. Check the Fargo-Moorhead Visitor and Convention Bureau for upcoming performances at fargomoorhead.org.

One of the nicest places to enjoy the peaceful Red River is 17 blocks south of Main Avenue. Here, tucked back behind residential streets, you'll find *Lindenwood Park* (1712 5th St. S; 701-499-6060; fargoparks.com), with spacious, wooded picnic grounds, playgrounds, bike and kayak rentals and trails, and 47 places to pitch a tent along this scenic oxbow.

Like Grand Forks, Fargo hums with pride when it comes to aviation. Check out the local heritage at *Fargo Air Museum* (1609 19th Ave. N; 701-293-8043; fargoairmuseum.org), which is at Fargo's Hector International Airport. Besides educating the public about aviation and North Dakotans' role in it, the museum celebrates the freedom, thrill, and exhilaration of flight and commemorates those who sacrificed their lives in times of war, from World War II to Afghanistan. On display is a DC-3 that served civilians as a transport and the military as a cargo and troop carrier during WWII. This one was based in Australia. A replica of the Wright Flyer, the first true airplane, was built at the museum in 2003 and has been rated as one of the best replicas of the Flyer in the US. Among the other aircraft that earned fame during WWII: a twin-engine B-25 Mitchell bomber and a P-51 Mustang, the war's premier allied fighter. Open 10 a.m. to 5 p.m. Tues through Sat; 10 a.m. to 1 p.m. on Sun; closed Mon. Admission is $10 for adults; $8 for seniors, military, and students; and $5 for kids 5 to 11.

If you take I-29 35 miles south through the Red River Valley, you'll reach Wahpeton and two more intriguing chapters of North Dakota history. ***Fort Abercrombie*** was the first permanent US military fort established in North Dakota and served as a gateway to the frontier from 1857 to 1878. Many considered it as a hub for several trails passing through the area. It was the only part of the state besieged by Dakota warriors for six weeks in the late summer of 1862, when the short but deadly US-Dakota War broke out in Minnesota. Only one original building remains, but blockhouses and the palisade wall have been reconstructed, and a museum helps bring that era to life. The museum is open 9 a.m. to 5 p.m. daily

skydive

If seeing planes has your adrenaline going or craving an ultra-rush, you can try a tandem skydive with Skydive Fargo (1040 19th Ave. NW Hangar #8, West Fargo). Call (701) 281-0149 or visit skydivefargo.com for more information.

BEST EASTERN NORTH DAKOTA FAMILY ATTRACTIONS

Fargo–Moorhead RedHawks
Newman Outdoor Field 1515
15th Ave. N
(701) 235-6161
fmredhawks.com

Red River Zoo
4220 21st Ave. S
(701) 277-9240
redriverzoo.org

Rheault Farm
2902 25th St. S
(701) 499-7788
fargoparks.com

Scheels
(701) 298-2918
scheelssports.com

Shipwreck Bay
Holiday Inn Fargo
3803 13th Ave. S
(701) 282-2700

Thunder Road Family Fun Park
(701) 282-5151
thunderroadfargo.com

AUTHOR'S FAVORITE FARGO SHOPS

Gallery 4
115 Roberts St. N
(701) 237-6867
gallery4fargo.net
Cooperative gallery with a variety of local art, from pottery and glass to jewelry and paintings. This gallery also has a "Made in Fargo" gift shop with smaller handmade gifts by North Dakota and Minnesota artists.

Kittsona
608 Main Ave.
(701) 936-0608
kittsona.com
Beautiful and trendy women's clothing, many local North Dakota and Minnesota brands, also sells home and gift items.

O'Day Cache
317 Broadway N
(701) 293-2088
odaycache.com
These Asian imports add up to beautiful decor, clothing, jewelry, housewares, furniture, and vibrant paper lanterns.

The Red Silo
12 Broadway N
(701) 478-3822
A collection of unique gifts, women's clothing, and home decor.

Revolver
627 1st Ave. N
(701) 235-2883
A mix of vintage clothes, jewelry, toys, and housewares.

Zandbroz Variety
420 Broadway N
(701) 239-4729
zandbroz.com
Best bet for beautiful stationery and pens, kitchenwares and cookbooks, jewelry, offbeat and retro kids' toys, and a great read, whether it's a brand new book or a rare vintage edition.

Memorial Day to Labor Day. Admission is $8, adults; $3 for children 6 to 14. For more information call (701) 553-8513 or go to history.nd.gov/historicsites/abercrombie.

Twenty miles southwest of the fort, check out the ***Bagg Bonanza Farm*** (8025 169th Ave. SE), near Mooreton. This 21-building farm is the sole remnant of the "king wheat" boom that started in the late 1870s when harvesting was mechanized, wheat farms were supersized, and railroads eagerly transported the bounty. Bagg Bonanza Farm was once a 6,000-acre operation—a fairly modest size for that era—but it's the last restorable Bonanza farm in the US and a National Historic Landmark. Guided tours are available from noon to 5 p.m. Fri through Sun, or by appointment. Open noon to 5 p.m. Fri to Sun, Memorial Day through Labor Day. Special events are scheduled throughout the season, including the annual Old-Fashioned Fourth of July Celebration. Admission is $5, adults; $2.50 for children 6 to 12. Concessions and a gift shop are on-site. For more information call (701) 274-8989.

Sheyenne Valley

Head an hour west of Fargo to reach **Valley City,** gateway to the Sheyenne Valley. Two of the valley area's most prominent features are not always found in North Dakota: trees and winding roadways. It's no surprise then that it became the **Sheyenne Valley National Scenic Byway** and one of the Midwest's most beloved fall treks with the valley dappled in vibrant shades of gold, yellow, and red. Of course, it's lovely and relaxing any season of the year as the road curves 68 miles from Lake Ashtabula to Lisbon.

The southern end of the byway, about 30 miles south of Valley City, heads toward **Fort Ransom** and **Fort Ransom State Park.** The community and park inherited the name of a frontier cavalry fort, which was established in 1867 to protect the settlers traveling between Minnesota and Montana. The park offers a variety of accommodations from three dozen campsites plus another 24 for those traveling with horses and, for those who want nicer places to rest, a farm house, two large yurts, a spacious covered wagon, and a cabin fit for two. Call (701) 973-4331 for more information.

Nowadays, the small Norwegian town of Fort Ransom is regarded as a scenic arts community. The **Ransom County Museum** covers regional history and has buildings form the past on its property. It's open 1 to 5 p.m. daily, Memorial Day weekend through Labor Day. Admission is $1 for adults. Call (701) 678-2045 for more information.

The **Sheyenne Valley Arts and Crafts Festival** is another popular attraction and takes place the last full weekend in Sept. Going strong since 1967, it now has 200 booths offering arts, crafts, and foods. Call (701) 973-4461 for more information.

Sodbuster Days takes place every summer during the second weekend in July and the first full weekend after Labor Day. Here you can revisit the horse-powered days of threshing, haying, and plowing, and homesteading activities from carding and weaving to silversmithing and blacksmithing. Wagon rides and entertainment round out the two weekends of living history. Admission is $10 which is good for both days. For more information call (701) 973-4331 or go to parkrec.nd.gov/events/sodbuster-days.

North of Fort Ransom, you'll also find tiny Kathryn with its 1900s main street and Clausen Springs Park, which is popular for camping.

Valley City in the heart of the byway ranks among the state's most beloved small-town destinations. Much of its charm comes from elegant and dramatic bridges—including the impressive **Highline Bridge.** At 3,860 feet long and 162 feet above the riverbed, the Highline Bridge is one of the longest and highest single-track railroad bridges in the nation. The first train officially crossed the trestle on May 12, 1908, and regular train service over the bridge began May 20. Because it was of vital importance in moving supplies and men, the bridge was closely guarded during both World War I and World War II to prevent sabotage.

You can learn more about the local history at **Barnes County History Museum** (315 Central Ave. N; 701-845-0966) or pick up a brochure on the bridges at the Rosebud Visitor Center (250 W. Main St.; 701-845-1891; hello valley.com).

Give yourself at least a few hours to stroll along the river and back and forth across the pretty bridges, many of which are on the campus of **Valley City State University.** Don't miss **Medicine Wheel Park** (medicinewheel .vcsu.edu) where strategically placed rocks create a 213-foot-diameter Native American solar calendar. Interpretive signs explain how it works, and you can catch celebrations here during the equinox and seasonal solstices. The park also has a dozen Native American burial mounds, a meridian calendar, and part of the North County National Scenic Trail that links North Dakota to Lake Champlain, New York.

Twelve miles northwest of Valley City, you can slow down the pace even more with a trip to the beaches by **Baldhill Dam and Lake Ashtabula.** This widened area of the Sheyenne River boasts 7 recreational areas where you can swim, fish, boat, picnic, and camp. It's fitting that Ashtabula means "fish river" to the Native Americans, since it is loaded with walleye, northern pike, yellow perch, black bullheads, and white bass. For more information, call (701) 845-2970 or visit mvp.usace.army.mil.

The **Valley City Federal Fish Hatchery,** one of two such facilities in the state, is also at the park. Call (701) 845-3464 for information.

Finally, if you want to grandly cap off a Dakota adventure, head about 70 miles southeast of Wahpeton to **Havana,** almost on the South Dakota border. Here you can nestle into the **Coteau des Prairie Lodge** (9953 141st Ave.; 701-680-1175; cdplodge.com). Perched on the gorgeous coteau which rises and stretches into South Dakota and Minnesota, the lodge serves up a pure, peaceful Dakota landscape and warm hospitality. Eleven guest rooms, each with its unique theme, are $140 per night. A suite which includes a kitchen and dining area is $200 per night. Farm tours can be arranged, or you can fish and observe birds at the nearby Tewaukon National Wildlife Refuge.

By going east of Valley City to exit 302 on I-94 and then south 14 miles on SD 32, you'll wind up at a former country schoolhouse housing the partnered businesses of the **Dakota Fiber Mill** and **Bear Creek Felting.** As the largest fiber arts mill in the state, this two-story brick school that was built in 1916 is the place for anyone who has anything to do with yarn. This is truly a full-service yarn business offering carding, spinning, washing, and felting services as well as classes. The owners hope to open the business with its retail shop and classes in the fall of 2020, and they are turning other areas of the large school into a bed-and-breakfast featuring 12 to 18 guest rooms, a dining area, kitchen, and a 5,000-square-foot event center. A herd of different types of sheep, goat, llama, and alpacas will be on the property. Call (701) 238-4003 or visit dakotafibermill.com or bearcreekfelting.com for more information.

Where to Stay in Eastern North Dakota

FARGO

Best Western Plus Kelly Inn and Suites
1767 44th St. S
(701) 282-2143
bestwestern.com
Moderate

Fargo Inn and Suites
1025 38th St. S
(701) 282-6300
fargoinn.com
Inexpensive

Hilton Garden Inn
4351 17th Ave. S
(701) 499-6000
hiltongardeninn3.hilton.com
Moderate

Radisson Hotel
201 N. 5th St.
(701) 232-7363
radisson.com
Moderate to expensive

GRAND FORKS

AmericInn by Wyndham
1820 S. Columbia Rd.
(701) 780-9925
Inexpensive to moderate

Best Western Harvest Inn and Suites
3350 32nd Ave. S
(701) 775-5000
bestwestern.com
Moderate

Canad Inns Destination Center
1000 S. 42nd St.
(701) 772-8404
canadinns.com
Moderate

C'mon Inn Hotel and Suites
3051 32nd Ave. S
(701) 775-3320
cmoninn.com
Moderate

Days Inn
3101 S. 34th St.
(701) 314-2997
daysinn.com
Inexpensive

Where to Eat in Eastern North Dakota

FARGO

The Boiler Room
210 Roberts Alley
(701) 478-1990
boilerroomfargo.com
Moderate

Cafe Aladdin
1609 32nd Ave. S
(701) 232-4200
cafealaddinfargomoorhead
.com
Moderate

Kroll's Diner
1033 45th St. S
(701) 492-2319
sitdownandeat.com
Inexpensive to moderate

Paradiso Mexican Restaurant
801 38th St. S
(701) 282-5747
paradiso.com
Moderate

SELECTED CHAMBERS OF COMMERCE

Carrington Area Chamber of Commerce
871 Main St.
Carrington 58421
(701) 652-2524
cgtn-nd.com

Fargo–Moorhead Convention & Visitor Bureau
2001 44th St. SW
Fargo 58103
(701) 282-3653
fargomoorhead.org

Greater Grand Forks Convention & Visitors Bureau
4251 Gateway Dr.
Grand Forks 58203
(701) 746-0444
visitgrandforks.com

Valley City Area Chamber of Commerce
250 W. Main St.
Valley City 58072
(701) 845-1891
valleycitynd.org

Wahpeton Convention & Visitors Bureau
1900 4th St. N
Wahpeton 58075
(701) 642-8559 or
(888) 850-9544
visitwahpeton.com

Wurst Bier Hall
630 1st Ave. N
(701) 478-2437
wurstfargo.com
Inexpensive to moderate

GRAND FORKS

Brick and Barley
9 N. 3rd St.
(701) 757-4012
brickandbarleygf.com
Moderate

Darcy's Cafe
1015 N. Washington St.
(701) 775-4050
Inexpensive

The Red Pepper
1011 University Ave.
(701) 775-9671
redpepper.com
Inexpensive

Rhombus Guys
312 Kittson Ave.
(701) 787-7317
rhombusguyspizza.com
Moderate

Index

A

Aberdeen, 1
Aberdeen Aquatic Center, 4
Aberdeen Convention & Visitors
    Bureau, 25
Aberdeen Railway Station
    Canteen, 7
Adams Homestead and Nature
    Preserve, 47
Adams Museum, 115
Alerus Center, 179
Along the Missouri River, 59
Alpine Inn Restaurant, 100
Al's Oasis, 64
AmericInn by Wyndham, 24, 122,
    150, 191
Anchor Grille, 79
Angostura Recreation Area, 110
Angostura Resort, 110
Annual Corn Palace Stampede
    Rodeo, 53
Aqua Addicts Ski Shows, 4
Arrowhead National Wildlife
    Refuge, 156
Arrowwood Cedar Shore Resort, 64
Art Alley, Rapid City, 92
Arts in the Park, 9
Austin–Whittemore House, 44
Avenue of the Flags, 96

B

Backyard Barbeque, 58
Badger Hole, 104
Badlands, 85
Badlands Astronomy Festival, 87
Badlands Dinosaur Museum, 138
Badlands Grill Restaurant and
    Bar, 173

Badlands Inn, 87
Badlands Loop, 87
Badlands Motel, 150
Badlands National Park, 84, 85, 86
Bagg Bonanza Farm, 178, 188
Baker's Bakery & Cafe, 123
Baldhill Dam and Lake
    Ashtabula, 190
Baltic, 31
Barefoot Resort, 123
Barnes County History
    Museum, 190
Basil Restaurant Sushi Bar and
    Asian Bistro, 151
Baum, L. Frank, 5
Bavarian Inn, 122
Baymont by Wyndham Mandan
    Bismarck Area, 150
Baymont Inn & Suites by
    Wyndham Sturgis, 123
Bear Butte State Park, 112
Bear Country USA, 95
Bear Creek Felting, 190
Beaver Creek Nature Area, 41
Belfield, 137
Belle Fourche, 118
Belle Fourche Chamber of
    Commerce, 124
Belle Joli Winery, 99
Ben Reifel Visitor Center, 87
Ben's Brewing Company, 58
Bergeson's Homestead, 39
Best Western Golden Spike
    Inn, 122
Best Western Harvest Inn and
    Suites, 191
Best Western Kelly Inn, 57
Best Western of Huron, 24

Best Western Plus Kelly Inn and
    Suites, 191
Best Western Ramkota Hotel, 24
Betty Engelstad Sioux Center, 180
Beulah, 145
Big Sioux Recreation Area, 39
Big Sioux River, 34
Big Tom's Diner, 79
biking, 94, 103
Birchtree Gallery and Framing, 16
birding, North Dakota, 156
Birnt Hills Trail, 143
birthplace of American Legion
    baseball, 10
Bismarck, 147
Bismarck–Mandan Convention and
    Visitors Bureau, 151
Black Elk Peak, 107
Black Forest Inn, B&B Lodge, 123
Black Hills, 95
Black Hills and Badlands Tasting
    Trail, 98
Black Hills Bagels, 125
Black Hills Burger and Bun
    Co., 123
Black Hills Mining Museum, 117
Black Hills Mountain Fest, 94
Black Hills National Forest, 85, 94
Black Hills Playhouse, 104
Black Hills Powwow, 91
Black Hills Powwow and Art
    Expo, 84
Black Hills Roundup Rodeo, 119
Black Hills Visitor Information
    Center, 89
Black Hills Wild Horse
    Sanctuary, 109
Black Hills Wine and Beer
    Trail, 98
Blarney Stone Pub, 150
Bluebell Lodge, 104

Blue Dog State Fish Hatchery, 12
Bobkat's Purple Pie Place, 123
Boiler Room, The, 191
Bonanzaville, 183
Botticelli's Ristorante Italiano, 125
Bottineau, 167
Bottineau Chamber of
    Commerce, 173
Bottineau Convention and Visitors
    Bureau, 151
Boutique 23, 147
Bramble Park Zoo, 3, 17
Bread Poets, 150
Brick and Barley, 192
Brickhouse Grille, 151
Bridge City Marina, 73
Bridges Restaurant & Lounge, 79
Broadway Bean and Bagel, 173
Brookings, 18
Brookings Area Chamber of
    Commerce and Convention
    Bureau, 25
Brothel, The, 116
Brown, Sam, 15
Buechel Memorial Lakota
    Museum, 82
Buffalo Gap National
    Grasslands, 88
Buffalo Ridge Resort, 17
Buffalo Rock Lodge & Cabins, 106
Buffalo Roundup and Arts
    Festival, 84
Buffalo Run Resort, 40, 57
Buford, 141
Buglin' Bull Restaurant & Sports
    Bar, 123
Bully Pulpit Golf Course, 140
Bumpin Buffalo Bar & Grill, 124
Burlington, 166
Burning Hills Amphitheatre,
    129, 130

Burns, Ken, 66
Bur Oak Diner, 58
Buryanek State Recreation Area, 63

C
Cafe Aladdin, 191
Cafe Brule, 44
Calumet Bluff, 50
Canad Inns Destination Center, 181, 191
Candy Co., 181
Capitol Christmas Trees, 67
Capitol Lake, 68
Capitol Rotunda, 67
Capitol Theatre, 6
Carlock, 63
Carrington, 160
Carrington Area Chamber of Commerce, 192
Carver's Cafe, 97
Cascade Falls Picnic Ground, 110
Casey Tibbs Rodeo Center, 69
Cattleman's Club Steakhouse, 79
Cave Hills, 120
Cedar Inn Family Restaurant, 173
Cedar Pass Lodge, 87
Centennial Trail, 103
Central North Dakota, 152
Central States Fair, 84
Chamberlain, 64
Chamberlain–Oacoma Area Chamber of Commerce, 78
Chapel in the Hills, 94
Charles Gurney Hotel, 49
Charlie's Pizza House, 58
Charlys Restaurant & Lounge, 79
Chase Lake National Wildlife Refuge, 156
Chateau de Mores State Historic Site, 129
Chef Louie's, 57

Chester Fritz Auditorium, 181
Cheyenne River Indian Reservation, 75
Cheyenne River Tribe's Grand River Casino & Resort, 74
Chief White Crane Recreation Area, 50
Children's Museum at Yunker Farm, 184
Children's Museum of South Dakota, 3, 18
Child's Play Toys, 34
chislic, 33
Chislic Festival, 42
CH Patisserie, 34
Christmas at the Capitol event, 67
Christopher, Warren, 142
Chubby Chipmunk, 92
Chubby Chipmunk Chocolates, 124
Chute Rooster Steak House and Lounge, 124
Circle B Chuckwagon, 100
Circle H Ranch, 63
City of Presidents, 92
Clarion Hotel Convention Center, 172
Clark, Charles Badger, Jr, 104
Clay County Historical Society Museum, 44
ClubHouse Hotel and Suites, 56
Cluckin' Good Chicken & BBQ, 58
C'mon Inn Hotel and Suites, 191
Codington County Heritage Museum, 17
Cogan House Bed and Breakfast, 52
Colonial House Restaurant & Bar, 125
Conqueror's Stones, 72
Corn Palace, 29, 52
Corn Palace Festival, 53

Coteau Cafe, 18
Coteau des Prairie Lodge, 190
Coteau des Prairies, 13
Cottonwood Bistro, 25
Country Apple Orchard, 38
Country Inn & Suites, 24, 57
Courtyard by Marriott, 57
Cowboy Cafe, 151
Cowboy Poetry Gathering, 133
Coyote Blues Village Bed and
    Breakfast, 100
Cramer Kenyon Heritage Home, 48
Crazy About Cupcakes, 58
Crazy Horse Memorial, 85, 101
Cross Ranch Nature Preserve, 145
Cross Ranch State Park, 145
Crossroads Hotel at Huron Event
    Center, 24
Crossroads Restaurant, 25
Crow Creek Indian Reservation,
    54, 64
Crow Peak, 114
Crow Peak Brewing Co., 99
Custer, 102
Custer Area Chamber of
    Commerce, 124
Custer, George A., 146
Custer National Forest, 120
Custer Resorts, 104
Custer State Game Lodge, 104, 106
Custer State Park, 85, 103
Custer Wolf, The, 123
Czech Days, 42

D

Dacotah Prairie Museum, 3, 4
Dahl Fine Arts Center, 93
Dairy Bar, 20
Dakota Brickhouse, 45
Dakota Cyclery, 134
Dakota Dinosaur Museum, 128

Dakota Discovery Museum, 29,
    53, 54
Dakota Fiber Mill, 190
Dakota Growers Pasta Co., 160
Dakotah Buffet, 173
Dakotah Lodge, 57
Dakotah Rose Bed &
    Breakfast, 173
Dakota Inn Bed and Breakfast, 16
Dakotaland Museum, 22
Dakota Sioux Casino, 24
Dakota Sun Gardens and
    Winery, 161
Dakota Sunset Museum, 77
Dakota Territorial Capitol
    Replica, 48
Dakota Territorial Museum/Mead
    Cultural Education Center, 48
Dakota Territory Air Museum, 166
Dakota Wesleyan University, 53
Dakota Zoo, 149
Dale and Martha Hawk Foundation
    Museum, 172
Darcy's Cafe, 192
Day County Museum, 11
Days Inn, 24, 191
Days of '76 Museum, The, 116
Days of ''76 (Rodeo and
    Parade), 84
D.C. Booth Historic National Fish
    Hatchery and Archives, 113
Deadwood, 114
Deadwood Chamber of
    Commerce, 124
Deadwood Gulch Resort, 122
Deadwood Mountain Grand, 122
Deadwood, series, 116
Deadwood Social Club, 114
Dell Rapids, 29
Dell Rapids History Museum, 30
Dells Theatre, 30

Dempsey's Brewery Pub, 26
Depot Pub & Grill, The, 58
Des Lacs National Wildlife
    Refuge, 167
Des Lacs River Valley, 167
De Smet, 21
Desperados Cowboy
    Restaurant, 100
Devil's Gulch, 30
Devils Lake, 158, 162
Devils Lake Convention and
    Visitors Bureau, 173
Dickinson, 138
Dickinson, Angie, 142
Dickinson Convention and Visitors
    Bureau, 151
Dinosaur Park, 93
dinosaurs, 90
Dock 44, 63
Dorothy Jencks Memorial
    Garden, 48
Dough Trader Pizza Company, 125
downtown Sioux Falls, 34
Drekker Brewing Company, 186

E
Eagle's View Bed & Breakfast, 79
Earth Resources Observation
    Systems (EROS) Data Center, 31
East Bank, 34
eastern North Dakota, 174
Easton Castle, 6
Eastwood Park, 166
Edwinton Brewery, 147
1880 Train, 98
1881 Custer County Courthouse
    Museum, 102
8th and Railroad Center, 35
Elixir Roasterie, 58
Elkhorn Ranch, 131
Elk Ridge Bed & Breakfast, 122

Elks Theatre, 93
Enchanted Castle, 138
Enchanted Highway, 138
Enigma, 91
ethnic festivals, 42
Eureka, 76
Eureka Pioneer Museum of
    McPherson County, 76
Evan's Plunge, 108
Everest Cuisine, 125
Expressway Suites, 150

F
Fall River County Historical
    Museum, 109
Falls Overlook Cafe, 32
Falls Park, 29, 32
Falls Park Visitor Information
    Center, 32
Fargo, 182
Fargo Air Museum, 186
Fargo Brewing Company, 186
Fargo, downtown, 184
Fargo Film Festival, 184
Fargo Inn and Suites, 191
Fargo–Moorhead Convention &
    Visitor Bureau, 192
Fargo–Moorhead RedHawks, 187
Fargo Theatre, 178, 184
Farmhouse Café, 130
Faulkton, 11
Fawick Park, 37
FestiFall, 47
Fighting Stallions, 68
Fireflour Neapolitan Pizza &
    Coffee Bar, 150
Firehouse Brewing Co., 91
Firehouse Wine Cellars, 91
Fireside Inn and Suites, 172
First Gold Hotel, 122
First Presbyterian Church, 21

Five Nations Arts Museum, 146
Flaming Fountain, 68
Flandreau, 21
FlatIron Historic Sandstone
    Inn, 122
Flood Memorial Marker, 182
Fool Soldier Band Monument, 72
Foote Creek B&B, 24
Forestburg, 55
Forestburg melons, 55
Former Governor's Mansion State
    Historic Site, 148
Fort Abercrombie, 187
Fort Abercrombie State Historic
    Site, 178
Fort Abraham Lincoln State Park,
    146, 149
Fort Berthold Reservation, 143
Fort Buford, 141
Fort Lincoln Trolley, 149
Fort Mandan, 145
Fort Meade Museum & Old Post
    Cemetery, 111
Fort Meade Recreation Area, 112
Fort Pierre National Grassland, 69
Fort Randall Dam Visitor
    Center, 62
Fort Randall Military Post, 62
Fort Ransom, 189
Fort Ransom State Park, 189
Fort Seward Historic Site and
    Interpretive Center, 159
Fort Seward Wagon Train, 160
Fort Sisseton State Park, 3, 12
Fort Thompson, 65
Fort Totten State Historic Site, 163
Fort Union Trading Post National
    Historic Site, 128, 140
Fort Union Trading Post
    Rendezvous, The, 133
fossils, 90

445 Martini Lounge, 91
Four Points by Sheraton
    Williston, 150
Frontier Museum, 142
Frontier Village, 155
Frost Fire Ski and Snowboard
    Area, 179

G

Gallery 4, 188
Garretson, 30
Gaslight, The, 125
Gather, 26
Gavins Point Dam, 50
Gavins Point Powerhouse, 50
George S. Mickelson Trail, 103
German-Russian Schmeckfest, 76
Gettysburg, 77
Giago, Tim, 83
Gingras Trading Post State Historic
    Site, 178
Gladys Pyle Historic Home, 3
G. L. Stocker Blacksmith Shop, 77
Gold Discovery Days, 84
Golden Buffalo Casino, 65
Good Earth State Park, 41
Good Old Summertime
    Festival, 21
Goosefest, 167
Goss Opera House, 17
Governor's Inn, 79
Gramma Sharon's Family
    Restaurant, 151
Granary Rural Cultural Center, 5
Grand Forks, 179
Grand Forks Air Force Base, 162
Grand Gateway, 123
Grand Opera House, 30
Grand River Casino & Resort, 75
Grassy Butte, 135
Great Bear Recreation Park, 38

Greater Grand Forks Convention &
Visitors Bureau, 192
Great Outdoor Store, 34
Great Plains Family Restaurant, 79
Great Plains Synfuels Plant, 145
Great Plains Zoo and Delbridge
Museum, 29, 39
Green Bean Coffeehouse, 125
Gregory County, 62
Grille 26, 58
Guadalajara, 25

H
Hampton Inn, 123
Hampton Inn and Suites, 24
Hangar Restaurant & Ace
Lounge, 25
Happy Times Carousel, 11
Hargens Gallery, 54
Harold Schafer Heritage
Center, 129
Haunted Forest, 4
Havana, 190
Hawktree Golf Club, 140
Hawthorn Suites by Wyndham, 173
Hebda Family Produce and Prairie
Gardens, 49
Heddy Draw overlook, 104
Heritage Center at Red Cloud
Indian School, 84
Hickok, Wild Bill, 115
High Country Guest Ranch, 100
Highlands Historical District, 6
Highline Bridge, 189
High Plains Heritage Center
Museum, 113
Hill City, 97
Hill City Chamber of
Commerce, 124
Hilton Garden Inn, 191
Historic Adams House, 115

Historic Bullock Hotel, 122
Historic Lantern Tour, 102
Hitching Horse Inn, 79
Hjemkomst Center, 185
Hjemkomst Viking Ship, 185
Holiday Inn City Centre, 57
Holiday Inn Express Hotel and
Suites, 24
Holiday Inn Rushmore Plaza, 123
Home Porch Gifts, 34
Homestake Adams Research and
Cultural Center, 116
Homesteader Day Harvest
Festival, 41
Homesteader, The, 79
Hotel Alex Johnson, 91
Hotel Donaldson, 184
Hotel Sturgis, The, 123
Hot Springs, 107
Hot Springs Area Chamber of
Commerce, 124
Howard Johnson Inn and
Suites, 79
Howe, Oscar, 54
Humpback Sally's, 147
Humphrey Drugstore, 23
hunting seasons, 8
Huron, 22
Huron Chamber & Visitors
Bureau, 25
Hutterite Colonies, 6
H. V. Johnston Cultural Center, 75
Hyatt House Minot, 173

I
Icelandic State Park, 176
Indian Creek Recreation Area, 72
Indian Museum of North
America and Native American
Educational and Cultural
Center, 101

Ingalls Homestead, 3
International Adventure Trail, 157
International Music Camp, 169
International Peace Garden,
    158, 167
International Ragtop Festival, 172
Ipswich, 7
Iron Mountain Road, 106

J
Jackson, Phil, 142
Jambonz Grill & Pub, 125
Jamestown, 155
Jamestown Tourism Center, 173
Jamestown Visitor Center, 158
JD's BBQ, 151
Jesse James Roundup Days, 30
Jewel Cave National Monument,
    85, 102
Jewels of the West, 99
Joachim Regional Museum and
    Prairie Outpost Park, 139
Joseph N. Nicollet Tower and
    Interpretive Center, 14
Josiah's Coffeehouse, Café and
    Bakery, 35
Journey, The, 90
juneberry ice cream, 168
Junior Paleontology program, 109
J.W. Parmley Museum, 7

K
Kaladi's Bistro, 58
Karl E. Mundt National Wildlife
    Refuge, 62, 75
Kathmandu Indian Cuisine, 58
K Bar S Lodge, 123
Kenmare, 167
Ken's Airboat Service, 8
Keystone, 96
Kirby Science Discovery Center, 38

Kittsona, 188
Klein Museum, 71
Knife River Indian Villages, 144
Knotty Pine Cabin, 122
K Restaurant, 35
Kroll's Diner, 191
kuchen, 76
Kulm, 152

L
La Hacienda, 25
Lake Agassiz, 174
Lake Alice National Wildlife
    Refuge, 156
Lake Andes National Wildlife
    Refuge Complex, 62
Lake Byron, 23
Lake Francis Case, 61
Lake Herman State Park, 27
Lake Metigoshe State Park, 167
Lake Minne-Eho, 4
Lake Norden, 10
Lake Oahe, 70
Lake Sakakawea, 128, 143
Lake Sharpe, 65
Lakeside Marina and Recreational
    Area, 160
Lakeview Meadow, 172
Lakeview Motel, 79
Lakota, Nakota, and Dakota
    Heritage Village, 97
La Minestra, 69
L'Amour Family Home Site, 158
L'Amour, Louis, 142, 156
Land of Oz, 3
Langenfeld's Ice Cream and
    Dairy, 16
Latchstring Inn Restaurant &
    Lounge, 114
Laughing Sun Brewhouse and
    Pub, 150

Laura Ingalls Wilder Pageant, 9, 21
Lead, 117
Lead Chamber of Commerce, 124
Lee, Peggy, 158
Legends in Light Laser Show, 101
Lemmon, 121
Lewis and Clark Interpretive
    Center, 145
Lewis and Clark Marina, 51
Lewis and Clark Recreation
    Area, 29
Lewis and Clark Resort, 51
Lewis and Clark Riverboat, 148
Lewis and Clark State Park, 143
Lewis and Clark State Recreation
    Area, 49
Lewis and Clark Trail, 140
Lewis and Clark Visitor Center, 50
Lillian and Coleman Taube
    Museum of Art, 165
Lincoln Borglum Museum, 97
Lindenwood Park, 186
Links of North Dakota, The, 140
Little Missouri Dining Room, 151
Lode Star Casino, 65
Lodge at Deadwood, The, 122
Long Lake National Wildlife
    Refuge, 156
Long X Visitor Center and
    Museum, 136
Lostwood National Wildlife
    Refuge, 157
Loud American Roadhouse, 125
Louis L'Amour Trail, 157
Lower Brule, 65
Lower Brule buffalo herd, 65
Lower Brule Indian Reservation, 64
Lowe's Garden Center, 166
Lund's Landing Lodge, 143

M
Maah Daah Hey Trail, 134
Madison, 27
Magic City Express, 165
Main Street Square, 90
Maltese Cross Cabin, 128, 131
Mama's Ladas, 34
Mammoth Site, 85, 109
Mandan, 146
Maple River, 186
Marina Grill, The, 51
Maris, Roger, 142, 185
Market on Phillips, The, 34
Matthews Opera House and Art
    Center, 113
Maverick Steaks and Cocktails, 24
McCall, Jack "Crooked Nose", 49
McCrory Gardens and State
    Arboretum, 18
McGovern Legacy Museum, 54
McKenzie County Heritage
    Park, 136
McKenzie County Tourism, 151
Medicine Wheel Park, 190
Medora, 128
Medora Musical, 128, 129
Medora Musical Welcome
    Center, 129
Medora Riding Stables, 132
Medora South Unit Visitor
    Center, 133
Mellette House, 17
Memorial Park & Garden, 93
Meridian Bridge, 48
Mickelson, George S., 68
Middle Border Museum and Case
    Art Gallery, 54
Midsommar Festival, 42
Mills, Billy, 83
Mineral Palace Hotel &
    Gaming, 122

Miner Brewing Company, 98
Minervas, 35
Minervas Restaurant and Bar, 24
Minot, 164
Minot Convention and Visitors
    Bureau, 173
Minot International Airport, 166
Minuteman Missile National
    Historic Site, 85
Missouri Flats Inn, 150
Missouri National Recreational
    River, 48
Missouri River, 59
Missouri–Yellowstone Confluence
    Interpretive Center, 141
Mister Smith's, 46
Mitchell, 52
Mitchell Convention and Visitors
    Bureau, 57
Mitchell Prehistoric Indian
    Village, 55
Mitchell Public Library, 54
Mobridge, 70
Mobridge Chamber of
    Commerce, 78
Mo-Rest Motel, 70
Mostly Chocolates, 94
Mountain, 178
Mountains to Prairies B&B, 122
Mount Coolidge, 104
Mount Moriah Cemetery, 116
Mount Rushmore National
    Memorial, 85
Mount Rushmore National
    Monument, 96
Mrs. Murphy's Irish Gifts, 34
Mund, Cara, 142
Museum @ Black Hills
    Institute, 99
Museum of Geology, 90

Museum of Wildlife, Science, and
    Industry of Northeastern South
    Dakota, 12
Mustang Sally's, 124
Myra Museum, 182

N
Naked Winery, 98
National Buffalo Museum, 158
National Field Archery Association
    (NFAA) Headquarters and
    Museum, 51
National Grasslands Visitor
    Center, 88
National Music Museum, 29, 44
Native American Day, 84
Needles Highway, 106
Newton Hills State Park, 47
Nichole's Fine Pastry, 185
Nick's Hamburger Shop, 19
Noble Inn, 173
Norsk Høstfest, 159, 164
North Dakota Birding Trail, 158
North Dakota Game and Fish
    Department, 137
North Dakota Heritage Center, 148
North Dakota Heritage Center and
    the Capitol Grounds, 149
North Dakota Mill and
    Elevator, 180
North Dakota Museum of Art, 181
North Dakota State Fair, 159, 164
Northeastern South Dakota, 1
Northeast South Dakota Celtic
    Faire and Games, 9
Northern Plains Indian Art
    Market, 36
Northern Plains Peoples
    Educational Center, 117
North Winds Lodge, 150
Norway House, 172

Norwegian Log Cabin Museum, 94

O

Oahe Dam, 65, 75
Oahe Days, 68
Oahe Visitor Center, 66
O'Day Cache, 188
OG Greens, 58
Oglala Lakota College Historical
    Center, 83
Oh My Cupcakes!, 58
Old Courthouse Museum, 29, 33
Old Danish Mill, 167
Old-Fashioned Cowboy Christmas,
    130, 133
Old Market Eatery and Bar, 18
Old Red Old Ten Scenic
    Byway, 148
Old Sod Post Office, 135
Old Style Saloon No. 10, 114
On-a-Slant Village, 146
Orchard Creek Cottages, 123
Orman Dam, 119
Oscar Zero, 162
Outlaws' Bar and Grill, 136
Oyate Trail, 61

P

Palisades State Park, 29, 31
Palm Garden Cafe, 24
Papa's Pumpkin Patch, 149
Paradiso Mexican Restaurant, 191
Paramount Wine Bar, 35
Parmley Western Land Office, 8
Patterson Reservoir, 139
Paul Nelson Farm, 78
Peacock Alley, 147
Pembina, 170, 176
Pembina County Historical
    Museum, 176

Pembina State Museum, 171,
    176, 178
Perky Pine Café, 124
Peter Norbeck National Scenic
    Byway, 106
Petrified Wood Park and
    Museum, 121
Pettigrew Home and Museum, 33
Pheasant Capital of the World, 7
Pheasant Restaurant and
    Lounge, 20
Phillips Avenue Diner, 35
Philly Ted's Cheesesteaks and
    Subs, 125
Pickler Mansion, 11
Pickstown, 62
Pierre, 65
Pierre Convention and Visitors
    Bureau, 78
Pierson Ranch Recreation Area, 50
Pine Ridge Indian Reservation,
    82, 83
Pioneer Days, 183
Pipestem Creek Bed and
    Birding, 161
Pipestem Dam and Lake, 160
Pirogue Grille, 147
Pizza Di Paolo, 58
Plains Art Museum, 185
Platte-Winner Bridge, 63
Plum's Cooking Store, 35
Pollock, 70
Powder House Restaurant, 125
powwow etiquette, 74
Prairie Berry Winery, 98
Prairie Edge & Sioux Trading
    Post, 92
Prairie Homestead Historic Site, 86
Prairie House Manor Bed and
    Breakfast, The, 24
Prairie Inn, 57

Prairie Sky Ranch, 13
Prairie Village, 29
Presidential Trail, 96
Pride Dairy, 168
Prime Time Tavern, 25
Pump House, 124
Putnam House, 161
Pyle House Museum, 23

Q
Quality Inn, 79
Quarry Days, 29
Queen Bee Mill, 32
Queen City Bakery, 35
Quilt Inn and Suites, 172

R
Rabbit Bicycles and Repair, 103
Radisson Hotel, 150, 191
Raging Rivers Waterpark, 149
Railroad Museum, 165
Ralph Engelstad Arena, 179
Ramkota Hotel, 79
Ramkota Hotel & Watertown Event
    Center, 24
Randall Creek Recreation Area, 62
Ransom County Museum, 189
Rapid City, 89
Rapid City Convention & Visitors
    Bureau, 124
Rapid City Downtown, 85
Rapid City's historic downtown, 90
Rapid City Urban Mountain
    Park, 93
Redlin Art Center, 3, 15
Red Pepper, The, 192
Red River Valley, 174
Red River Zoo, 187
Red Rock Restaurant, 125
Red Rock River Resort, 108
Red Rooster Coffee House, 6

RedRossa Italian Grill, 79
Red Silo, The, 188
Red Steakhouse, 46, 58
Red Trail Vineyard, 186
Regent, 138
Reifel, Ben, 83
Reptile Gardens, 95
Revolver, 188
Rheault Farm, 187
Rhombus Guys, 185, 192
Richardton, 139
Riverfront Event Center, 57
River's Edge, 58
Riverwalk, 165
Rocket Motel, 122
rockhounding, 88
Rolla, 169
Rollout Bike Rentals, 4
Ronald Reagan Minuteman Missile
    State Historic Site, 162
Roosevelt Park Zoo, 165
Rosalie's Restaurant, Bakery and
    Lounge, 25
Rosebud Indian Reservation, 82
Rose Stone Inn, 30
Roughrider Days Rodeo, 133, 138
Rough Riders, 130
Rough Riders Gift Shop, 131
Royal River Casino, 21
Royal River Casino and Hotel, 24
Roy Lake State Park, 12
Ruby House Restaurant, 125
Rug and Relic, 35
Rushmore Hotel & Suites, The, 123

S
Sage Creek Grille, 123
Sage Meadow Ranch, 110
Sake Japanese Restaurant, 25
Sammy's Restaurant & Omelette
    Shop, 24

Samuel H. Ordway Jr. Memorial
    Preserve, 10
Sanaa's, 35
Sand Lake National Wildlife
    Refuge, 9
Sanford Lab Homestake
    Visitor, 117
Santee Sioux Powwow, 21
Sauerkraut Days, 154
Scandinavian Heritage Center, 164
Scenic Tour, 102
Schadé Winery, 40, 99
Scheels, 187
Scherr Howe Arena, 71, 75
Schmeckfest, 42
Sculptor's Studio, 97
SculptureWalk, 36
Sertoma Butterfly House and
    Marine Cove, 38
Shadehill Recreation Area, 120
Shady Rest Motel, 122
Shakespeare Garden and Anne
    Hathaway Cottage, 55
Sheila Schafer Gallery, 129
Sheps Canyon Recreational
    Area, 110
Sheyenne Valley Arts and Crafts
    Festival, 189
Sheyenne Valley National Scenic
    Byway, 189
Shipwreck Bay, 187
Sica Hollow State Park, 13
Sidewalk Arts Festival, 38
Silk Road Cafe, 58
Silverado Franklin Historic Hotel &
    Gaming Complex, 115
Silverado Grand Buffet, 124
Silver Mountain Resort &
    Cabins, 123
Sioux Falls, 32

Sioux Falls Convention and
    Visitors Bureau, 57
Sioux Falls Outdoor Campus, 39
Sioux River Folk Festival, 47
Sisseton Chamber of
    Commerce, 25
Sitting Bull Monument, 73, 75
Sitting Bull Visitor Center, 150
Sky Dancer Hotel & Casino, 172
sky-diving, 187
Sky's Fine Dining, 180
Slim Buttes, 120
Smith, Tama, 135
Smith–Zimmermann Heritage
    Museum, 29
Smoking Mule, The, 79
Snake Creek Recreation Area, 63
Sodbuster Days, 189
Souris River Brewing, 173
South Dakota Agricultural Heritage
    Museum, 20
South Dakota Air & Space
    Museum, 89
South Dakota Amateur Baseball
    Hall of Fame, 10
South Dakota Art Museum, 3, 19
South Dakota Cultural Heritage
    Center, 67, 75
South Dakota Discovery Center
    and Aquarium, 68, 75
South Dakota Film Festival, 9
South Dakota Korean & Vietnam
    War Memorial, 68
South Dakota Missouri River
    Tourism, 78
South Dakota National Guard
    Museum, 68
South Dakota School of Mines and
    Technology, 90
South Dakota's State Capitol, 67
South Dakota State Fair, 3, 9, 22

Southeastern South Dakota, 27
Southeast South Dakota
   Tourism, 57
Spearfish, 112
Spearfish Canyon Lodge, 113, 123
Spearfish Canyon National Scenic
   Byway, 113
Spezia, 35
Spirit Mound, 46
Standing Rock Indian
   Reservation, 75
Standing Rock Reservation, 149
State Capitol, Bismarck, 147
Stavig House Museum, 15
Steever House Bed and
   Breakfast, 56
St. Joseph's Cathedral Historic
   District, 33
St. Mary's Catholic Church, 139
St. Mary's Cemetery, 152
St. Mary's Church, 152
Stockyards Ag Experience Barn
   and Plaza, 32
Stone Faces Winery, 98
Storybook Island, 93
Storybook Land, 3
Storybook Land Festival, 9
Storybook Land & Wylie Park, 3
Strasburg, 154
Strawbale Winery, 40
Sturgis, 111
Sturgis Motorcycle Museum & Hall
   of Fame, 111
Sturgis Motorcycle Rally, 111
Stutsman County Memorial
   Museum, 160
Sue the T-rex, 121
Sullys Hill National Game
   Preserve, 163
Summer Creek Inn and Spa, 123
Super 8 Motel, 24

Sylvan Lake Lodge, 104, 106, 124
Sylvan Rocks Climbing School and
   Guide Service, 105

T
Tally's Silver Spoon, 91
Tastee Treet Drive-In, 58
Tatanka: Story of the Bison, 117
10 North Main, 165
Termesphere Gallery, 113
Terrace Park, 37
Terry Peak Ski Resort, 118
Theodore Roosevelt National Park,
   128, 135
Theodore Roosevelt National
   Park's Painted Canyon, 132
Theodore's Dining Room, 151
Thomsen Center Archeodome, 55
Three Affiliated Tribes
   Museum, 144
Thunder Road, 4
Thunder Road Family Fun
   Park, 187
Tibbs, Casey, 69
Tin Lizzie, 124
Toasted Frog, The, 180
Tobacco Garden Bay, 143
Tobacco Gardens, 128
Tobacco Gardens Resort and
   Marina, 143
Tokyo Japanese Cuisine, 58
Totten Trail Historic Inn, 163
TownePlace Suites by Marriott, 24
Trailshead Lodge, 118
Trapper's Kettle, 137
Tri-State Museum, 119
Tucker's Walk Vineyard, 40
Turtle Mountain Band of Pembina
   Chippewa, 170
Turtle Mountain Indian
   Reservation, 171

Turtle Mountains, 158, 171
Turtle River State Park, 182
Turtle Town Confectionary, 125
Twisted Pine Winery, 99
221 Melsted Place Bed &
    Breakfast, 177

U
Union Grove State Park, 47
University of North Dakota, 181
University of South Dakota, 43
USS *South Dakota* Battleship
    Memorial, 37

V
Valiant Vineyards, 40
Valley City, 189
Valley City Area Chamber of
    Commerce, 192
Valley City Federal Fish
    Hatchery, 190
Valley City State University, 190
Valley of the Giants Trail, 41
Val's Cyclery, 165
Vérendrye Monument, 66
Vermillion, 43
Vermillion Area Tourism, 57
Visitor Center (Storybook Land), 3
Visit Spearfish, 124
Visual Arts Center, 37
Volksmarch, 101

W
Wahpeton Convention & Visitors
    Bureau, 192
Walhalla, 178
Wall Drug, 88
Walrus Restaurant, The, 151
Ward County Historical
    Society Pioneer Village and
    Museum, 166

Ward's Store and Bakery, 25
Washburn, 145
Washington Pavilion, 29
Washington Pavilion of Arts and
    Science, 36
Watertown, 15
Watertown Area Chamber of
    Commerce and Convention and
    Visitors Bureau, 25
Watertown Confectionery, 16
Watford City, 133, 136
Waverly Steakhouse & Lounge, 26
Webster, 11
Welk Homestead State Historic
    Site, 155
Welk, Lawrence, 49, 142, 155
West Boulevard, 93
western North Dakota, 126
western South Dakota, 80
West Whitlock Recreation Area,
    75, 77
White Butte, 131
White Eagle, 83
White House Café, 173
Whitestone Hill Battlefield Site, 152
Whitlock Bay Salmon Spawning
    Station, 78
Whitlock Bay Walleye
    Tournament, 78
W. H. Over Museum of Natural
    and Cultural History, 43
Widman's Candy Shop, 181
Wild Caving/Spelunking Tour, 102
Wilde Prairie Winery, 40
Wildlife Loop Road, 103
wild prairie rose, 178
Williston, 135, 141
Williston Brewing Company, 151
Williston Convention and Visitors
    Bureau, 151
Williston Steakhouse, The, 151

Williston Tourist Information
    Center, 143
Willow Springs Cabin B&B, 123
Wind Cave National Park, 107
wineries, 40
wine trail, 40
Wingate by Wyndham
    Bismarck, 150
Wishek, 154
"World's Largest Buffalo"
    sculpture, 155
Wounded Knee, 82
Wounded Knee Museum, 89
Wounded Knee National Historic
    Landmark, 83

Wrangler Inn, 79
Wurst Bier Hall, 192
Wylie Park, 4
Wylie Park Campground, 4

Y
Yankton, 48
Yankton Convention and Visitors
    Bureau, 57
Yellowstone Trail, 7

Z
Zandbroz Variety, 36, 188
Zesto Shop, 79